OSC

Figuring Genre in Roman Satire

AMERICAN PHILOLOGICAL ASSOCIATION
AMERICAN CLASSICAL STUDIES
VOLUME 50

Series Editor
DONALD J. MASTRONARDE

Studies in Classical History and Society
MEYER REINHOLD

Sextus Empiricus
The Transmission and Recovery of Pyrrhonism
LUCIANO FLORIDI

The Augustan Succession
An Historical Commentary on Cassius Dio's "Roman History"
Books 55–56 (9 B.C.–A.D. 14)
PETER MICHAEL SWAN

Greek Mythography in the Roman World
ALAN CAMERON

Virgil Recomposed
The Mythological and Secular Centos in Antiquity
SCOTT MCGILL

Representing Agrippina
Constructions of Female Power in the Early Roman Empire
JUDITH GINSBURG

Figuring Genre in Roman Satire
CATHERINE KEANE

Figuring Genre in Roman Satire

Catherine Keane

OXFORD
UNIVERSITY PRESS

2006

OXFORD
UNIVERSITY PRESS

Oxford University Press, Inc., publishes works that further
Oxford University's objective of excellence
in research, scholarship, and education.

Oxford New York
Auckland   Cape Town   Dar es Salaam   Hong Kong   Karachi
Kuala Lumpur   Madrid   Melbourne   Mexico City   Nairobi
New Delhi   Shanghai   Taipei   Toronto

With offices in
Argentina   Austria   Brazil   Chile   Czech Republic   France   Greece
Guatemala   Hungary   Italy   Japan   Poland   Portugal   Singapore
South Korea   Switzerland   Thailand   Turkey   Ukraine   Vietnam

Copyright © 2006 by American Philological Association

Published by Oxford University Press, Inc.
198 Madison Avenue, New York, New York 10016

www.oup.com

Oxford is a registered trademark of Oxford University Press

All rights reserved. No part of this publication may be reproduced,
stored in a retrieval system, or transmitted, in any form or by any means,
electronic, mechanical, photocopying, recording, or otherwise,
without the prior permission of Oxford University Press.

Library of Congress Cataloging-in-Publication Data
Keane, Catherine.
Figuring genre in Roman satire / Catherine Keane
    p. cm.—(American classical studies; v. 50)
Includes bibliographical references.
ISBN-13 978-0-19-518330-6
ISBN 0-19-518330-4
1. Verse satire, Latin—History and criticism. 2. Literary form—History—To 1500
3. Literature and society—Rome. 4. Social problems in literature. I. Title.
II. American classical studies; no. 50.
PA6056.K37   2006
871'.070901—dc22   2005023766

9 8 7 6 5 4 3 2 1

Printed in the United States of America
on acid-free paper

Preface and Acknowledgments

In quoting from Horace, Persius, and Juvenal, I have relied mainly on the *Oxford Classical Texts* edited by Edward Wickham and H. W. Garrod (1912), and Wendell Clausen (1992). Quotations from the fragments of Lucilius refer to Warmington's Loeb Classical Library text (1967). All translations, except where otherwise noted, are my own.

While researching, writing, and editing this work I received crucial support of various kinds from the Department of Classical Studies at the University of Pennsylvania, the A. W. Mellon Foundation, the Classics Departments at Northwestern University and Washington University in St. Louis, and the Loeb Classical Library Foundation. I also owe a debt to Cathy Marler for assistance with clerical and logistical matters, to the editorial board of the APA Monographs Series for its support and attention, to Maria Sarinaki for creating the index, and to Oxford University Press–USA, especially Elissa Morris, Eve Bachrach, and Gwen Colvin, for guiding the book through the publication process.

The individuals who read part or all of this manuscript at different stages, and whose advice continues to help me, include Ryan Balot, Joseph Farrell, Kirk Freudenburg, Erin McGlothlin, Bridget Murnaghan, Bill Ray, Ralph Rosen, and my former fellow Ph.D. candidates from the University of Pennsylvania, who along with the department faculty made the best research community that anyone could want. Some have put in considerable effort over the long term to provide me with useful advice, support, and good conversation about satire, especially Susanna Braund, John Henderson, and Dan Hooley.

Finally, I thank my colleagues at Washington University, my immediate and extended family, and my friends in St. Louis and other parts, who have enthusiastically awaited the publication of this book. All of them helped to make it happen with their unconditional support and prudent advice.

Contents

Introduction   3

1. The Theatrics of Satire   13

2. Satiric Attack   42

3. Satire and the Law   73

4. Teaching Satire   105

Conclusion: Observing Romans   137

Notes   143

Bibliography   165

Index   175

Figuring Genre in Roman Satire

Introduction

OVERVIEW

Writers of satire strike many different poses, ranging from conservative to transgressive, constructive to malicious. Horace, Persius, and Juvenal, the verse satirists of ancient Rome, use particularly diverse and colorful methods to practice their moral and social criticism. Such inconsistency of authorial perspective and agenda might be said to obfuscate, or even to preclude, a coherent generic theory; it has certainly fueled a long scholarly debate about satire's essential nature. As a literary form, satire challenges readers on many levels, even prompting questions about its own historical origins and rhetorical aims. Indeed, more so than with other genres, we tend to feel more comfortable when we shift from talking about satire as literature to describing it as a kind of social practice. Satirists expose, perform, attack, punish, and instruct. In other words, they mimic society's existing methods of criticism, correction, and entertainment in creating their literary texts. Models for the satiric procedure have been identified, by the Roman poets and their readers alike, in theatrical performance, in physical violence, in legal process, and in teaching.

These comparisons beg to be investigated, for they speak volumes both about the genre of satire and about the society that created it. They suggest that satire's reputation as the "wholly Roman" genre (*tota nostra*, in Quintilian's judgment; *Inst.* 10.1.93), is justified not just because Roman authors developed the literary form, but because satire mirrors or channels Roman society's most treasured institutions. This book identifies and aims to explicate two intertwined ways in which satire engages with social practices and behaviors. In explicit ("programmatic") declarations, the poets outline a multifaceted critical strategy that derives from theater, violence, law, and teaching. But programmatic commentary is only one manifestation of satire's mimetic generic theory. In their representations of social life, Horace, Persius, and Juvenal give considerable attention to the institutions that shaped Roman culture between the first century BCE and the second century CE, including its theaters, arenas, courts, and educational traditions. In creating a critical picture of society, then, the satirists examine the very acts that they claim to perform in a metaphorical sense with their texts. The narrative tapestry created in the process brings out many aspects of satire-like procedures of exposure and judgment—not just their corrective and constructive functions, but also their dangers and flaws. Satire does not treat its social models any more gently than it does other topics.

Satire dramatizes its own generic theory in demonstrating its close and reciprocal relationship with Roman social practices. The four chapters of this study uncover four encoded and interlocking accounts of the genre's origins and purposes, all embedded in the selective and subjective satiric picture of the world. Each social model for satire constitutes a programmatic motif, which the individual poets explore and nuance as they progress through their work. Throughout, the conventional satirist figure acts as both critic and subject. This introductory chapter lays out a theoretical account of satire's mimetic and composite generic formula, and explains the role of the satirist figure within it.

PROGRAMMATIC PROVOCATIONS

It is common to define satire as a synthesis of procedures with varying aims and styles, such as "attack, entertainment, and preaching."[1] This compound type of definition usefully takes into account satire's variety of rhetorical postures (fierce, ironic, moralistic, and so on), a manifestation of the genre's debt to drama, rhetoric, and other literary modes.[2] But analogous descriptions offered by the Roman poets themselves indicate that speaking style is only one dimension of their performance. In programmatic discourse, we see four satiric functions articulated, which are best described as imitation or replication of existing social practices. The *Sermones* ("chats") of Horace, mild though they may seem, explore satire's full range. Horace describes his genre's second-century CE founder Lucilius as a successor to Greek comic dramatists (1.4.1–5), and correspondingly imagines himself as a performer on stage (1.10.76–77). Other Horatian images emphasize a more aggressive function, comparing the satirist to a violent bull (1.4.34) and his work to a sword, with which he threatens critics (2.1.39–41). Horace relates satire to the legal scene as well, posing as a defender of flouted laws (1.4) but also recognizing that satire might be construed as illegal slander (2.1). Finally, he famously compares his satire, a mode of criticism that employs humor, to the pedagogical strategy of bribing pupils with cookies (1.1.24–26). This same range of contexts—theatrical, combative, legal, didactic—is also conjured by Horace's successors. Persius styles himself as a script-writer (*Satire* 1.44), a violator of his audience's ears (1.107–108), a vigilante social commentator (1.112–114), and a pupil and proponent of Stoic ethics (*Satire* 5). Juvenal, for his part, compares his work to dramatic production (*Satire* 4.1–2) and more specifically to tragedy and spectacle (6.634–637, 14.256–264); his inspiration is the metaphorical-sword-wielding Lucilius (1.165); and he both laments flouted laws (1.158–159) and risks punishment himself (1.155–157). Moreover, Juvenal's complaints about the deterioration of traditional morality (1.87, 147–149) imply that he has a moral-didactic program as well.

Satirists, then, do not just describe, distort, and criticize social life. They claim to intervene in it as well—at least in an indirect manner through their texts. The functions that they pretend to adopt have never been used as a framework for an analysis of the genre, although the connections repeatedly proposed between satire and drama, violence, law, and teaching suggest a coherent and rich generic theory. It is clear how these four practices might be conceived as influencing satiric social criticism. Drama, like satire, is a literary form that employs the persona (in the word's concrete sense, the actor's mask); it also provides stock images and social themes that fit well into satire's entertaining narrative vignettes. Comic drama in particular is associated with exposure and mockery of human folly and vice, which constitutes another connection with satire.[3] The nonliterary models reflect this moral or corrective program in other ways. Violence and law are both used in society as means of punishment and social control. Correspondingly, the genres of ancient blame poetry feature many programmatic images of violence,[4] while legal process offers a more refined model for the textual and often subtle satiric "prosecution" of vice. Teaching is the ostensible purpose of ancient diatribe, another ancestor of satire; even if we do not accept the thesis that for every vice it condemns, satire recommends an opposing virtue,[5] we may still believe that the genre's criticisms have the potential to edify.

Satire's models—both individually and as a group—import complications as well.[6] For one thing, they combine to create a hybrid form, varied in technique and agenda. While satire already shares elements with theater in being a literary form, its advertised connections to violence, law, and education have the very different effect of anchoring the genre in rituals of social and political life. Even the nonliterary models make an odd group; to note one possible clash, "attacking" and "teaching" might strike us as programs that are too different to cooperate. Furthermore, while the metaphors contextualize the satirist broadly in the cultural arenas in question, the exact position that he takes in each arena is not consistent. According to the passages surveyed above, the satirist may act as dramatist, performer, or spectator, assailant or victim of violence, jurist or criminal. Finally, the metaphorical representations of satiric criticism are not proffered solely in order to defend or valorize the genre. Satirists do not simply highlight the benefits that their work can bring to society, but often allude, via the programmatic metaphors, to less palatable effects and motivations that readers might well be disposed to entertain.[7] In their project of self-definition, the poets do not aim solely to disarm detractors (by claiming, for instance, to practice inoffensive or indirect criticism). Rather, they lay out satire's aetiology—a biased and subjective story, to be sure, but one that is comprehensive in its own way.

In their self-referential discussions, the satirists juxtapose images that may either harmonize with or repel one another. Consequently, they encourage readers to wonder how the metaphors may be understood to work, both separately and in combination. Satiric programmatic language employs the same rhetoric of "inquiry and provocation" that is seen in the genre's treatment of moral issues.[8] The metaphorical descriptions of satire occur most frequently in the conventional apologia, where the poet defends his work to a skeptical or hostile interlocutor.[9] Some images are presented by those interlocutors, and framed as criticisms. But they are just as much creations of the satirist. The apologia is a rhetorical fiction over which the poet has complete control; by introducing issues that he wishes the reader to consider, he helps to shape his own reception.[10] Satire shares this strategy with ancient comic drama, both the abusive "Old" and the milder "New" and Roman traditions. A comic parabasis or prologue may read superficially as commentary external to the play, but in reality it is a particularly manipulative part of the performance.[11]

In the apologia, even when a poet does not explicitly accept a particular characterization of his genre, the image that has been introduced has power. It becomes a motif and a source of "provocation" in satire's programmatic discourse. The fact that the apologia is a carefully contrived performance makes it difficult to believe that the satirists would hold up challenging or unflattering descriptions of themselves only to tame or bury them in a harmonious generic formula. Yet the modern assessments of satire as a balanced combination of styles or functions often seem designed to tone down the more troubling associations of each element. A similar effect is created by theories that, following Dryden, separate examples of satire into two polarized modes—the urbane "Horatian" and the aggressive "Juvenalian." Besides failing to account for ambiguous cases, this kind of classificatory scheme resists recognizing the genre's intrinsic complications, and effectively neutralizes the two poles identified by treating them as predetermined complements.[12] If applied to the conception of satire as social practice, such a scheme would ease the apparent tensions between alternative social models such as "attack" (which sounds malicious and extreme) and "teaching" (which has a more altruistic and refined ring). This study presumes, however, that the satirists deliberately cultivate such tensions. The inherent complexities of the models, and the relationships between them, generate satire's most striking effects and its most meaningful interpretive difficulties.

The metaphorical language of the satiric apologia introduces alternative versions of the genre, and raises further questions about the mimetic relationships in question. For it plugs satire into real-world activities and institutions that are themselves complex, socially and politically charged, and culture-defining. In what particular respects are we to imagine satire performing, attacking, prosecuting, or teaching, and what do we need to know about those activities themselves—both in their particularly Roman forms, and more broadly construed—in order to grasp what satire itself is and does? What kinds of relations exist between these models that would explain their cooperation (and meaningful conflict) in the theory of satire? And considering the genre's variety of methods and material, how can we form a coherent theoretical picture at all?[13]

I address these questions by using satire's programmatic metaphors as interpretive lenses through which to read, and reread, the genre. Metaphor is a common, even unconsciously used, device in the theorizing of genre (as in literary "family trees" and generic "formulas"). But it may be used as a stepping stone to deeper questions about the nature of literature.[14] In programmatic discourse, satire is aetiologized as a derivative or offshoot of existing practices in society, which we may see in turn as kinds of nonliterary or proto-satire. To understand their value to the literary form, we must examine their workings more closely—but specifically as the poets envision them.

READING SATIRE'S CONTENT

In the work of Horace, Persius, and Juvenal, representations of Roman society—the nonprogrammatic part of satire—abound with images of the genre's social models in action. Characters in satire perform in and watch plays and shows, fight with one another, punish offenders and transgress against the law, teach and learn. I argue that the satirists write these accounts in order to explore in more depth, and illustrate more vividly, aspects of their genre that are referenced in programmatic gestures.

Many scholars now regard traditional generic subject matter as a site for cryptic, self-reflexive commentary. This approach has become common in the interpretation of Roman comedy, owing to its metatheatrical element, and especially in the study of late Republican and early Imperial poetry, with its complex intertextuality and literary-critical codes.[15] Several recent studies reveal that Roman satire shares an intricate self-reflexive program with other ancient genres. To summarize the most influential discussions, satire's abundant images of food can be read as symbolizing alternative recipes for the genre itself, discussions of pedagogy open up questions about satire's own methods of teaching, and a journey narrative can cryptically relate the eclectic formation of the satiric genre.[16] From these studies we may conclude that satiric narratives and images are not mere static reflections of generic principles, but vehicles for working out those principles discursively, over the course of entire poems or books.

A metaliterary approach has thus far been applied to particular satiric themes and poems, but it is a valuable tool for understanding satire's broad range of chosen subjects. In any given poetic genre we may envision a connection between (ostensibly external) subject matter and text, as each genre presents a "model of reality" as seen through its own particular lens.[17] In satire, this relationship is vividly captured in a well-known programmatic statement of Juvenal's: since the dawn of humankind, "whatever people do—their prayers, their fears, their anger, their pleasures, their joys and goings-on—is the fodder of my little book" (*quidquid agunt homines, votum, timor, ira, voluptas, / gaudia, discursus, nostri farrago libelli est*, 1.85–86). As readers have noted, this is something of an exaggeration of Juvenal's actual narrative scope.[18] But as a description of the satiric genre, the claim carries an intriguing implication. Satire (*satura*, "fullness" or "miscellany") is composed of the "fodder" (*farrago*) that is human experience. Genre feeds on, and becomes identical with, subject matter.[19] Juvenal's tag conveys the idea that satire's subjects are not simply stock material to be trotted out, but a source of inspiration and even emotional energy for the poet.

A study of satire's social contexts and models can thus take a cue from the Juvenalian passage. The satirists assert in programmatic contexts that their work is inspired by four specific practices with critical aims. The programmatic claims are substantiated in the poets' representations of Roman life, where those satire-like practices feature prominently. We should not view this as a coincidence, as if the poets were merely documenting all topics of Roman social life.[20] As Henderson has argued, the generic satirist figure is not an objective observer but a constructed subject in his own right, who effectively defines his own concerns when he focuses on particular social groups and conflicts.[21] According to this view, the genre's model of reality adds to and complements explicit programmatic remarks and creates a richer picture of the poet himself. And while many recurrent themes adumbrate the world view of the satirist (dining, patronage, rustic life, sexual behavior, greed), no set of themes is more directly related to his constructed social identity than the practices on which satiric criticism is modeled. Programmatic metaphors set up a reciprocal relationship between satire and major Roman institutions, which plays out as satire both imitates and interrogates those institutions.

An approach to genre that rests on the identification of important themes runs the risk of treating genre as a static construct and ignoring its dynamic evolution.[22] Recognizing this, I will regard the satiric text as an ongoing narrative—if not in the strict sense that characterizes epic or historiography, in the sense of a sequence of discussions and stories that build on one another and convey a feeling of dramatic time. This narrative continuously brings forth revelations about the genre itself. Like the love elegist, the satirist spins out an extended account of experiences and reactions that exhibit his genre's nature.[23] Significantly, our first extant book of satire, Horace's *Sermones* 1, reflects the internal thematic and sequential coherence typical of the Augustan poetry book.[24] That text is a paradigm for the subsequent tradition, in which book arrangement and intertextuality enrich generic construction. Satiric apologiae do not establish a static or prescriptive generic theory, but set in motion a theory that is adaptive and dynamic.

I organize this study around satire's models, rather than as a chronological survey of the individual poets. My aim in doing so is to show that each model has its own discernible history in the tradition, and exerts a unique influence on satiric representation. The satirists present as many models of reality as they claim social functions. At the same time, the thematic orientation of this book allows a more detailed and rich picture of each poet's work to become visible. The individual satirists stand out not only by virtue of their particular contributions to the evolution of each theme, but also in their striking uses of satire's models, individually and in combination, to develop and refine the theory of the genre.

PERFORMANCES OF THE SATIRIST FIGURE

The primary goal of this study is to incorporate satire's professed social functions into our theoretical picture of the genre. In the process, however, I hope to refine our understanding of the poet figure, another focal point in recent scholarship. The generic satirist figure who promotes and explores his roles in society is of course a separate entity from the historical authors of satire. I follow the now-standard view of the satiric speaker as a dramatic character, with a personality conjured mainly through rhetorical techniques.[25] But I prefer not to use the label "persona" ("mask") that was the trademark term of late-twentieth-century satire criticism. Traditionally, persona scholarship has emphasized rhetorical elements of the satiric performance, the verbal cues that reveal the fictionality of the satiric speaker. Meanwhile, other potentially important aspects of the satiric performance have been somewhat neglected. It is useful to take into consideration the broader view of the literary persona adopted by scholars of other poetic genres. The lyric persona, it has been argued, is more than a means of distancing author from text; it is a pose that defines the poet as a product of, and agent in, his society. When a lyric poet invites his audience to share in grief, enjoy obscenity, or claim *urbanitas*, he is simultaneously taking on a culturally constructed role and helping to define the values of his social group.[26] This interpretation of the persona is no more biographically based than the strictly rhetorical view, but it takes into account the social dimension and Roman context of the poet's performance.

Metaphorical programmatic descriptions of the satiric genre suggest that the poet figure has a social identity—or more accurately, a range of social identities. The satirist becomes, at different moments, a stage performer or spectator, a fighter or victim, a jurist or criminal, a teacher or scholar—all roles that entail more than verbal performance. Moreover, these are practices that Romans employed in order to organize their world and define themselves within it. When he assumes one of these roles, the satirist takes on responsibility for a culturally significant enterprise. Certainly, looking at programmatic references alone, it is difficult to perceive the depth and implications of the satirist's adopted poses. But the poet has other ways of imagining his interactions with society. In narrative and descriptive contexts, alter egos for the satirist figure act out aspects of his work. Their tactics, successes, and failures reflect back on him, in addition to filling out the genre's critical picture of Roman society.

Because the satirist figure is a specifically Roman character, it is impossible to ignore the influence of historical context on the poses struck by the individual satirists. Horace wrote during the dramatic early years of Octavian's consolidation of power, Persius during the infamously paranoid rule of Nero; Juvenal's generation lived through the last of several sinister reigns in the first century CE. Writers in each period were clearly concerned with the effects of the imperial political structure on literature. Freudenburg has recently argued that the three satirists style themselves as victims of the decline of *libertas* (free speech), lamenting the loss of the "original" satiric method embodied in the Republican Lucilius.[27] The present study aims at complementing such diachronic analyses with a view of satire's contemporary and longstanding influences. In more than one way, the satiric genre lives up to Quintilian's characterization, acting out and evaluating Roman beliefs and anxieties. The poses adopted by Horace, Persius, and Juvenal connect satire to enduring Roman institutions, and even to more ancient practices such as violence and social organization. The picture of the genre that emerges certainly has a historical dimension, as each poet selectively and self-consciously develops the programmatic themes of his predecessors. But the literary-historical narrative that they create has as much to do with poetic self-promotion as it does with historical and political change. Because satire professes to be topical, its evolution is usually studied as a phenomenon shaped by history; yet like other ancient poets, its authors also build a highly subjective and tendentious account of their genre's origins and development.[28]

MAKING SATIRIC HISTORY

The readings in this book will show that theater, violence, law, and teaching make rich and problematic models. There is ample room in satire for the poets to nuance the images that are presented in programmatic passages. We learn in satiric images of social life that dramatic performance has hidden and sometimes deleterious effects, that perpetrators of violence have vulnerabilities of their own, that the law can disappoint as often as it corrects, that a teacher's authority is mutable. In addition, the models generate further complications (and so more interesting characterizations of satire) by occasionally blurring into one another. Violence can take the form of a ritual performance; legal process shows glimpses of its more primitive and harsh origins; teaching has its theatrical aspects and its dangers. These discoveries all reflect back on the satirist figure himself as he executes his twofold agenda of mimicry and critique. Satire's method of self-definition does not simply defend the genre, but also exposes its occasional destructive effects, failures, and dubious mechanisms.

This collective, aetiological account of satire begins in the poets' programmatic debates. Although each poet modifies the apologia in ways that evoke his particular historical circumstances and introduce his own perspective on the genre, they all use conventional argumentation, language, and imagery. In each chapter, I first examine the language and presentation of the apologiae themselves, identifying the key themes and provocations associated with the social model in question. These observations guide my subsequent readings of the extended, and encoded, commentary to be found elsewhere in satire. As each chapter shows using a different lens, the satirist and (more frequently) his alter egos in society act out satiric functions and witness their effects. The chapter discussions therefore put less emphasis on the individual poems as satires per se, treating specific ethical or cultural problems, than on the broader, metaliterary narratives in which they participate. Both approaches, of course, are equally useful to our understanding of this poetic genre.

Chapter 1 examines the model that inspired the persona theory, although it immediately becomes clear that drama provides more than just "masks" for the poets. The dramatic analogy for satire emphasizes the latter genre's critical function, its placement of subjects before the community with the poet posing alternately as dramatist, performer, and spectator. The satirists seem intrigued by the operation of theater because it engages participants both emotionally and cognitively, it encourages critique and self-critique from viewers, and it stratifies society on stage and in the audience. Satiric gestures to drama also reveal the satirists' willingness to take on the negative associations of their chosen social analogues. Roman prejudices are bound to be aroused by a satirist figure who puts himself on a metaphorical stage or excitedly witnesses society's "shows."

Like theater, physical violence and legal process can take the form of performances, though they have rather different objectives. Metaphorical satiric attack aims to punish and mock, while satire's "prosecutorial" function represents a more sophisticated approach to correction. Chapters 2 and 3 examine these two models in turn, showing how the satirists represent the mechanics of Roman society's own methods of attack and punishment. Satiric violence is typically aimed at deviant behavior; in this sense it bears a resemblance to the regulatory, staged violence of sacrifice and spectacle, which marks out victims in order to stabilize the rest of the community. But such practices have their perils: they highlight the insecurity of those who wish to mark out Others, as well as exposing them to retaliatory attack. Satire acknowledges that perpetrators of regulatory violence hold a precarious place.

Some of the same dangers appear where satire allies itself with law, a force that is revealed as having roots in raw violence. Moreover, the law has more than one problematic role in satire's programmatic discourse. It is not only a model for the satiric judgment of vice, but a real-world context for the genre, imposing restrictions on the satirist figure. The defining force that is the law propels the satirist into an ongoing quest for a suitable climate for his work. This quest itself, not any resolution of it, sums up the genre's legal identity; new and fruitful contexts for satiric discourse continuously arise as the poets explore the law's allure, its restrictions, and its disappointments.

The same models appear in the work of all three satirists, attesting the theoretical coherence of the tradition, but each poet uses and examines them in a distinctive way. Horace, in this study, lives up to his image as an often self-undermining ironist. His alter egos act out both the constructive and the unsavory aspects of satire's evolution and social functions. The image of satire produced when Horace himself appears as an "acting" character is similarly ambiguous. In contrast, Persius conducts famously subtle and elliptical interrogations of ethical ideas. His dialogues and diatribes hold the programmatic metaphors up for scrutiny, revealing their inherent paradoxes in ways that prevent simple characterization of his own satiric agenda. Juvenal, who revives and aggressively develops satire's narrative component, uses scenes of "daily life in ancient Rome" to dramatize his work's functions and effects—both constructive and destructive. He also contrives programmatic images and narrative scenarios that merge satire's functions together in provocative ways.

The individual satirists thus make distinctive contributions to the unfolding history of the genre. This is a self-conscious enterprise, in which the poets both allude to the traditions of their predecessors and promote themselves as innovators. Both positive and negative characterizations of satire are employed to this end. For example, while Horace draws heavily on comic devices himself, he depicts the satire of Lucilius as an antitheatrical endeavor. The chapter that he contributes to satire's "theatrical history" thus highlights his own contribution as a novel step forward. In a similar way, Juvenal responds to his predecessors' ambiguous attitudes to violence by bringing out more engagingly the potential for humor in images of attack and deformity. When he employs vivid and troubling images that resist a sanitized satiric theory, Juvenal promotes his work as the most morally challenging in the satiric tradition.

The self-promotional purpose of apologiae and of metaliterary vignettes and images is especially manifested in the satirists' treatment of education, the subject of chapter 4. The satirist figure's pose as a teacher draws attention to the satiric text as a practical product offered to the outside world. The didactic relationship is therefore also a relationship between text and engaged reader, and so the poets seem to be positioning themselves in literary tradition, not only in the social world. This has self-undermining effects, as the narratives about teaching embedded in satire point up the transitory nature of the pedagogical—and so the satiric—career. Didactic and literary success for the author also means transformation into a completed text, which is fated to be critiqued and even replaced.

The teaching theme is the one that depends most heavily on the genre's autobiographical fictions, an element that has more typically been a starting point in studies of satire. I deliberately postpone analysis of the genre from this angle, in order to show that metaphorical readings of the satirist figure point us to a more comprehensive understanding of the authorial *ego*. The prevalent notion of the satiric speaker as a rhetorical agent, distinguished by the verbal style of his criticism, fails to take into account the whole range of social contexts that shape the genre. The author figure must be viewed as a participant in the definitive institutions of his society. His multiple social roles combine to fashion his authorial perspective.

Although Roman satire developed in a challenging, and changing, political context, a consistent generic program is visible in the work of its authors. The satirist figure plays a double role of subject and critic, thereby affording his readers a unique and interested view of Roman social and political life. Meanwhile, he also encourages readers to develop an analytical and critical view of satire. In their project of self-presentation, Horace, Persius, and Juvenal operate on the principle that any publicity is good publicity, embracing even images that cast their genre in an unflattering light. Their investigation of satire's social origins and its potential positive and negative effects on society is a built-in part of the genre's critical mission.

The four accounts uncovered in this book overlap and interconnect, exhibiting satire's own complexity. It is fitting that satire, the "stuffed" genre, would present multiple narratives of its creation and development, none of which can be seen as entirely independent from the rest. Nevertheless, this investigation has its logical beginning with the model that reflects satire's primary status as literature.

1

The Theatrics of Satire

The persona theory treats the speaker in satire as a performer distinct from the author. Scholars understand the poet to be speaking through a variety of masks (e.g., "angry" or "ironic") when he attacks or mocks society. The device of the persona offers disguises to the satirist, but it is only an entry point into the multiple connections between satire and drama. This chapter will bring out the other aspects of the relationship, taking the first crucial steps away from a basic rhetorical view of the satiric persona toward a more vivid picture of the satirist figure's roles. Drama's appeal as a model derives from various aspects of its broader social function and its reception as literature. Like satire, drama puts human behavior on display before the community. It provides examples of grand, humorous, and bawdy narrative episodes and language, all of which are useful to the satirists in their agenda of entertaining and moralizing. And because much Greek and Roman drama was performed in agonistic contexts, with authors competing before judges, patrons, and public, dramatic authors often engage in self-referential and self-defensive discourse, to which the satirists look for inspiration when they express their own aims to readers. These connections are manifested in the two bodies of evidence examined in this chapter: the satiric programmatic discussions that feature versions of the dramatic analogy, and the satiric model of the world, in which drama plays a considerable role.

Like the other representations of satire examined in this study, the dramatic analogy is highly flexible. Satire may be compared to particular genres (comedy, tragedy, mime) or to spectacles of the nonliterary type (races, games, combat). The satirist may identify himself as a dramatist, a performer, or a spectator of events. He may also take a more distanced and utilitarian stance, employing dramatic images and exempla in his ethical arguments. Drama is a versatile tool. But it is also a tool with ambiguous power, as the satirists themselves are the first to acknowledge. They investigate drama as a social practice, highlighting its inner workings, its effects on spectators and readers, and its relation to other cultural institutions. The entire complicated perception of drama in Roman society is conveyed in satiric representations. This leaks into satire's generic identity and invites critical assessment from readers.

The material that I examine here illustrates the dialogic relationship between satire and each of its models that will be seen in subsequent chapters as well. These relationships establish satire's identity as the quintessential Roman genre, which is shaped and inspired by key Roman institutions. In the present case as elsewhere, the satirists' imitative approach is not purely pragmatic. The poets do "use" drama, but it exerts power over them as well. With every new revelation that they produce about drama's power and its ideological baggage, their genre seems to become more enmeshed with its model.

MASKS OF THE SATIRIST

Claims about satire's dramatic nature posit a variety of relationships between the two literary spheres, often in an interrogative or ambiguous manner. Some sources assert that satire actually derives in some way or other from dramatic genres. The historian Livy refers to early dramatic performances in Rome, which he calls *saturae*.[1] The satirists themselves point to literary-historical and thematic ties between their work and the genres of comedy and tragedy.[2] These particular models bring very different styles, ethical concerns, and other associations to satire. Their impact will be more fully understood after I analyze the satiric representations of drama later in this chapter, but it is useful to begin by surveying the poets' more explicit claims.

Horace is our primary source for the idea that Roman satire descends from Athenian Old Comedy. He claims that his predecessor Lucilius followed the playwrights Eupolis, Cratinus, and Aristophanes in attacking individuals with complete freedom of speech (*libertas*, *Sermones* 1.4.1–7). Horace also notes that Old Comic diction exhibits a variation in tone that all careful poets should emulate: "Those men who wrote Old Comedy had their success from this; in this they should be imitated" (*illi scripta quibus comoedia prisca viris est / hoc stabant, hoc sunt imitandi*, 1.10.16–17).[3] Framing his relationship with comic models in more personal terms, Horace reveals that he brings "Plato . . . Menander, Eupolis, and Archilochus" along to his country retreat (2.3.11–12). Although this glimpse at Horace's bookbag tantalizes more than it clarifies his literary agenda, the list of the poet's literary "companions" (*comites*, 12) continues the programmatic motif of a relationship between Roman satire and Greek comic genres. The mention of Eupolis echoes Horace's comic genealogy of satire in 1.4, while the iambic Archilochus and the New Comic playwright Menander suggest diverse comic influences.[4]

One of the curious paradoxes attached to satire is the idea that this "wholly Roman" genre could be a descendent of the genre that died with classical Athens. The claim lends to satire the reverend status of an otherwise inimitable literary and social practice, while glossing over significant differences in form, production, subject matter, and political context.[5] The fourth-century CE grammarian Diomedes, most likely drawing on Horace's remarks, confidently describes satire as a "a kind of poetry among the Romans . . . composed in the manner of Old [Greek] Comedy for the purpose of carping at people's vices" (*carmen apud Romanos . . . ad carpenda hominum vitia archaeae comoediae charactere compositum*).[6] But the self-evident connection that the grammarian identifies is not expressed so clearly by Horace's successor in satire. Persius, in his own first *Satire*, assures his audience that if they like Eupolis, Cratinus, and Aristophanes, they will also like his poetry (1.123–125). In this way he stops short of positing a literary genealogy or even a shared social agenda, suggesting a more subtle basis for the comparison.

Comic drama also provides a useful model for satire's historical development, as demonstrated by Horace's respective characterizations of Lucilius and himself. The same poem that begins with the comparison of Lucilian invective and Old Comic *libertas* goes on to point to the gentle social criticism typical of New Comedy as a model for Horace's own satire. This relationship is illustrated in the portrait of the poet's own moralizing father, modeled on the old-fashioned *paterfamilias* of Terentian comedy in particular.[7] *Sermones* 1.4 thus constructs an account of comic drama's evolution to which satire's own development is meant to be compared.[8] This prompts readers of satire to adopt a classificatory mindset as they approach the genre and compare its individual authors. Such a hint is made not just when Horace draws a dichotomy between works inspired by Old and New Comedy, but in Juvenal's comparisons of his satire to an entirely different dramatic model, tragedy. The sixth *Satire* of Juvenal, devoted to the flaws and crimes of women, culminates in accusations of routine murder. The satirist acknowledges that his high-flown language and tales of crime smack of tragedy, although his examples are taken from real life (634–638). Similarly, Juvenal compares his story of Egyptian cannibalism in *Satire* 15 to the crimes memorialized in tragedies—although the poet boasts that his story is more heinous because the guilty party is an entire *populus* (29–31). In both passages, Juvenal draws a comparison between his genre and tragedy, under the pretext of noting some fundamental differences (real crimes are worse than legendary ones; tragedy can only be about individuals).

As the moralizing comic father of *Sermones* 1.4 is replaced in Juvenal 1 by the image of a burning, bellowing Lucilius, who frightens rather than amuses his audience (165–167), so Juvenalian satire overall invites comparison with more high-flown genres. Critics have readily classified Juvenal's satire as a tragic counterpart to Horace's comic version.[9] But like Horace's tendentious literary-historical narrative in *Sermones* 1.4, Juvenal's programmatic gestures engage audience expectations about genre and tradition, rather than imposing a simple descriptive label. The ambiguities in the comparison made in *Satire* 6 show the way to a more nuanced picture of the relationships between satire and dramatic genres. That passage actually takes the form of a complicated rhetorical question, which does not receive a thorough answer:

> fingimus haec altum satura sumente coturnum
> scilicet, et finem egressi legemque priorum
> grande Sophocleo carmen bacchamur hiatu
> montibus ignotum Rutulis caeloque Latino?
> nos utinam vani.

> Surely I'm inventing this, with my satire taking up the high tragic boot,
> and I've passed the boundary and law set by my predecessors
> and am reveling in Sophoclean bombast to produce a poetry
> alien to Rutulian mountains and the sky of Latium?
> I *wish* I were making it up. (6.634–638)

As it is framed here, the comparison between satire and tragedy can only be accepted by an especially compliant reader. In itself, Juvenal's question, with its multiple verbs, participles, and adjectives, is ambiguous. Just how does Juvenal, and/or his interlocutor, conceive the relation between his satire and tragedy, and the generic transgression involved? Has he in fact passed beyond a *lex operis*? Is tragic subject matter in fact alien to Italy? The rhetorical presentation leaves all of this unclear. Juvenal's allusion to tragedy, via the words of the imaginary critic, places the responsibility for assessing the comparison on readers. Readers, for their part, must consult their understanding of tragedy's origins and workings in order to evaluate this characterization of Juvenalian satire. They may come to the conclusion that the series of claims are far from accurate. There is certainly no known generic *lex* that specifically forbids Juvenal to treat the subjects he does, and tragedy—which after all, like satire, addresses serious ethical and political matters—was one of the first literary genres produced in Rome.[10] Yet the very invitation to classify Juvenal's satire, clearly so different from Horace's, as "tragic" could also prompt readers to tailor or simplify their views of tragedy and comedy.

The system of classical dramatic forms provides a vocabulary for the criticism of satire that hinges on perceived differences between dramatic genres. By comparing their work with one or more types of drama, the satirists engage readers' preconceptions about both satire and drama at once. This makes the work of classifying satire more dependent on issues of reception and criticism, and consequently more charged and subjective; where there are gaps or disagreements about critical issues, there is more potential for these issues to seep into satire's generic space.

Comparisons based on specific genres, however, are only one manifestation of the analogy between satire and drama. After all, it is possible to use the labels "comic" and "tragic" to refer only to poetic style or tone, without hinting at the full theatrical context in which comedy and tragedy were produced. The satirists actually play up a deeper connection between their work and dramatic performance in general: they pose as directors, performers and spectators in a world that they cast as "dramatic." Burns dubs this practice "theatricality," and argues that it is guided by perception rather than intention or real circumstances:

> Theatricality is not . . . a mode of behavior or expression, but attaches itself to any kind of behavior perceived and interpreted by others and described (mentally or explicitly) in theatrical terms. These others are more aware of the symbolic than of the instrumental aspect of any behavior which they feel that they can describe as theatrical . . . theatricality itself is determined by a particular viewpoint, a mode of perception.[11]

The Roman satirists construct a world where actions and utterances, including their own, are viewed as performances or responses to performances. Imaginary theater supplements the influence of real theater, spectacle, and dramatic literary traditions in the satiric representation of human affairs.

As the vivid dialogues staged in many satiric poems illustrate, satire is a dramaturgical project.[12] A number of the satirists' programmatic comments play up the performative aspects of satiric critique or of human behavior. Persius, for one, suggests that he is a kind of dramatist. The poet argues with a hostile interlocutor for one-third of his first *Satire* before freely admitting that he has invented this character and put words in his mouth: "Whoever you are, whom I have made to speak from the opposite side" (*quisquis es, o modo quem ex adverso dicere feci*, 44). The satirist here acknowledges his role as the creator of all speaking parts in his poems; this associates his work both with forensic rhetoric and with drama, two spheres of ancient literary culture that were intimately related. The ancient commentary compares Persius' address to his character to a device of mime and comedy.[13] By breaking the dramatic illusion, Persius represents the writing of satire as a dramaturgical endeavor. This is certainly a valid programmatic announcement, given the multitude of speakers who appear in the *Satires* often to the confusion of editors.[14] Only in the fourth *Satire* does the poet give explicit instructions to his reader to imagine the poem as a dramatic dialogue, when at the outset he identifies its two speakers as Socrates and Alcibiades (1–3). But Persius' direct address to his interlocutor in the programmatic dialogue of *Satire* 1 draws attention to the pervasive dramaturgical element of his genre.

Juvenal advertises his role as dramaturge as well. With the weary-sounding introduction to *Satire* 4, "here comes Crispinus again, and I often have to summon him to play his role" (*ecce iterum Crispinus, et est mihi saepe vocandus / ad partes*, 1–2), Juvenal poses as a dramatist who must retell historical events using the actual participants as actors. The memory of his schooling that Juvenal presents at 1.15–17 foreshadows this aspect of his work as satirist; Juvenal recalls being trained in declamation, an activity that involved reconstruction of historical scenarios and role-playing.[15] While in *Satires* 6 and 15 Juvenal compares the subject matter of his satire to tragic plots, at the opening of *Satire* 4 he fleshes out the dramatic analogy slightly by pointing to the mechanical process behind his reenactment ("staging") of events.[16] This technique operates in the most colorful *Satires*: for example, in *Satire* 2, Juvenal parades sexual deviants as if on stage, appealing to his Roman audience with a combination of titillation and moralizing.[17]

Satirists also pose as performers, as distinct from behind-the-scenes dramatists. This conveys the idea that their work itself is subject to direct critical view. Horace, claiming that a small and enlightened readership is enough for him, declares "for it is enough that the knights applaud me, as the brazen Arbuscula said, scorning the rest, when she was hissed at" (*nam satis est equitem mihi plaudere, ut audax / contemptis aliis explosa Arbuscula dixit*, 1.10.76–77). The mime actress to whom Horace compares himself makes a strange and undignified model, but her appearance is memorably and significantly placed at the end of book 1. This instance of self-presentation, instead of giving the satirist figure the insulated status of dramatic author, subjects him to the associations of performance. In a far more melodramatic image, Juvenal speculates that satirizing powerful individuals may earn him the punishment of death in the arena (1.155–157). Like Horace, Juvenal imagines himself on view before his public and his targets, as if satire's exposing function were being inverted to make the poet a victim.[18] As subsequent chapters will discuss further, the Juvenalian case involves not only exposure, but also violence and punishment, and so represents several of satire's social models merged and focused on the satirist figure himself.

Finally, satire's subject matter is sometimes represented as inherently dramatic, rather than as raw material shaped by the poet. Horace imagines that the dinner party of Nasidienus, which he himself missed, was better than a public show ("I would have preferred to witness no shows more than these," *nullos his mallem ludos spectasse*, 2.8.79). The description attributes a theatrical quality to a ritual of everyday life; it also expands the sense of "theater" to include the whole range of entertainments offered at Roman public festivals (*ludi*). Likewise, Juvenal draws his readers along by contending that human behavior makes a better spectacle than anything offered at the festivals (14.256–264).[19] As in *Satire* 6, Juvenal is contrasting the real-world subject matter of his poetry with relatively tame dramatic performances, and even implying that the ready-made spectacle of everyday life needs no modification by a dramatic artist.

These programmatic references, which connect satire to specific dramatic genres, and to performance broadly construed, invite examination of other appearances of drama in satire. When Horace, Persius, and Juvenal represent theatrical activity or employ other dramatic references in their arguments, they are treating a subject close to their own enterprise. Performance and spectatorship are modes of play and criticism that satire imitates. Nevertheless, the satirists examine these practices with a critical, analytical eye, not merely trotting out convenient references, but exploring the functions and effects of theater itself. Their narratives and vignettes develop the portrayal of the playful, critical, and punitive functions of theater to which they allude in programmatic references.

This investigation is enriched by our knowledge that the theater itself held an ambiguous place in the minds of Romans. The elite Roman attitude toward theater and spectacle was split between appreciation for the moral and political utility of performance, and suspicion of the practice and its participants.[20] On the one hand, tragic and comic plays, as part of the educational curriculum, were understood to have moral uses; the culture's taste for performance created a mechanism for politicians to sponsor festivals and curry favor; even the assembly and arrangement of the populace could give off an air of orderliness and enable communication of sorts between people and officials (and, by the late first century BCE, emperors in particular). On the other hand, such assemblies could provoke unrest; plays could send out subversive messages troubling to those who held power; and actors themselves were regarded by many with suspicion or contempt. On the broader social level as well, the theater (especially comic theater) served the dual function of providing fantasy and escape for the audience while working to reinforce the normal social hierarchy.[21] Theater thus acted out two opposed but closely associated desires of the community—for liberation and for stability. Each dramatic performance presented opportunities for the conflict and the resolution of these desires.

Were satire's agenda one of simple moralizing, satirists might appeal only selectively to drama as a model—emphasizing drama's edifying content, for example, instead of the ambiguous aspects of its production and reception. But as part of a general program of self-scrutiny and self-exposure, the satirists probe, and implicate themselves in, all aspects of the theater and its reception in Rome. Drama makes a useful model for them precisely because it is so politically and morally charged and troubling; it is both a vehicle for exposure of social problems and a fertile target for satire's own exposing mission. The satirists especially play up the potential for drama's functions to overlap with other practices related to satire—violence, legal process, and teaching—while never simplifying or sanitizing the meaning of any one of these practices.

IN VOLGO ET SCAENA

Horace's use of drama in his self-presentation has a dimension and subtlety that is best appreciated through an examination of the Arbuscula reference in *Sermones* 1.10. The poem itself serves as Horace's formal self-defense, as author and protégé of Maecenas, at the close of his first book of satire. The image of Horace as Arbuscula (76–77) resonates in curious ways with other aspects of the poet's self-portrait, showing that the analogy can generate tensions and ambiguities. For one thing, it comes shortly after Horace has stressed, in two ways, that his satire is *not* drama. Defending his careful work and discriminating audience, he declares that his little-known poems will not "return again and again to be watched on stage" (*nec redeant iterum atque iterum spectanda theatris*, 39). Next, he lists the current masters in Roman poetic genres, beginning with Fundanius the comic playwright (40–42); this list ends with Horace's explanation that he himself has chosen to write in a genre with no living master. Nevertheless, this is followed by an image of the poet as Arbuscula, a dramatic performer.

Horace's particular choice of model is also striking—and not only because Arbuscula is a woman, standing for Horace even as he describes his elite male social and literary world. She is also a *mima*. While mime was a popular form of entertainment even among the elite of the late Republic and the Augustan period (as attested by Cicero's praise of the same Arbuscula),[22] it still had a reputation as a low genre. Not only is this the sort of performance that *did* appear in theaters "again and again," but Horace specifically compares himself to the actress herself, rather than a writer (an analogy that might make more sense). Actors and especially *mimae* had a dubious status in Roman society. Thus the anecdote has an odd ring at a moment where Horace is arguing that he belongs in Maecenas' group of literati, and at the end of a book in which he has so carefully narrated and illustrated his intimacy with that group. However convenient the sketch for illustrating Horace's point about audience taste, the comparison undermines the poet's ostensible agenda in the passage: to solidify his hard-won social and literary status.

The critical message in the anecdote is also relevant to Horace's self-presentation. Arbuscula is scorning a large part of her audience, content with the section that has applauded her instead of hissing. This emphasizes that the theater is a place of public judgment and, inevitably, dissent; in turn, this aids Horace's defense of his anticipated small readership. By identifying himself with a performer and expressing the desire for a discriminating audience, he give his boast the color of a Terentian prologue, in which an actor defends and promotes the playwright.[23] But the *mima* is a special alter ego that gives the poet a particular edge as critic. By suddenly getting on stage, as it were, Horace takes on a resemblance to a figure whom he derides at the opening of the same poem. At 1.10.5–6, Horace criticizes those who value his predecessor Lucilius for his wit alone, pointing out that "by that reasoning, I'd also have to admire the mimes of Laberius as if they were fine poems" (*nam sic / et Laberi mimos ut pulchra poemata mirer*). It is noteworthy that Horace chooses as an example of a mime writer the knight who was compelled by Julius Caesar to act in one of his own pieces as punishment for his criticisms, and who used the opportunity to criticize Caesar again from the stage.[24] His temporary humiliation ironically gave Laberius the power to criticize; this ambiguous status is not unlike the posture that Horace takes when he styles himself as a *mima*.

Horace's provocative choice of alter ego exposes some of the aesthetic, ethical, and political complexities of drama, and associates them with satire. In other theatrical scenes in the *Sermones*, Horace uses his genre's dramatic affiliations as a vehicle for creating a more complex picture of satire. He performs the duty of a satirist by representing drama three-dimensionally, as it were—by pointing up not only its potential edifying purpose, but its dubious participants, its divided reception, and its occasional misuse. By association, satire's own critical postures and procedures are put on display for its readers to critique. The theatrical perspective influences each satirist's model of the world. But a unique feature of Horace's theatrical satire, and a consequence of the strong presence of this poet's *ego*, is that the satirist figure himself acts out many of theater's functions and its problems. This satirist exhibits a knee-jerk Roman prejudice against performers even though he elsewhere allies himself with them; he borrows convenient ethical exempla from drama but also acts as an exemplum and a target of sermons; and he condemns ill-applied theatrical logic while using the same logic himself.

While he styles himself as a performer, Horace also encourages a moral interpretation of theatrical activity that follows the typical Roman elite prejudice against actors and other performers. Actors in the Roman world attracted suspicion, a phenomenon that Edwards has discussed at length. Their marginal social status was paradoxically empowering: they performed in a space where power structures and cultural beliefs could be challenged, while they themselves had no status to lose. They were also proverbially sexually desirable, a sort of hybrid of the prostitute on display and the adulterer lurking in the home; by the same token, they were viewed as living in the thrall of the passions that they simulated and aroused in others.[25] This makes performers, especially those in low genres such as mime and farce, suitable "extras" in *Sermones* 1.2, where Horace criticizes irresponsible erotic dalliances. Even the poem's opening, a prelude to the discussion of sexual matters, conjures a self-contained social world of *mimae*, musicians, and other entertainers and peddlers, all in mourning for one of their own[26]:

> ambubaiarum collegia, pharmacopolae,
> mendici, mimae, balatrones, hoc genus omne
> maestum ac sollicitum est cantoris morte Tigelli.

> The companies of flute-girls, the potion-sellers,
> beggars, mime actresses, jesters—this whole species is
> wretched and distressed at the death of the singer Tigellius.
> (1.2.1–3)

Divorced from the performance context in which they may actually exert power over their audience, these characters appear only as emotional and dissolute, reflections of the prejudice against their professions. A hint of the same prejudice is seen in the lecture on madness delivered to Horace by the Stoic Damasippus (*Sermones* 2.3). Damasippus holds up a number of appropriate exempla of madness from tragedy and comedy: Orestes (132–141), Ajax and Agamemnon (187–223), Agave (303–304), and the conflicted comic lover debating with his slave (259–271).[27] But he also cannot resist trotting out an anecdote about a drunken tragic actor as an example of obliviousness (60–62). Asleep onstage, Fufius turned his audience into participants in his humiliation, and rendered his tragic dream scene (he was playing the sleeping Iliona) merely ridiculous. His public failure makes him an especially good exemplum.

In drawing on the theater for ethical material in two very different ways, Damasippus echoes the more obviously mixed perspective of the poet. While performers are easy satiric targets, the ethical content of drama is valuable currency for a moralist. Horace employs many stock types from comedy in vignettes about social behavior and human motivation; examples are the bumpkin (1.3.29–32), the stern father (1.4.105–120; cf. 48–56), the spendthrift and the miser (1.2.4–22; cf. 1.1.41–99), the adulterer (1.2.38–46 and 127–133, 2.7.53–67), the cheeky slave (Davus, the primary speaker in 2.7, who shares his name with one of Terence's slaves), and the parasite (2.7.36–39, 2.8.21–24).[28] Comedy's stock characters represent particular vices, foibles, or misguided attitudes. But Horace does not take a strictly utilitarian approach to the ethical content of drama. He, too, acts as a dramatic subject, and with largely unflattering effects. In the diatribe poems, *Sermones* 1.1–3, Horace may be in rhetorical control, but he is also an inept philosopher, the comic *doctor ineptus*.[29] As he takes more passive dramatic roles in the "self-incriminating" book 2, he appears more and more to be under the control of the dramatic world that he has created.[30] The parade of stand-in satirists, other *doctores inepti*, puts the procedure of satiric moral criticism on display for the reader's amusement in ways that monologues by the satirist cannot.

Meanwhile, Horace himself becomes a target of satire, subject to lectures first from the Stoic Damasippus (2.3) and then from the slave Davus (2.7). Both encounters are set in the period of the Saturnalia holiday, a time that encourages role-reversal. Damasippus foregrounds his competitive stance toward the satirist by noting at the outset that Horace is not using his literary (and largely comic) models well: "What was the point of packing Plato with Menander, Eupolis, and Archilochus, of bringing along such impressive companions?" (*quorsum pertinuit stipare Platona Menandro, / Eupolin, Archilochum, comites educere tantos?* 11–12). Horace's arsenal of *comites* sits idle, and Damasippus takes advantage of his lapse to construct his own form of *sermo*, laced with exempla from the stage. The second lecture delivered against Horace's flaws constitutes a different kind of reversal which pushes Horace further into a subject role under the control of drama. Davus is not only a new *doctor* but a character straight from comedy, taking advantage of the rules of the Saturnalia to lecture his master (4–5). Although he is technically Horace's property—both literally and in the sense that he is a piece of the poet's comic arsenal—he temporarily overpowers his master and frames him as a comic parasite (32–42) and adulterer (46, 53–61).

The literary performance that begins, in *Sermones* 1.1, with the diatribist Horace actively constructing and participating in a dramatic world evolves, as if organically, into a drama that features Horace as a character. In the final poem of book 2, this shift of control is represented in the dominant role of Fundanius, the comic poet also named in 1.10. Horace's own position is markedly passive and marginal; he has been excluded from the comic event that was Nasidienus' dinner party, and depends on his friend for an account. An even more powerful figure from the world of comedy than Davus, Fundanius shapes Horace's experience of a drama that he did not witness firsthand.

Horace's embrace of the comic world at the beginning of the *Sermones*, like his self-identification with Arbuscula, has far-reaching consequences. The poet's staged displacement is an important subtext of the *Sermones*, also manifested in his approach to the themes of violence, law, and teaching (cf. chapters 2, 3, and 4). But this development is certainly not an earnest demonstration of a real loss of control; it is Horace who gives rhetorical power to his speakers, and reduces his own.[31] Drama is not just the satirist's literary or ethical property; it encourages payment in kind from Horace, in the form of his own satire.

Even the assertion of authority and discrimination with which Horace concludes his most confident apologia implicates him in the flawed comic world of the *Sermones*. Arbuscula the *mima* offers to Horace a useful retort to critics: "It is enough that the knights applaud me, as the brazen Arbuscula said, scorning the rest, when she was hissed at" (*satis est equitem mihi plaudere, ut audax / contemptis aliis explosa Arbuscula dixit*, 1.10.76–77). In the context of Horace's boasts about his discriminating friends, this attitude seems appropriate. But it also echoes an earlier passage with a very different message. The foolish miser conjured at 1.1.66–67 sees his lifestyle in theatrical terms, and justifies his behavior in this way: "The people hiss at me, but I applaud myself at home" (*populus me sibilat, at mihi plaudo / ipse domi*). This character's adoption of a theatrical perspective is guided by his self-interest and not by an interest in his own enlightenment; his case is paradigmatic for the diatribes. But at the end of the book, in response to analogous circumstances, Horace and his alter ego use basically the same logic. To be sure, Arbuscula gets her confidence from the approval of a discriminating audience, but there is still a noticeable symmetry in thought with the earlier passage. The theatrical perspective has wide applicability, and no stable moral utility.

Horace's foregrounding of his debt to drama and theatricality has one more important effect: it is his means of promoting his unique contribution to the satiric genre. When Horace portrays his targets as comic characters, he is engaging in a stripping down of status and dignity that depends on the Roman elite conception of theatrical performance as akin to prostitution.[32] His work achieves the same end as the phenomenon of the "noble mime," (*mimus nobilis*, a type that appears at Juvenal 8.198–199). At first glance, it seems as though Horace is imitating the Lucilian satiric procedure of "stripping off the hide" (*detrahere . . . pellem*)—exposing the foul nature that people hide under a façade.[33] This description of Lucilius' work is Horace's own, and appears in the programmatic opening poem of *Sermones* 2:

>. . . est Lucilius ausus
>primus in hunc operis componere carmina morem,
>detrahere et pellem, nitidus qua quisque per ora
>cederet, introrsum turpis ...
>
>. . . Lucilius first dared
>to compose poems in this genre,
>and to tear away the hide in which everyone went about in public
>looking shiny and clean, though foul within . . .
>(2.1.62–65)

Clearly both Horace's method, and the method that he ascribes to his predecessor, aim to debase and debunk. But a closer reading of the passage above sheds a different light on Horace's strategy. The process that Horace imagines Lucilius to have employed is actually inverted in the *Sermones*: instead of stripping off a façade, Horace clothes his targets in comic garb. Meanwhile, Horace seems to be representing Lucilius' attacks (whether accurately or not) as an antitheatrical endeavor—that is, tearing apart people's acts was the Republican satirist's mission.³⁴ This idea is picked up in an equally suggestive image a few lines later. Horace goes on to conjure a picture of Lucilius delivering his satire for his friends "away from the crowd and the theater" (*a volgo et scaena*, 71). *Scaena* has a metaphorical sense here, referring to public life,³⁵ but Horace's use of the term underscores the point communicated in the earlier passage: the agenda of Lucilius was to oppose dishonest social theater.

For Horace, theatricality itself—the orchestration and enactment of everyday drama—is the satirist's work. Theatricality is an enabling mode for this poet, not an insidious societal practice that he must sabotage and break down. Even when adopting drama as a model means importing all the problems of its reception and implicating oneself in that world, this is clearly Horace's choice. Satire becomes dramatic in every sense of the term recognized by Roman society. By writing this new version of satire into the genre's history (which necessitates rewriting the formula of the Lucilian project), Horace creates a paradigm that his successors must address. Persius and Juvenal each add to the dramatic definition of satire, expanding and nuancing Horace's model of social theater.

PRIVATE VIEWINGS

While Horace converts his satire to a performance subject to criticism, another option for the dramatist-satirist is to reinvent drama itself to better fit his intended satiric mode. This is the approach of Persius, who is overall less self-mocking than Horace, although no less fascinated with his genre's ambiguous social models. Persius uses the Horatian theatrical paradigm selectively and innovatively. Twice in his first *Satire*, the poet points to a connection between his satire and drama. He admits to writing the various parts in his programmatic dialogue ("you whom I made to speak," *quem . . . dicere feci*, 44), acknowledging that satire imitates drama's form. He also claims that admirers of Old Comedy will also like his satire (123–125), obliquely recalling the literary-historical association outlined in *Sermones* 1.4. These brief programmatic comments read almost like a capsule summary of the earlier poet's use of drama in defining his genre, at once evoking the involved discussions and numerous vignettes of drama in the *Sermones*, and condensing them into a synopsis that on the surface looks rather simple.

Persius' abbreviation of so many Horatian discussions and images parallels the more subtle theatrical landscape of his *Satires*. The busy dramatic world of the *Sermones* is gone, including, for the most part, comic exempla used for moralizing purposes. Where Persius does present such an exemplum, Hooley senses an effort at emotional realism that resists a reductive moral interpretation. Describing a lover's agonized hesitation at his girlfriend's door (5.161–174), Persius synthesizes Horatian, Terentian, and elegiac material, but he also produces a psychologically authentic portrayal of inner struggle with the potential to elicit sympathy rather than mockery.³⁶ Hooley's impression that Persius aims to reinvent and recontextualize this literary *topos* (recalling the way that Lucilius allegedly undid social theatricality) is supported by the poet's treatment of dramatic matters elsewhere. In Persius, the most salient difference from Horace is his relocation of drama from its public context into a private transaction between reader and text. The experience of drama that Persius depicts in his *Satires* is a personal, intense internalization of dramatic texts, not a public and communal event featuring a large cast of performers.

Such is the impression that Persius creates with the curious image of his ideal audience near the end of *Satire* 1. While Horace's capsule history of Old Comedy evokes a public performance context ("they marked [criminals] out with great freedom of speech," *multa cum libertate notabant*, 1.4.5), Persius imagines someone diligently reading the comedians, pale from concentration (*palles*, 124). The functional similarity between the genres is not made explicit: Persius does not follow Horace in positing that satire shares a public and punitive function with Old Comedy, but only declares that an enlightened reader will enjoy both. Even the image of private enjoyment is puzzling, for the passage mixes terms referring to reading with others referring to hearing: "Look at this [poetry] too, if you have an ear for something more refined; let my reader's ear be cleansed and fired by [Old Comic texts]" (*aspice et haec, si forte aliquid decoctius audis / inde vaporata lector mihi ferveat aure*, 125–126).[37] This hypothetical reader seems to transform the experience of reading a written text into a private recitation, which still preserves the fiery tone of Old Comedy (even in textual form, Cratinus is "bold," *audaci*, and Eupolis "angry," *iratum*, 123–124). But any sense of public performance (including a recitation scenario, the context of Persius' own entrance into the literary scene) is definitely missing. What has happened to the Horatian literary history, in which the Old Comic poets were conjured up in their original, socially valuable performance setting (*notabant*, 1.4.5)? The image that Persius presents is very different. It emphasizes just how dead Old Comedy is, at least as far as its performance context is concerned—dead long before Lucilius appropriated its social function or Horace adapted its diction; imagined as a set of canonical texts rather than as live, topical productions. The allusion to Horace is indisputable, but much has been elided or disguised.

When we consider how Persius represents drama elsewhere, it becomes apparent that Old Comedy's relegation to textual form is part of a larger pattern. Persius treats the subject of poets and their work in the first *Satire*, particularly love poetry and epyllion; dramatists, however, are virtually absent. Two archaic tragedians do appear in a sense: Accius is equated with the "veined" book that holds his plays (76), and Pacuvius with his "warty" drama on Antiope (77–78). While we can almost see the pulpits, the readers, and the audiences of love poetry and epyllion, and especially the intense physical responses of the listeners,[38] actual dramatic works appear only in material form in this poem. As much as this emphasis on public recitation reflects the realities of the first century CE, there may also be a programmatic agenda underlying Persius' treatment of the topic in this poem, and specifically a message about drama and its relation to satire. It is clear that in contrast to the well-attended recitations of tired imitation-Alexandrian poetry, images of the dissemination of satire emphasize the private: he will have no readers, or maybe two (lines 2–3); he has decided to whisper his words into a ditch (119–120). The picture near the end of the poem of a discriminating reader poring over the triumvirate of Old Comedy seems to be reinforcing the message that Persius, like Horace in *Sermones* 1.10, wants and expects a small readership. But what has happened to the other significant quality of drama—the assembly of speakers and voices—on which Persius draws to script his apologia? One may well expect that kind of dynamic, or for that matter the presence of an audience, to have some part in this satirist's representation of drama.

An actor does appear toward the end of Persius' book, but his method of performing is surprising. At the opening of *Satire* 5, musing upon the conventional poet's wish for a hundred mouths, Persius imagines such poets actually eating their poetry instead of producing it: "What great lumps of solid poetry are you cramming in, that require the labor of a hundred throats?" (*quantas robusti carminis offas / ingeris, ut par sit centeno gutture niti*? 5–6). Shifting to the subject of tragic poetry in particular, Persius pictures an actor eating his part: the "pot [of tragic texts] will boil often to be dined on by the dull Glyco" (*olla . . . fervebit saepe insulso cenanda Glyconi*, 8–9). This constitutes a crude joke on the particular tragic stories of Procne and Thyestes (named in line 8), both of which feature acts of cannibalism. But the representation of the actor's function itself is an absurd demystification, and, as with the poets, a counterintuitive one: Persius describes Glyco consuming or absorbing the tragedies, rather than delivering them to an audience. Even Glyco's name (glykōn, "sweet") evokes consumption, and his performance reads like greedy fixation on the texts (*saepe . . . cenanda*).[39] Here, now that Persius is finally alluding to an element of performed drama—namely, an actor—he figures the act of performing, or at least of learning the drama, as an inwardly directed process.

The inept Glyco can point us to a better understanding of Persius' adoption of Old Comedy as a shadowy model in *Satire* 1. The satirist's ideal audience is someone deeply engrossed in reading. The pallor of the hypothetical reader reflects not merely his single-minded diligence, but the enthusiasm and emotion that he feels while absorbed in books[40]—a mirror of the poets' own passion (*audaci, iratum*). Even though he is not witnessing a real performance, the reader of Old Comedy is still captured by the text—perhaps even more so than he would be in a theater, since he must imagine the action and dialogue himself. This recalls Persius' reference to his interlocutor (*quem . . . dicere feci*). That passage clues us in to a key feature of Persian satire: as dramatist-satirist, Persius seems to act out all the parts in his polyphonous poems. Some scholars have interpreted *Satire* 3, which features an earnest Stoic and an ill-tempered and lazy student, as a dialogue between the poet's "higher" and "lower" selves.[41] One critic comments that Persius gives his many characters a rather uniform speaking style.[42] The *Satires* are full of speakers with different social positions and attitudes, and yet the dramatic structure around them is quite transparent. As he admits in his programmatic dialogue, Persius acts all of the parts that he creates.

The theme of self-scrutiny that the *Satires* use as a refrain puts this theatrical model to work in the moral sphere. The first advice that the satirist gives is to avoid external evaluators and exempla: "Do not look outside yourself" (*nec te quaesiveris extra*, 1.7). The challenge is internal evaluation, which necessitates playing critic and object (or viewer and performer) at once. Persius' poem on prayer, *Satire* 2, exposes not the "vanity of human wishes" that Juvenal's tenth *Satire* makes its theme, but the practice of uttering false prayers that cover secret, greedy hopes. Persius revives the Lucilian project (as represented by Horace) of stripping away shining exteriors, but he performs this work in a private setting, proposing that one's own conscience should be the most fearsome judge. *Satire* 4 also warns of the dangers of looking for external objects of criticism, instead recommending a "descent into oneself" (*in sese . . . descendere*, 23). The dialogue between Socrates and Alcibiades, punctuated with quotations of other zealous social critics, adroitly exposes the human tendency to look for targets "out there" in society.[43] The satirist's ventriloquism thematizes the act of criticism while confounding the reader's attempt to organize, attribute, and interpret that criticism. The poem concludes with the injunction to "live with yourself" (*tecum habita*, 52), echoing the formulas at 1.7 and 4.23. Persius' model of dramatic self-scrutiny constitutes an alternative to the public stage of Horatian theatricality.

The reader at 1.123–125 is ready for this process, for he is able to bring dead drama back to life in his head. His private excitement contrasts directly with that of the gushing, performing audiences of bad poetry earlier in that poem, who seem to attend recitals just so that they can be seen reacting.[44] His careful reading also contrasts with the method of Glyco the actor, whose repeated devouring of texts only adds to his air of dullness. All acts of reading and performance are internal processes in Persius, but there is a right way and a wrong way to engage with texts. Curiously, the readers in *Satire* 1 who are held up as antitheses to the reader of Old Comedy also inappropriately combine literature with eating: the satirist advises them to limit themselves to "the Edict in the morning, and 'Callirhoe' after lunch" (*mane edictum, post prandia Callirhoen*, 1.134). Texts (and subliterary ones at that[45]) are forced to fit around these readers' gastronomic programs, rather than holding primary importance; moreover, while they consume literature on a full stomach, Persius' reader approaches his texts with open, cleansed ears (*vaporata . . . aure*, 1.126).

But there is still more programmatic value in Persius' ideal reader. His quiet entrancement over the Old Comic poets recalls Horace's deficiencies as a reader in *Sermones* 2.3: Damasippus points out there that the now unproductive satirist has packed his books, including Eupolis, in vain (11–12). That Horace, the real author of Damasippus' accusation, is reluctant to "use" these models may indicate that he recognizes the tensions between them.[46] But this does not preclude the possibility that Persius is rewriting the account of Horace's stalled reading program in order to promote himself. Where Horace leaves us with the image of the books still packed and waiting to be read, Persius' ideal reader dives in.

Persius further enhances his reader's desirability by concealing his actual feelings and thoughts, just as he obscures the precise relationship between Old Comedy and satire. The abbreviated allusion to the Horatian generic history of *Sermones* 1.4 and 1.10 becomes a tendentious reminder of Horace's paralysis as a reader (at least as portrayed in the Saturnalian *Sermones* 2, a book to which Persius alludes frequently). This new satirist gives us a reader so engaged that he is growing pale, so entranced that he does not explain to us why his reading material matters so much. Tantalizing his readers with the idea that they may find such excitement themselves, Persius ends his programmatic poem with an invitation to the wise, and a dismissal of the rest. Satire, like drama when it falls into the right hands (literally), becomes an opportunity for private reflection, even private self-critique.

THE MIRRORS OF DRAMA AND SATIRE

Persius converts the Horatian theatrical mode to a unique hybrid of text and performance. His successor, in an expansive move that we will see replicated in different ways with each model for satire, redirects the dramatic analogy back to a performance context. In the poems of Juvenal, the dramatic analogy appears in the greatest variety of forms, with the satirist figure taking different positions at every turn. Juvenal poses as a dramatist at times, but he also often calls attention to his own performance as if he were an actor; at other times, he pretends to be a mere spectator of human affairs, which already resemble theatrical productions. In Juvenal, too, many images of performance—more than in his predecessors—adumbrate theories of drama that in turn reflect on his satire. Satiric alter egos from the world of the theater offer explanations of how playwriting, acting, and spectatorship work. In a sense Juvenal provides the fullest explanation of what an affiliation with drama can mean for the satirist. It is he who most closely scrutinizes satire's trademark device, the persona. He also problematizes the interpretation of drama, and delves into the psychology of the audience, where Horace only categorizes viewers and Persius concentrates on describing physical responses. This critique of drama reflects Juvenal's investment in the dramatic aspects of his own work and his willingness to subject that work to critical scrutiny.

Juvenal suggests that he regularly assumes the role of dramatist: "I often have to summon Crispinus to play his role" (*Crispinus . . . est mihi saepe vocandus / ad partes*, 4.1–2). This gesture directs us to consider how Juvenal's satiric subjects imitate—or even rival—dramatic plots. Other comparisons have similar aims. Nero, a representative of the debased modern nobility, was a second Orestes in that he, too, murdered his mother, although the motives of the two men differed (8.215–221).[47] Human affairs, especially behavior driven by greed and ambition, are more entertaining than plays or games (14.256–264). The tale of an entire village's cannibalistic frenzy is more shocking than tragedies concerned with similar crimes (15.29–31). Each of these allusions to drama and theater—or to other types of entertainment, in a noteworthy expansion of the programmatic metaphor—hangs on the idea that drama and real life share the same subject matter, while also declaring that reality offers more sordid and disturbing material.

Juvenal's allusions to satire's dramatic qualities recall two functions of drama explored by the previous satirists: its ethical utility (expressed in Horace by the parading of exempla and the references to theater as a site of judgment), and its entertainment value (suggested by the applause of Horace's audiences and the engagement of Persius' reader). Yet Juvenal does not highlight these functions in his apologia. In *Satire* 1, Juvenal professes a number of motives for his literary project. Because everyone else in Rome is churning out poetry, he might as well make a contribution (1–18); he also cannot restrain himself from complaining about current conditions (30–31, 63–64), and he longs to punish the criminals who freely parade about Rome (158–159). These claims about the role of satire, ranging from cynical to ambitious, do not indicate that the genre has an entertainment value or that it could offer anything to readers who are not directly involved in the crimes Juvenal describes. The cognitive aspects of composing and viewing drama, and so of composing and reading dramatic satire, are not explicitly cited. To discern a Juvenalian theory of drama, it is necessary to examine the depictions of performance elsewhere in the *Satires*.

The real dramatists in Juvenal's *Satires* do not tell us much about the matter. Although images of the theater are frequent, the poets behind the scenes seldom appear. Some of Juvenal's irksome literary contemporaries are authors of comedies and tragedies (1.3 and 4–6), and of course some tragic poets appear in the bleak *Satire* 7 on the literary professions. But the latter group of authors is hungry, helpless, and silent, and the works they write are simply meal tickets, not meaningful in themselves (12, 72–73, 87). In that poem, Juvenal concentrates more on poets' thwarted desires and sterility than any artistic or didactic intentions. There is even less indication here of the motives and mechanics behind the creation of drama than in Persius *Satire* 5.

More prominent, however, is the element of everyday theatricality. The *Satires* feature an array of characters with a keen sense of the dramatic aspects of social life. In dwelling in his first *Satire* on the ritual nature of urban Roman experience—for example, the daily greeting of patrons by their clients (the *salutatio*, 1.95–126; cf. 3.126–130) and the march of rich men and their retinues through the streets (1.32–48)—Juvenal emphasizes that Romans are constantly engaged in a performance of identity. In a variation on this theme, some characters in subsequent poems strategically cultivate false images of themselves. The pathics attacked in *Satire* 2 hide their true nature under rugged exteriors (2.1–15; cf. the stingy patron Virro in *Satire* 9), Domitian hides his own crime of incest while playing the stern censor (2.29–33), and the same emperor's courtiers avoid incurring his displeasure by acting as *amici* (4.72–75). Legacy hunters make flattery their livelihood (12.93–130); cheaters pose as pious and honest (13.75–119). In these cases, the satirist counters the hypocrisy of his targets by in turn putting them on display in a drama of his own design. Juvenalian satire fights unsavory theatrical behavior with the equally theatrical procedure of exposure and humiliation. In this sense, Juvenal may be seen as hybridizing the Lucilian approach that Horace describes at 2.1.62–65, and Horace's own method of putting targets on a metaphorical stage—namely, the fictional vignettes of his satire.

But if this strategy of exposure underlies much Juvenalian narrative, there are exceptions visible in characters whose theatrical perception of life—whether they direct, perform, or observe others—is fascinating enough to the satirist to become an object of study in itself. This is certainly true of one character who takes on the role of dramatist and has made an art of his theatrical approach to social relations. In *Satire* 5, Juvenal imagines his addressee, the poor client Trebius, appearing at his patron's home for a dinner, only to be enlisted in a private show. A malicious literary descendant of Horace's Nasidienus, the host Virro is a metaphorical dramatist whose *cena* renders his clients unwilling performers. The parade of puny dishes that he presents to his clients are shadows of his own rich meal—an unequal banquet, *cena inaequalis*, that dramatically metaphorizes the gap in their status over and over with each course.[48] The cheap wine that inaugurates the clients' meal ensures that they will be actors and not just spectators, for they instantly break out in a brawl (26–29). Their humiliation is clinched and their compliance in the degrading ritual fully exposed when they receive a final course of rotten apples, described as being fit only for performing monkeys (153–155).[49]

Virro's motive, as Juvenal imagines it, is entertainment: "What comedy, what mime is better than a wailing gullet?" (*quae comoedia, mimus / quis melior plorante gula?*157–158).[50] The host's approach to directing combines *Schadenfreude* with the skills of a tragedian or comedian—who must, after all, understand human nature enough to calculate how people will react to their environment and treatment. But his procedure and Juvenal's participation create a different effect from that of the other "exposing" poems cited above. First, the poem that frames the drama retains the social hierarchy established by Virro. Readers are directed to laugh not at the vicious host, but at the client, who is drawn into his game. Second, the process of translating *cena* into performance is made to seem more sinister by Juvenal's omission of any reference to the primary or internal reception of the show. While Virro orchestrates the drama and would seem to be its intended audience, we never actually glimpse his reaction. The host is pictured only as hands holding fine cups (37–39) and a stomach reacting to the food and wine (49). His pleasure, if there is any, seems to derive from his work as dramatist, not from amusement at the product. Instead, the poem pulls in both the humiliated client and Juvenal's readers to be spectators to Virro's creation. In this case, then, the satiric poet acts only to transmit a character's theatrical behavior to his own reading audience, without subjecting that character to exposure or reversal. Juvenal and his alter ego do nothing to oppose the status quo. Virro's poetic function suggests that satiric directing can be employed to torture the already downtrodden, and not just to orchestrate a subversive exposure of powerful and guilty individuals. Like the comic slave awaiting his inevitable beating,[51] Trebius is the victim in an intricately dramatized social hierarchy. The satirist's identity as dramatist takes on a sinister edge when we appreciate the metapoetic significance of the *cena* poem.

The ambiguous ethical function of satiric theatrics is also manifested in the alter egos who imitate Juvenal's other dramatic functions. The satiric role of performer, already shown to link satire's generic identity to complex social issues in the case of Horace and the *mima*, underlies the modern persona theory, which has been especially influential in criticism of the highly rhetorical and versatile Juvenal. Appropriately, this satirist, who stars as an actor in the drama of his five books by adopting a colorful series of personae, is also the satirist who has the most to say about actors, their methods, and their motives. In his portrayals of actors at work, Juvenal illuminates the workings of the satiric persona as well.

The conduct of actors is a predictable and rich target for Juvenal, even more so than for Horace. Besides enjoying a nauseating popularity among Roman women (6.63–81, 396–397), performers engage in mimicry, a practice that typically attracts intense suspicion from conservative Romans.[52] Juvenal's scrutiny of actors in the *Satires* makes him seem aligned with this conservative attitude, while at the same time excessively prurient about his subject. These effects together mark Juvenal's commentary on acting as telling instances of self-exposure.

Juvenal delivers his most vehement attacks on the behavior of actors—and all mimics—in the voice of Umbricius, the narrator of *Satire* 3, who has decided to abandon a changed Rome. An old-fashioned native, Umbricius resents Rome's easy adoption of customs from the Hellenized East. The immigrants who have flooded the city have inspired the population to adopt their style of dress (67–68), intensifying the already theatrical element of life in Juvenal's Rome.[53] But the influence of Easterners, according to Umbricius, goes still deeper: a native skill at flattery and dissimulation has promoted immigrants to the top of the social hierarchy at the expense of "true" Romans, who are naturally guileless. "The whole nation [of Greece] is a comedy" (*natio comoeda est*, 100), and when actually performing on stage, Greeks seem to take on the identities of even the female characters that they play (93–97). Meanwhile, in the theatrics of social life, while offering insincere flattery "is certainly allowed and praised among us . . . they [Greeks] are believed" (*haec eadem licet et nobis laudare, sed illis / creditur*, 3.92–93). The description of the talent of the typical "hungry Greekling" (*Graeculus esuriens*, 78) is intriguing:

> . . . rides, maiore cachinno
> concutitur; flet, si lacrimas conspexit amici,
> nec dolet; igniculum brumae si tempore poscas,
> accipit endromidem; si dixeris "aestuo," sudat.
> non sumus ergo pares: melior, qui semper et omni
> nocte dieque potest aliena sumere vultum
> a facie . . .

> . . . If you laugh, he shakes with a greater
> cackle; he weeps, if he glimpses a friend's tears,
> though he isn't sad; if in wintertime you ask for a brazier,
> he puts on a mantle; if you say "I'm hot," he sweats.
> So we aren't equal: he fares better, who always, every
> night and day, can put on a face borrowed from
> someone else . . .
> (3.100–106)

Because he can effectively reproduce the emotions and even the physical sensations of his audience, a potential patron, the Greek damages the chances of an honest native Roman at gaining the same man's attention. Umbricius is motivated in his complaint by resentment at being edged out of the competition, but he shores his position up with a deeper moral objection. This kind of acting makes a participant of the spectator. The Greek employs a mimetic strategy that is dishonest and manipulative, even threatening to his audience's integrity and self-possession. The patron will no doubt be drawn deeper and deeper into a reciprocal relationship as he sees his feelings mirrored. Umbricius' suspicion appears to stem from the idea that "the dangerous qualities inherent in acting are those qualities inherent in human nature, deceit, irreverent mimicry and the power to arouse in others passions and emotions normally controlled."[54]

The complaints of Umbricius have special import in the context of satire, and in this poem in particular. This speaker is well equipped to recognize the Greek's methods because he is himself a dramatic performer, delivering a declamation-style tirade. Ancient rhetoricians knew that artificial representation of emotion was essential to successful oratory.[55] If we remember the persona theory's basic assumption that the satirist is a performer, we must sense the irony in Juvenal's portrayal of the angry, melodramatic Umbricius, whose speech features common tactics for conveying emotion such as rhetorical questions and overgeneralizations.[56] The performing Greek is a reflection of his creator, Umbricius, much in the same way that Virro in *Satire* 5 functions as a reflection of the dramatist-satirist. Moreover, the actor's methods ultimately point back to the techniques used by the satirist himself throughout his work. We might imagine Juvenal responding to the trials of downtrodden Romans as the Greek responds to a grieving friend (*flet . . . nec dolet*). Whenever Juvenal humors a complaining acquaintance (*Satires* 9, 13) or adopts the cause of a pauper (*Satire* 5, and indirectly in *Satire* 3), he behaves much as the Greek does. Every persona that the satirist adopts is manufactured in an attempt to identify with some disenfranchised or disgruntled party.

The description of the Greek prompts two especially powerful ideas about the practice of satiric performance. First, Juvenal gives the impression that the Greek's acting is manipulative because it is parasitic, drawing on the existing feelings of his audience (*aliena sumere vultum / a facie*). Umbricius focuses on the Greek's use of those tactics rather than on their actual effects—at least, we never actually see the patron's face, the arousal that is key in Burns' description of acting. The Greek surely aims to gratify his companion by replicating his feelings, however, and Umbricius implies that he meets with success. If applied to the scenario of satiric performance, this idea would suggest that Juvenalian satire merely serves as an emotional mirror, generating feelings that the reader already possesses or desires to see exhibited in someone else. Reading satire—"watching" the actor-satirist perform—looks more like a self-seeking activity than an attempt to learn from another's perspective.

Second, the Greek's agenda is pragmatic and involves assuming whatever emotion or attitude is required by the situation. He is versatile and attentive to his audience, guided by his need to please. This is a programmatically meaningful point in that it differs greatly from the morally oriented idea of satiric performance that has shaped some persona criticism. Some examples of persona scholarship reflect the assumption that the poet himself is morally enlightened and disapproves of the baser characters that he "plays."[57] This idea is fraught with problems in itself, since while an actor need not feel the emotions of his characters, he also need not feel the opposite to be said to be acting.[58] The passage on the Greek—which represents an unscrupulous and manipulative individual adopting a more sympathetic persona—should be sufficient to demolish the assumption that someone who plays a "bad" character must himself be "good."

Virro the dramatist represents a sinister kind of dramatic technique and thus casts a negative light on the simple analogy of satirist as dramatist. Similarly, the passage on the Greek, if read as a commentary on persuasive, emotive speech, undermines the image of satiric performance as a morally driven enterprise. Juvenal experiments with many personae throughout his corpus, but his very versatility underscores his resemblance to a group that is a frequent target of his. Far from reassuring us as to his harmlessness and sensible perspective behind the masks, Juvenal uses this alter ego to demonstrate that we cannot make any confident assessment of the real motives of the performing speaker. Like *Satire* 5, this case challenges the moral interpretation of satire's dramas.

At the same time, Juvenal's *Satires*, like Horace's *Sermones*, still acknowledge that theatrical events and spectacles can be sites of communal moral judgment. Large gatherings at the theater, amphitheater, and circus encourage the audience both to critique the shows and to discuss other social and moral matters. Juvenal mentions the theater as one venue where gossip is shared and judgment is passed on reprobates (11.4). In *Satire* 8, where he condemns the phenomenon of the *mimus nobilis* and the example set by Nero, the satirist rebukes both the members of the nobility who humiliate themselves on stage (183–188, 192–210), and the *populus* that endures such disgraceful proceedings (189–192). In both cases Juvenal assumes the perspective of an audience member, either picking up the topic of the spectators' chatter (*Satire* 11) or offering a critical response to the shows that they watch (8).

The moral impact of scandalous performance is conveyed, albeit hyperbolically, in two parallel passages in *Satire* 8. First, recalling a nobleman's performance in a mime that featured the crucifixion of a bandit, Juvenal declares that the performer deserved real crucifixion for shaming himself so (187–188). Turning to the stage career of Nero, the satirist deems the emperor's performances a more worthy justification for his eventual overthrow than his tyrannical behavior (221–223). Both judgments, in rather circular fashion, convey the gravity of theatrical disgrace by imagining the crime converted into punishment. The *mimus nobilis* should find his mock-cross replaced by a real one, and the performing *princeps* should be remembered in history as a perverted Orestes. The satirist takes over the role of thinking, judging spectator himself. In envisioning revenge, he draws on and commemorates the offending performances.

Juvenal also identifies with spectators of everyday theatricality. In *Satire* 5 he imagines Trebius indignantly watching (*spectes*) the showy presentation of the two meals (120–121); the *indignatio* of the client recalls the satirist who watches Rome's parade of criminals and hypocrites ("indignation makes my verse," *facit indignatio versum*, 1.79). In *Satire* 13, contemplating the fraud perpetrated on his addressee Calvinus, Juvenal observes that his friend's slippery debtor is ostentatiously "acting a mime" (*mimum agit*, 110) when he denies responsibility. Detecting dissimulation in others is another function of the spectator-satirist.

Satire 1 sets up the metaphor of the satirist as spectator by depicting the poet standing at the crossroads, making frantic notes about what he sees (63–64). This pose represents the satirist as spectator in a much more explicit way than do previous images in the tradition. Horace, although he does imagine himself watching metaphorical *ludi* at 2.8.79, mainly uses the generic theatrical audience as a symbol of public judgment (e.g., the miser in 1.1 and Arbuscula in 1.10). Juvenal, however, positions himself among spectators and shows especial curiosity about the psychology and the social role of the audience. In examining and even identifying with other viewers, he brings out the transforming nature of spectatorship. Like play production and mimicry, watching theater is not simply a moral or cognitive process; it can also turn a spectator into a participant.

The first twenty lines of *Satire* 8 play on this theme, in one of Juvenal's most creative experiments in satiric spectatorship. The poem's subject is the visible decline in virtue among the Roman nobility, and at first Juvenal invites his reader to do the observing. He seems to lead his audience through the statue-filled atria of noble families, an effective backdrop for a lecture on the betrayal of ancestral virtues. Crumbling portraits of ancestors symbolically reflect the erosion of the virtues that they represent, and so the satirist may point to them as evidence.[59] But the observing goes both ways. Because they are not enlisted as moral examples, the anthropomorphic portraits become more like degraded spectators themselves, amplifying the disgrace of their descendants by bearing witness to it. Helplessly fixed in place, they resemble the indifferent *populus* at the theater with its collective "hard face" (*frons durior*, 189). But the *populus* has chosen to take on that quality; the ancestor portraits are powerless except as participants in the public humiliation of their families. In turn, they wear the signs of decline.

Human audiences at real theatrical events and spectacles, however, have the ability to emote and to judge. The revealing emotional and intellectual experience of audience members fascinates the satirist, who is himself a professional spectator. In highlighting this aspect of Roman social experience, Juvenal takes his cue from a Horatian passage that mocks and criticizes the behavior of contemporary theater audiences. The *Epistle to Augustus* (2.1) is concerned with the relationship between authors and their audiences, and in his discussion of dramaturgy Horace singles out unappreciative theatergoers for criticism. The current taste for spectacle, the poet laments, means that more attention is paid to costumes, even to spectacular entr'actes, than to the poetry of drama. This phenomenon is a worthy subject for philosophical contemplation:

si foret in terris, rideret Democritus, seu
diversum confusa genus panthera camelo
sive elephans albus volgi converteret ora,
spectaret populum ludis attentius ipsis
ut sibi praebentem nimio spectacula plura . . .

If he were on earth, Democritus would laugh,
whether a mixed creature such as a panther crossed with a camel,
or a white elephant, attracted the eyes of the crowd,
and he would gaze with more interest at the people than at the games themselves,
since they would offer him more spectacles by far . . .
(*Ep.* 2.1.194–198)

While these audience members believe themselves to be spectators only, they are the object of an anthropological examination by Democritus, conjured from four centuries earlier. The philosopher and the poet, scornful of the general disrespect for poetic art, bring to mind a comic convention. As in the Arbuscula passage in the *Sermones*, Horace evokes the prologues of Terence, where the playwright regularly beseeches the audience to pay careful attention to his craft. The Democritus scene especially recalls the two prologues of *Hecyra*, which complain of the play's unfortunate history of competition with gladiators and tightrope walkers.[60] Horace invites his own readers to adopt Democritus' amused perspective on spectators, to choose a critical gaze over rapture with the visual treats on stage.

Juvenal adapts Horace's image of Democritus at the beginning of his tenth *Satire*, asking what the same philosopher would think if he were to lay eyes on contemporary Rome (28–46). The figure of Democritus, who is understood to represent the distanced and mocking persona that Juvenal adopts in book 4,[61] is worth a closer look. Juvenal follows Horace in pointing to Democritus' trademark laughter at human folly (cf. Sen. *Dial.* 9.15.2), but it is also noteworthy that the passage echoes the theatrical context of Horace's Democritus scene.

While Juvenal's philosopher is not at the theater, he does observe the *pompa circensis*, the parade that precedes the *ludi Romani* with all its shows. This is described in terms suggestive of performance, in the tableau of the sumptuously dressed praetor with a toga that hangs in "curtains" (*aulaea*, 39).[62] But the perspective that distinguishes philosopher from mass audience in Horace is not so clear in Juvenal. Where Horace's Democritus, with his intent gaze (*spectaret . . . attentius*, 197), directs the reader to look critically at the theater audience, Juvenal's becomes something of a spectacle himself, "shaking his sides with unceasing laughter" (*perpetuo risu pulmonem agitare*, 33; the laughter continues at 47 and 51). We are aware of Juvenal's philosopher standing amused at his doorstep (29–30) much as we are encouraged to envision the satirist himself taking notes at the crossroads in Satire 1. Juvenal's Democritus also lacks the theatrical innovativeness exhibited by his Horatian counterpart, for instead of cleverly creating his own spectacle, he observes what is deliberately designed to catch his eye, a procession that politicians have orchestrated in order to impress.[63] This reconfiguration of the Horatian passage puts Democritus in a more scripted, less autonomous role. It also encourages us to assimilate the observing satirist to the theatrical audiences that he depicts elsewhere. Distanced, cognitive criticism does not seem to be an option.

The citizens of Juvenal's Rome are also players in organized spectacles, devoted, as the famous line puts it, to bread and circuses (10.81). That memorable tag is certainly a criticism of popular taste, but its surrounding context tells us more about the nature of this mass spectatorship. According to the satirist, this phenomenon is a result of the people's loss of a role in elections:

> . . . iam pridem, ex quo suffragia nulli
> vendimus, effudit curas; nam qui dabat olim
> imperium, fasces, legiones, omnia, nunc se
> continet atque duas tantum res anxius optat,
> panem et circenses.

> . . . For a long time now, since we stopped selling
> votes to anyone, the populace has let go its cares; for that body that once
> gave out commands, magistracies, legions, all of that, now reins
> itself in and excitedly longs for two things alone,
> bread and circuses.
> (10.77–81)

Juvenal's account of the end of elections under Tiberius resembles that of his contemporary Tacitus, who takes the senatorial point of view and dismisses the traditional campaigns as nothing but tedious vote-peddling.[64] But the satirist's cynical reference to campaigning is embedded in a trenchant comment about politics, spectacles, and the masses. Once the steward of political power, the *populus* now concentrates on the dole and entertainment.[65] But Juvenal's account of the transformation of that *populus* is highly overdetermined and transparent, airing several conflicting justifications for the political rearrangement. It is described first as a willing rejection of responsibility on the people's part (*effudit curas*), then as a move toward self-restraint or compromise (*se continet*), then as a plunge into unrestrained desire (*duas tantum res anxius optat*). This shifting reflects the artificiality of the ideological justifications themselves, cultivated by the more powerful sectors that control the masses' political role. But the connection of these characterizations with the increasing importance of the shows is extremely significant.[66] We are made to see that spectacle in Imperial Rome has been given a vital political function, in that it may be serving several needs: taming ambition, drowning resentment, or enabling the enduring elite characterization of the masses as appetite-driven.

Like Democritus in the same poem, the *populus* in *Satire* 10 has been drawn into a disempowered, scripted theatrical role; both become consumers of performance, rather than independent agents or critics. Juvenal again characterizes the Roman masses as spectators in the next *Satire*, where he praises his peaceful domestic retreat over the mad scene of the city. While the poet is settling in for an unpretentious dinner, "today the circus holds all of Rome" (*totam hodie Romam circus capit*, 11.197). On the surface, Juvenal appears to be defining himself in contrast to this throng; he prefers a small gathering, with recitations of Homer and Vergil as "entertainments" (*ludos*, 179). But when the satirist envisions the scene outside, he does so with enough detail to erode some of this distance. In his digression on the circus (193–202), we glimpse the flag waved at the beginning of the race, the green tunics of the favored team, the praetor dressed as if for a triumph (like the one that attracts Democritus' gaze in *Satire* 10), the emotional reaction of the crowd when their favorite team loses, the young men and their female companions in the stands. We even "hear," with Juvenal, the roar of the crowd (*fragor aurem / percutit*, 197–198). The color, noise, and excitement of this faraway scene is brought right into the satirist's home and undercuts his claim to be detached from it all. Juvenal's vivid, lingering vision of the circus defines him as a Roman subject.

The message that spectatorship transforms is reinforced by the behavior of particular spectators in Juvenal, who are participants in the larger, flawed world, not detached observers. The rant of Umbricius, *Satire* 3, is replete with accounts of metaphorically theatrical Roman social life, in addition to commentary on real theatrical experiences. In Rome, simply attending the theater requires one to perform one's social identity—or in the case of Umbricius, to stand aside while others take center stage in doing so. The poor man's experience at the theater encapsulates everything that Juvenal complains is wrong with Rome in *Satire* 1: the rich sons of pimps, auctioneers, gladiators, and trainers loudly demand the front seats reserved for equestrians, pushing the poor away (3.153–158). Umbricius goes on to imagine a corresponding scene in the innocent countryside, where theatergoers focus on the stage itself rather than on their status and appearance:

> . . . ipsa dierum
> festorum herboso colitur si quando theatro
> maiestas tandemque redit ad pulpita notum
> exodium, cum personae pallentis hiatum
> in gremio matris formidat rusticus infans,
> aequales habitus illic similesque videbis
> orchestram et populum . . .
>
> . . . Even when the solemnity
> of festival days is observed in the grassy
> theater, and a well-known after-piece returns
> to the stage, and the gaping of a pale mask
> frightens a rustic baby in its mother's lap,
> you will see there equality in dress, and the
> front and back seats looking alike . . .
> (3.172–178)

The sober uniformity of the assembled rustic population reflects its innocence of urban corruption; this is the ostensible point of interest for Juvenal. Other details, however, are brought out in subordinate clauses. The play that the country people view is "a well-known after-piece" (*notum exodium*, an Atellan farce) that is returning to the stage (*redit*) and the uncomplaining audience. A baby—who aptly embodies the community's innocence, while making a strange representative of its theatrical tastes—is frightened by an actor's mask.

Umbricius frames the scene as a fantasy of austere Roman ideals. But does that mean that the country people also represent the best approach to spectatorship, one that Umbricius or the satirist is claiming to emulate? If so, the scene's embedded message about satire would be a curious one. The audience is uncritical, content with repeat performances of old stories about ogres, gluttons, and buffoons (the stock characters of farce). The one individual response that is magnified for our examination is the fright of a baby in its mother's lap, a decidedly emotional and reflexive reaction. The country people's approach to spectatorship may be morally informed—inasmuch as they dress neatly, eschew status-consciousness, and appreciate what is put before them—but it is not cognitive. Innocence means negligible, or indecipherable, critical reflection. If this population represents the attitude of the satirist, we might infer that he approaches his own material with a naive credulity and a set of rather dull critical tools.

There is an alternative model in a much savvier audience that appears in a later passage. Ironically, however, this latter group is a target of the satire rather than an object of praise. In *Satire* 6, Juvenal begins his argument against marriage by surveying Rome for suitable women. One of the first places that he visits is the theater, for—as Ovid also implies at *Ars* 1.89–100—women's behavior there conveniently displays their character. The catalogue of women's names and reactions gives the impression that Juvenal has carefully observed his subjects:

THE THEATRICS OF SATIRE 39

> ... cuneis an habent spectacula totis
> quod securus ames quodque inde excerpere possis?
> chironomon Ledam molli saltante Bathyllo
> Tuccia vesicae non imperat, Apula gannit,
> 65 sicut in amplexu subito et miserabile longum.
> attendit Thymele: Thymele tunc rustica discit.
> ast aliae, quotiens aulaea recondita cessant,
> et vacuo clusoque sonant fora sola theatro,
> atque a Plebeis longe Megalesia, tristes
> 70 personam thyrsumque tenent et subligar Acci.
> Urbicus exodio risum movet Atellanae
> gestibus Autonoes, hunc diligit Aelia pauper.
> solvitur his magno comoedi fibula, sunt quae
> Chrysogonum cantare vetent, Hispulla tragoedo
> 75 gaudet: an expectas ut Quintilianus ametur?

> ... Do all the blocks of seats hold one
> safe object of love, one you might pick out?
> When soft Bathyllus dances the part of Leda with gestures,
> Tuccia can't control her bladder; Apula gives out a sudden and
> 65 pathetically long squeal, as if she were being embraced.
> Thymele is riveted: the country girl Thymele is learning.
> But other women, whenever the curtains come down and are stored
> and only the courts are busy while the theater sits empty and closed,
> during the wait from the Plebeian games to the Megalesian, these sadly
> 70 cling to the mask and staff and tights of Accius.
> In an Atellan farce Urbicus elicits a laugh with the gestures
> of Autonoe; he is the pauper Aelia's favorite.
> These women pay a high price to undo the belt of a comedian; others
> keep Chrysogonus from singing, while Hispulla enjoys a tragedian;
> 75 whom do you expect them to love—Quintilian?
> (6.61–75)

In the world described in the misogynistic *Satire* 6, theatrical performances grant just one more opportunity for women of all social types to engage in fantasy and, when one thing leads to another, adultery. The satirist claims that he learns all he needs to know about women just by watching them watch plays.

But in examining and describing the women, Juvenal lets us see just how much they resemble himself when he watches the spectacle of Roman society. The similarity in the emotional tendencies of both parties is visible enough: Tuccia's literal incontinence, a response to the actor named climactically at the end of the previous line, parallels Juvenal's own emotional discharge onto his writing tablets at 1.63 (cf. his overpowering emotions at 1.30, 45, and 79).[67] Beyond the women's visceral response, too, there is an analytical perceptiveness at work that resembles the satirist's. While the women are wild about shows, they are not exactly susceptible to dramatic illusion. They like watching the performances because of their lust for the men underneath the costumes, not because of the illusions that these actors create. The women are even content to dream of actors in the off season and fondle their disembodied and decontextualized props. Ironically, in this regard the women, intent on removing the actors' costumes, come closest to the perspective of the satirist watching social theater. Like Juvenal examining and exposing hypocrites and criminals, they look past the illusion itself and fixate, with strong emotion, on the mechanics of the production. But perceptive power akin to the satirist's seems, in this case at least, to come at the price of one's moral integrity.

Juvenal has a close-up view of the behavior of spectators. It is tempting to believe that he is even symbolically present in the two audience scenes, in the form of the mask (*persona*, 3.175, 6.70). Because the *persona* simulates a human face, it adds to the sense that these spectators are themselves being put on display, their behavior absorbed and transmitted by the mask's always-open eyes and mouth.[68] This double function of the mask sums up the concentration of dramatic roles in the satirist figure, who observes, performs, and is observed himself. It also points to the mirroring effect of satiric drama: the satirist looking out at the country audience, sees a version of his own moral strictness and ready emotion, while the women in the city show the same perceptiveness and prurience expressed by the poet in *Satire* 6. The reverse is equally true, for each audience's response to the *persona* reflects its own nature. One mask elicits a response that is naïve, morally pure, and fearfully noncognitive; the other arouses its decadent viewer, who is at once resistant to illusion and overly addicted to its visceral effects. This tantalizing dichotomy of methods of viewing characterizes satire's own reception. The impact of satire depends on the perspective and desires of the reader, who might fear the genre (*Sermones* 1.4.33, Juvenal 1.165–167) or find its lurid revelations titillating.[69] Such indeterminacy is inherent in the dramatic analogy, and as the next chapters show, it is replicated in other programmatic images drawn from cultural institutions.

The dramatic analogy attracts the satirists by offering a convenient ethical and literary language for their use. But the transaction pulls each poet into an intense dialogue of genres. Horace acts out his own absorption into his theatrical world. Persius redefines drama to make it mirror his private satiric procedure. Juvenal's own satire shares drama's moral and political complications. While the three poets express a variety of judgments on the practice that inspires them, one theme is prevalent: theater is a space in which all participants act out their social and moral identities. When they turn their attention to the stage, audiences exercise moral judgment; by organizing themselves to reflect society's hierarchy, audiences perform for others. In this way, theater serves as a perfect model for satire, which constructs exemplary performances of its targets, stirs both the emotions and the analytical faculties of its readers, and thereby creates an occasion for its audiences to judge their own beliefs and desires.

In these functions, theater also overlaps with two other practices that the genre mimics: corrective violence and legal process. The next two chapters will examine these models, which are imagined to practice moral judgment on different levels. While the satirists invite us to participate in their own versions of corrective attack and prosecution, they embrace and utilize the theoretical problems that underlie those practices rather than selecting their most idealized features.

2

Satiric Attack

While satire in its theatrical mode makes entertaining examples of everyday behavior, the genre has other ways of using its misbehaving targets to gratify readers. Besides parading and exposing vice, satirists may strike back at it—metaphorically. The satiric process is often likened to physical aggression. Satirists attack, bite, and lash; their work is scathing, cutting, and piercing. Physical violence is just under the surface in literary satire, but the exact relationship between the two practices requires some untangling to be understood. To this end, two theoretical formulations have been especially influential in modern satire criticism. Elliott's theoretical history of satire argues that the genre derives from primitive spells and curses that were designed to harm enemies; literary satire is the evolved, refined manifestation of those same impulses.[1] Freud's analysis of jokes posits a more immediate, rather than a historical, connection between humor and harm. The pleasure granted by a "tendentious" joke, Freud argues, stems first from the channeling of aggression into economical wit, and then from the bond formed between teller and audience, which is based on mutual hostility toward the joke's victim.[2] According to both theories, the impulse to violence is masked and transformed by language and wit. Satire is described figuratively as deferred or muted violence, a product of societies that have learned to disguise raw aggression.

While violence may be deferred, muted, or replaced in the production of verbal abuse, there is a fundamental and persistent association between the two practices. The Roman satirists acknowledge this connection by incorporating images of physical attack into their programmatic statements and debates. The poets write violence first into satire's history, by depicting its founder Lucilius as a warrior armed with metaphorical weapons, and then into the genre's contemporary public image. In their apologiae, they portray themselves as alternately perpetrating and suffering assault. Of course, a satiric poet may practice violence only in the form of words. But the metaphor itself opens up questions about the relationship between verbal and physical attack, and about the value of attack that aims at correcting or punishing faults. The satirists' programmatic commentary invites a deeper look into their richly drawn representations of human behavior. Satire is loaded with images of aggression, dramatizing processes that the poets are imagined, in programmatic contexts, to perform and to experience. Satiric narratives bring out the social charge that is packed into corrective violence and mockery tinged with violence.

Satirists sometimes envision their most criminal targets suffering for their crimes, and so practice a species of verbal assault that may be described as "mirroring-punishment."[3] But not all images of violence in satire can be parsed in this way. Various others, involving a range of sympathetic and unsympathetic character types, crop up in narratives about punishment or social control. In these contexts, the observing satirists expose the intentions and consequences of regulatory violence. Rather than simply punishing offenders, the attacks serve to construct the social boundaries that separate assailant from victim. The practice of satiric characters, in turn, mirrors the genre's own function of making difference through figurative violence.

I take the useful phrase "making difference" from Bogel's study of English Augustan satire, which sheds light on some aspects of the ancient genre. Bogel begins with the premise that satire presents a fictional and subjective version of reality, selecting targets that reflect the fears of the satirist and his social milieu. The root of these fears, he argues, is not the perceived difference, but the perceived sameness and proximity, of undesirable groups. The satirist's job is to combat such ambiguity and assimilation by clearly marking those groups as different:

> Satirists identify in the world something or someone that is both unattractive and curiously or dangerously like them, or like the culture or subculture that they identify with or speak for, or sympathetic even as it is repellent—something, then, that is *not alien enough* . . . The "first" satiric gesture, then, is not to expose the satiric object in all its alien difference but to *define* it as different, as other: to make a difference by setting up a textual machine or mechanism for producing difference . . . [This act is not] the recognition of difference but . . . anxiety about proximity or sameness or identification and . . . the consequent production of difference.[4]

The idea that satiric mockery and blame are aimed at making and reinforcing difference, rather than simply reflecting historical reality, also underlies recent studies of the Roman genre, especially those focusing on its representation of sex and gender. The satirist has been likened to the ithyphallic god Priapus, whose literary role is to mark out sexual deviants and women, typically threatening them with rape.[5] This reflects broader patterns in the construction of Roman masculinity; the satirist defines himself as an aggressive male by defining the feminine and the passive as deviant.[6] In satire, Roman values and prejudices intersect with a unique set of genre-building strategies. But many effects of this intersection have yet to be explored.

The concept of satire as a ritual of separation associates the genre with the violence of ancient sacrifice. While factional bloodshed threatens society, sacrifice, in which an outsider is designated to represent that threat, restores order by rendering the scapegoat "different" and so uniting the warring groups.[7] In ancient Rome, this basic strategy was employed to mark out Others in contexts outside the sacrificial. These practices used violence that was sometimes literal and sometimes verbal. Our growing understanding of how the Romans processed images of violence and physical disfigurement in organizing the world around them can inform the interpretation of satire. The practice of humor in Republican oratory is marked by a uniquely Roman perspective on deformity; opponents may be branded as deviant based on their physical traits.[8] Similarly, a set of self- and community-constructing strategies underlies Roman discourse about public spectacles featuring combat and grotesque sights. For the Romans, performances of violence generated and reenacted conflict as an apotropaic device to prevent real political discord.[9] The act of organizing and regulating the world was ritualized in practices such as mockery, the display of deformity, and arena violence.

Considered in this light, the metaphorical violence enacted by satire and the literal violence that it frequently narrates take on deeper generic and social significance. Satiric attack is a vehicle for marking out groups that are dangerously close to the satirist. But the genre also adds another layer of self-consciousness to this process, which this chapter aims to illuminate. Bogel writes that satirists "ask us to meditate on the problematic intricacies of identification and difference by which we define our own identities and our relation to others of whom we cannot fully approve or disapprove."[10] This invitation to "meditate" about mechanisms of making difference seems an implicit invitation to examine satire as well. The genre lives up to its reputation as quintessentially Roman by striving to make difference in Roman fashion, but it simultaneously fulfills its critical function by exposing its own workings, its vulnerable areas, and even its potential to fail.

This chapter will identify first programmatic images, and then representations of social behavior, that feature regulatory or mocking violence. As was seen to be the case with dramatic images, the satirists shine a revealing light on the violent practices that inspire them. Their examinations show that aggression generates both pleasure and danger for those who engage in it, although it is not always successful at regulating and making difference. Such procedures must be properly orchestrated. Satiric violence, like its social analogues, constantly runs the risk of becoming a kind of unresolved, perpetual, reciprocal violence. The tendency of the genre to shift between these two types is a persistent factor in its programmatic and narrative discourse.

Horace puts forth the idea that raw violence is an ancestor of the satiric procedure, one that is always threatening to return. It was humankind's original mode of interaction, designed to organize society and to brand offenders. Scenes of more muted or humorous violence recognize this original purpose, while also pointing up the motives and the costs of attack. The mixed value and effects of such violence are also exposed by Horace's successor. Persius highlights his authorial role as perpetrator of verbal violence. He describes his morally corrupt subjects as violated bodies, whose self-inflicted violence is a kind of failed attempt at self-definition. But Juvenal conducts the most elaborate critique of regulatory violence, one that is appropriately public and institutionalized to harmonize with the public, performative setting of his satiric attacks. He both indulges his audience with the gratifying effects of ritualized violence, and reveals the fragility of the system that promotes the practice. The exposure of society's methods of making difference amounts to an exposure of satire itself.

ANIMAL, MARTIAL, AND MEDICAL IMAGES OF THE SATIRIST

A wide range of programmatic images depict the satirist figure engaged in metaphorical violence. The *topos* is reminiscent of the Greek iambic tradition,[11] but the Roman satirists are clearly looking to Lucilius as well. His thirtieth book seems to have included an apologia poem pitting the satirist against a hostile victim-cum-critic, as suggested by the complaint "you delight in spreading abroad in your discourses [or satires, *sermones*] these things about me" (*gaudes cum de me ista foris sermonibus differs*, fragment 1085 W). Several fragments grouped with this one contain more colorful and metaphorical images that resemble later programmatic descriptions of satire. A speaker begins to admonish Lucilius, "now, Gaius, since you lash and wound us in your turn" (*nunc, Gai, quoniam incilans nos laedis vicissim*, 1075 W); possibly the same offended speaker adds, "and you split me apart by slandering me in many *sermones*" (*et maledicendo in multis sermonibus differs*, 1086 W).[12] Another fragment suggests torture of a quasi-medical nature: "You may clean me out entirely, and pluck me, and singe me, and vaunt, and harass me" (*totum purges devellas me atque deuras / exultas . . . et sollicites*, 1088–1089 W). Even an impressionistic reading of these fragments reveals the importance and the range of metaphors of violence in Lucilius' construction of satire. Whether he is referring to his work alone or to an exchange of criticism between satirist and victim, Lucilius supplies provocative images of verbal violence as physical attack, torture, and even a sadistic cosmetic procedure.

This fragmentary evidence is supplemented by the later satirists' account of their genre's original functions. Horace imagines Lucilius "scouring the city with much salt" (*sale multo / urbem defricuit*, 1.10.3–4), drawing out a common metaphor (wit as salt) to conjure a painful procedure.[13] The corresponding image of Lucilius in *Sermones* 2.1 is still more graphic: in a violent twist on the theatrical metaphor, the poet dared to "tear away the hide in which everyone went about in public" (*detrahere . . . pellem . . . qua quisque per ora / cederet*, 64–65). The metaphor recalls an Aesopian fable about an ass dressed in a lion's skin, who is exposed by a gust of wind.[14] While the means of exposure in the two accounts are different, the moral messages and the scenarios of humiliation are similar. Like the image of Lucilius scouring the city, the description in

Sermones 2.1 intimates that there is a social value in satiric violence: it cleanses, or at least exposes, corruption.

In Persius' capsule history of satire, the violent procedure of the genre's *inventor* is both more invasive and more self-sacrificing: "Lucilius cut into the city—including you, Lupus and you, Mucius—and cracked his molar on those men" (*secuit Lucilius urbem / te Lupe, te Muci, et genuinum fregit in illis*, 1.114–115). Persius adjusts Horace's constructive metaphors to emphasize further the pain caused by satire, and also implies that the satirist inadvertently inflicts damage upon himself (*et genuinum fregit in illis*).[15] When Lucilius reappears in Juvenal, he has grown from a pair of jaws to an even more vivid character, driving a metaphorical chariot through the field of satire (1.19–20). The champion of *libertas* burns, bellows, and brandishes his verses like a sword, inspiring fear in the guilty:

> ense velut stricto quotiens Lucilius ardens
> infremuit, rubet auditor, cui frigida mens est
> criminibus, tacita sudant praecordia culpa.
>
> Whenever blazing Lucilius bellowed as if
> drawing a sword, the listener whose mind was chilly with crimes
> blushed, and his guts sweated with silent guilt.
> (1.165–167)

In all of these images, satiric violence is equated with the socially beneficial exposure of vice and crime.

Horace, Persius, and Juvenal imagine Lucilius daring to punish the guilty with metaphorical violence. Their collectively composed image of Lucilius highlights several interesting aspects of satiric violence in its imagined original form. First, it may overlap with arguably more sophisticated agendas such as the display of wit and the theatricalization of everyday life (as expressed in Horace). Second, it may harm not only the hearers or victims but also the attacking satirist (in Persius). Third, it sometimes has a muted quality (Lucilius' drawn sword in Juvenal, the mere sight of which causes fright).

The images of an aggressive Lucilius are visions of satire's past, and are complemented by the satirists' representations of their own work. Horace works to construct a subtler style of satiric attack than that of his predecessor, one that both alludes to and balances his fiercer iambic persona in the *Epodes*.[16] Compared with these models, Horace's satiric persona is mild, but it is also infused with a colorful vocabulary of indirect and remembered poetic violence. By creating distance between his satiric and iambic personalities, while still evoking the violent functions associated with iambus, Horace communicates the idea that iambic aggression is inherent in and necessary to satire's image. A glance back at the three satirists' representations of Lucilius can help us to understand why. The imagined raw original version of the genre is both a valuable precedent and a liability for the post-Lucilian satirists, who indicate that they are restraining their own attacks in the face of the more limiting political conditions of the early Principate.[17] This recurrent claim represents satire's historical evolution in two different ways: as a laudable progression away from violence, and a lamentable loss of original vigor. Seen in this light, both the valorizing and the negative versions of satiric violence have costs and benefits.

Horace entertains two key questions: How can the genre participate in civilized society? How ought satiric violence relate to pleasure? In *Sermones* 1.4, the satirist's imaginary interlocutor compares the poet to a mad bull ("he's got hay in his horns; get far away," *faenum habet in cornu: longe fuge*, 34). This accusation compounds a potentially unflattering comparison of satirist to bull (an animal that has associations both with iambographers and with their victims[18]) with a claim that the satirist is mad as well. The same interlocutor also attempts to paint the satirist as malicious ("you enjoy doing harm . . . and you do this with perverse zeal," *laedere gaudes . . . et hoc studio pravus facis*, 78–79). Accusing the satirist of taking pleasure (*gaudium*) in the distress of others raises the possibility that satire transgresses even the limits of *urbanitas*, sophisticated irony.[19]

When representing his own satiric project, Horace is exploratory and discursive rather than declarative; the above characterizations of satire come in the form of questions and accusations. This is the nature of the satiric apologia, which explores the possible boundaries and rules of satire. The dramatic time of book 1 allows us to see these provocations as influencing subsequent narrative experiments. The suggestions made by Horace's interlocutor in 1.4, though temporarily deflected, will receive a more extended and nuanced response in later scenes employing violence. In the explicitly programmatic realm, too, the violent imagery lingers. Horace's innocuous self-description at the end of *Sermones* 1.4 does not end up eliminating the imagery of violence from his generic profile. In 2.1, a poem that will be examined in more detail in chapter 3, the poet appropriates and embraces some of the old accusations in defending his work to the jurist Trebatius.[20] In a question reminiscent of the animal comparison of 1.4.34, Horace likens his satire to methods of self-defense in nature: "The wolf attacks with his teeth, the bull with his horns; how are they taught if not by instinct?" (*dente lupus, cornu taurus petit: unde nisi intus / monstratum?* 52–53). While it reinforces the earlier comparison of the satirist to an aggressive animal, this defense also echoes the debate context of *Sermones* 1.4 by highlighting the satirist's own vulnerability to criticisms ("attacks") from others. In this light, satire appears as a self-defensive tool.

Horace encourages the self-defense interpretation a second time in *Sermones* 2.1. When Trebatius advises him to avoid causing offense with his verses, the poet likens his pen to a sheathed sword that he uses only when threatened:

>. . . sed hic stilus haud petet ultro
>quemquam animantem et me veluti custodiet ensis
>vagina tectus: quem cur destringere coner
>tutus ab infestis latronibus?

> . . . but this pen will hardly attack anyone living
> without provocation, and will protect me like a sword
> kept in its scabbard; why would I try to unsheathe it
> if I'm untouched by hostile thugs?
> (2.1.39–42)

While this description of satire is a variation on the earlier accusations that focus on Horace's alleged malice or madness, it also uses the argument of self-protection. Ironically, the image of the sword-wielding satirist comes in a poem that contains a *recusatio*, a refusal to write martial epic (12–15). It is unclear what "thugs" (*latronibus*) might come after the poet: they could be smarting targets of previous poems (those who "hate poets," 1.4.33), his critical readers (2.1.1–4), or those who envy his social connections (to which he alludes at 2.1.74–78). In any case, these are all attacks that result directly or indirectly from Horace's writing, a fact that colors the innocent claim of self-defense with irony. The martial metaphor can be tweaked to valorize the poet's agenda, although it is not fully justified here.

Horace's presentation of his train of thought subtly undercuts his claim to be an innocent lover of peace. First, line 40, which begins with an assurance of nonviolence, ends surprisingly with the appearance of a metaphorical weapon (*ensis*). The emphatic, spondaic enjambment of "kept in its scabbard" (*vagina tectus*) then tames the image, only to lead playfully to an imagined unsheathing (*cur destringere coner?*). A hint of sexual symbolism in the passage (and the poem in general) constructs the ideal satirist as an aggressive male, brandishing his phallus-pen in order to refute the criticism (in lines 2–4) that his verses lack vigor.[21] But even if we resist pursuing that association, the image of the tentatively aggressive Horace is a striking dramatization of satire's ambivalent relationship to violence. As the sword appears, disappears, and reappears, we sense that the satirist is debating with himself about the appropriate level of aggression for his satire, and is making sure that we are aware of his range. The wavering sword is the link between the two poles of gratuitous violence and reluctant self-defense.

This is not the first instance in *Sermones* 2.1 in which Horace brings out satire's provocative and playful aspects. Earlier in his argument with Trebatius, the satirist flippantly compares his work to practices motivated by intoxication and pleasure:

> quid faciam? saltat Milonius, ut semel icto
> accessit fervor capiti numerusque lucernis;
> Castor gaudet equis, ovo prognatus eodem
> pugnis; quot capitum vivunt, totidem studiorum
> milia: me pedibus delectat claudere verba
> Lucili ritu . . .

> What can I do? Milonius starts dancing whenever
> the excitement arises in his addled head and the lamps seem to multiply;
> Castor rejoices in horses, his twin brother in boxing;
> there are as many thousands of pursuits as there
> are individuals; as for me, I enjoy enclosing words in feet
> in the manner of Lucilius . . .
> (2.1.24–29)

This group of analogies associates the poet's writing with drunkenness (*fervor*) and the delight (*gaudium*) of a horse trainer and a boxer. Horace emphasizes his pleasure in versifying (*me . . . delectat claudere verba*), as if merely arguing the merits of poetry itself as a pastime. This suppresses the critical nature and the potential harmful effects of the satiric genre—aspects that are only alluded to in another case of enjambment, the clarification "in the manner of Lucilius" (*Lucili ritu*). So positioned, the spondaic phrase playfully reopens the debate of *Sermones* 1.4 on the functions and effects of Horace's critical method. Despite Horace's superficial protests, it appears that satiric attack and satiric pleasure may be one and the same.

Persius further broadens the range of the violence metaphor to create new, but equally ambiguous, representations of satire's social value. In his first *Satire*, as in *Sermones* 1.4, it is a critic who paints the genre as metaphorically violent ("But why this need to scrape tender ears with biting truth?" *sed quid opus teneras mordaci radere vero / auriculas?* 107–108). The charge that critical poetry might cause pain for its audience echoes Horace's sly concession that "there are those who like this kind of poetry very little, since most people are worthy of blame" (*sunt quos genus hoc minime iuvat, utpote pluris / culpari dignos*, 1.4.24–25).[22] Persius' own formulation, strikingly physical in contrast to its Horatian counterpart, also emphasizes a double effect on the reader. Satire can be at once uncomfortable and beneficial. The description approaches a medical metaphor, which in later examples of the genre is a common programmatic device. English satirists of the sixteenth and seventeenth centuries compare their texts to surgeon's scalpels, cauterizing irons, and purging medicines, among other metaphors denoting less constructive aggression.[23] In Persius, the image of scraping conjures philosophical austerity. The verb *radere* reappears in the list of the Stoic-trained satirist's functions at 5.14–16: Persius is "clever at scraping at degenerate ways" (*pallentis radere mores / doctus*, 15–16). Similarly, a scrupulous Stoic is said to have "washed his ear with biting vinegar" (*Stoicus . . . aurem mordaci lotus aceto*, 5.86), in this case undertaking to heal himself. While the philosophical associations quite literally sanitize the violent actions of Persian satire, the images of corporal violation have a lingering impact. The affected body parts, the ears, feature prominently in the literary and moral criticism of Persius, tying the metaphor at 1.107–108 into the larger, corrupt world described in the *Satires*.[24]

Like Horace, Persius further complicates the already double-edged picture of painful, corrective satire when he admits that writing gives him pleasure. Persius laughs at human behavior ("I cackle," *cachinno*, 1.12; cf. "this [ability to laugh] of mine," *hoc ridere meum*, 122). His confessions echo the charge against Horace at *Sermones* 1.4.78 (*laedere gaudes*). Woven into a programmatic discussion that also describes satire as physical assault (*radere auriculas*, 107–108), these images of mischievous pleasure direct the reader to link satiric amusement with satiric violence.

Persius' other often-cited description of his work in *Satire* 5, delivered in the voice of his teacher Cornutus, has a similar effect. In the space of two lines, Cornutus describes his pupil's satire as "scraping at degenerate habits" (*pallentis radere mores*, 15) and as "transfixing fault in a gentlemanly game" (*ingenuo culpam defigere ludo*, 16). The two images make a pointed juxtaposition—appropriately, as they follow directly upon the reference to the poet's *iunctura acris* (5.14), which means just that. The list of satire's functions is itself a "sharp joining," rattled off in a way that hardly veils the paradoxes contained within it.[25] Persius demonstrates that pleasure can derive from corrective violence—at least for perpetrator and audience. He seems to invite his reader to join him in the metaphorically violent *ludus* that is satire.

Juvenal eschews such subtle pleasures in favor of more direct and visceral satisfaction. From his first words in *Satire* 1, he appears to be getting back to his genre's crudest origins as imagined by Elliott. It is not on Juvenal's agenda to heal society with his "attacks." Writing satire, he declares, is his way of retaliating against boring poets ("will I never strike back?" *numquamne reponam?* 1). The aggressive example of Lucilius is a precedent for Juvenal's own explosion of anger. It is difficult for him to hold back, "*not* to write satire" (*difficile est saturam non scribere*, 30); he will perform this act in public, standing in the very crossroads (*medio . . . quadrivio*, 63–64). There seems to be no doubt about the poet's intentions. Thus, when a challenging interlocutor does surface to address Juvenal, he issues not an accusation but a warning. With this, the conventional images of satiric violence are decisively transformed. The most graphic image of violence in the programmatic tradition is also noteworthy for the fact that it features the satirist not as perpetrator, but as a victim of powerful men whom he has offended:

> pone Tigillinum, taeda lucebis in illa
> qua stantes ardent qui fixo gutture fumant,
> et latum media sulcum deducit harena.
>
> Defame Tigillinus, and you'll burn as part of that torch
> in which men stand burning and smoking with transfixed throats,
> and which draws a broad furrow through the middle of the sand.
> (1.155–157)[26]

The image of the satirist's punishment, which blends physical violence with degradation,[27] caps the evolution of the programmatic language in two spectacular ways. First, it redirects satiric violence entirely, underscoring, more than Horace or Persius do, the vulnerability of the practicing satirist to retaliatory attack when his verses offend the wrong people. Second, it transforms the metaphorical violence of the programmatic tradition (scouring, stripping, biting) into the most literal and irreversible form possible.

Juvenal's vision ironically celebrates the role of violence in the satirist's identity and experience. The punishment both dramatizes the poet's own work (it is swift, ruthless, and designed for public view) and memorializes his guilt (as he is transformed into a torch and makes his mark on the sand of the amphitheater[28]). Satiric attack comes back to haunt the poet himself, converting satiric author to victim, exemplum, and spectacle all at once. The poem's last description of the satirist, also presented by Juvenal's interlocutor, imagines him as a warrior who belatedly regrets his leap to action. While Horace surprises his critics with the metaphorical sword he has previously kept hidden, the satirist is the one to be surprised in Juvenal 1. His interlocutor envisions him standing helmeted as the trumpet sounds (168–170), like an unwilling combatant who has been thrust into the arena and the city's gaze. Juvenal backs away from this prospect with a promise to attack only the dead (170–171), but the threats against him have left their mark on his image. The entire process of satiric violence becomes, for Juvenal's reader and his punisher's audience, the subject of scrutiny. The image is a fitting climax not just to Juvenal's high-flown program poem, but to the entire tradition of violent programmatic images presented by his predecessors.

The satiric tradition represents a spectrum of violent processes, which exhibit jarring relations and contradictions. The apparent conflicts between these processes are a key part of satire's self-definition and of the reception that the genre encourages. While there is a dynamic of accusation and defense in programmatic debates, both the positive and the negative associations of satiric violence are the satirists' own creation. As Bogel puts it, the satiric apologia "is best understood not as a metasatiric comment on satire but as one of the mode's chief conventions," no more "outside the text" than satire's other material.[29] In other words, just as satiric narrative constructs a model of the world, the satirists' programmatic debates construct, rather than reflect, their genre's public image.

By appreciating the complexity of the former, we can more readily understand how the latter contributes to satire's self-presentation. In the three satirists' depictions of violence, the tensions raised in programmatic discussions persist and indeed become more perceptible. Each poet, in his own way, maps the problems identified in satiric violence onto the larger arena of Roman social life. In staging acts of violence, each satirist exposes and consequently undermines the boundary-drawing agenda that underlies much regulatory violence. Horace accomplishes this primarily by inserting himself into violent contexts as a participant or observer, while Persius and Juvenal use their satiric targets as case studies. The three satirists also explore the possible connections between violence and humor or pleasure, frustrating any attempt by their readers to draw a line between the projects of attack and entertainment.

FACING THE PAST

Horace's first book of satire is a story about evolution and difference. *Sermones* 1 dramatizes the poet's self-definition in relation to characters around him and to influences from his past.[30] The book also provides an account of human history that acknowledges the impact of the past on the present. In 1.3, Horace argues against the extremist Stoic view that all crimes are equal. He invokes the Epicurean theory of utilitarian justice, asserting that human culture (not nature, as the Stoics hold) has devised sensible laws for dealing with a range of offenses. But Horace's version of this argument looks back to less refined phases of history. As he tells it, violence was the first method that human beings used to relate to one another, and its purpose (much like the law's would be) was to organize society:

> cum prorepserunt primis animalia terris,
> mutum et turpe pecus, glandem atque cubilia propter
> unguibus et pugnis, dein fustibus, atque ita porro
> pugnabant armis quae post fabricaverat usus,
> donec verba quibus voces sensusque notarent
> nominaque invenere; dehinc absistere bello,
> oppida coeperunt munire, et ponere leges,
> ne quis fur esset, neu latro, neu quis adulter.

> When living creatures crept out of the newly made earth,
> a dumb and ugly herd, they fought over acorns and dens
> with their nails and fists, then with clubs, and then later
> with weapons which need had eventually devised,
> until they found verbs and nouns with which to give sense
> to their cries and their feelings; then they began to refrain from
> war, to build towns and to establish laws,
> that no one should be a thief, a bandit, or an adulterer.
> (1.3.99–106)

This account culminates in the birth of the civilized practices of language and law. But it also offers several hints that violence was absorbed, rather than replaced, by the more advanced methods of regulation. First, as Horace tells it, the original purpose of violence was to create boundaries and hierarchies in nascent human society (*glandem atque cubilia propter . . . pugnabant*)—foreshadowing the labeling and controlling functions of language and law. Second, much as the *animalia* in the first line turn out to be—evolve?—into human beings, violence itself experiences an evolution of its own. The primitive humans learned to fight with their nails, fists, clubs, and finally proper weapons (*unguibus et pugnis, dein fustibus, atque ita porro / pugnabant armis*).[31] The progression of ablatives of means, accompanied by alliteration on *p*, enhances the dramatic momentum in this phase of the story. Horace emphasizes the humans' gradual perfection of methods of attack. In this light, language, which appears in the next line (*donec verba . . . nominaque invenere*), begins to look like an extension of violence, a new invention that took over the regulatory functions of weapons. The same can be said for law, which is here represented as the primary result of the discovery of language. While an optimistic reading of the passage would draw a solid line between early physical violence and the civilized laws that appear at the climax of the account, the possibility lurks that there are actually links between these phases. Fish has asked this question in an examination of modern law and rhetoric: "Could it not be said that [legal] procedure rather than doing away with force merely masks it by attenuating it, by placing it behind a screen or series of screens?"[32] Horace's sketch of human history gives support to this view. His account shows a series of increasingly sophisticated organizational agendas being layered over a natural impulse to violence.

This subtext of Horace's evolution narrative has implications for his self-presentation as satirist. It points to the links not just between violence, speech, and law, but between these practices and satire. For one thing, the cave-people's progress, achieved by means of fingernails, speech, and moral reflection, mirrors Horace's own social progress as narrated in *Sermones* 1.[33] Moreover, the particular transitions in the evolution narrative evoke the broader development of the satiric genre. After *usus* helped them to make advances in weaponry, humans continued in this utilitarian agenda, developing language in order to articulate their feelings (*verba quibus voces sensusque notarent / nominaque invenere*). The verb *notare*, appearing near the subsequent explanation of the origin of laws (*ne quis fur esset, neu latro, neu quis adulter*), echoes a better-known and explicitly programmatic passage from the *Sermones*. Less than forty lines later in the book, Horace describes the authors of Old Comedy—the literary ancestors of Lucilius—as public censors for the city of Athens:

> si quis erat dignus describi, quod malus ac fur,
> quod moechus foret aut sicarius aut alioqui
> famosus, multa cum libertate notabant.
>
> If anyone deserved to be criticized, because he was a scoundrel or a thief,
> because he was an adulterer or a murderer or otherwise worthy of
> ill repute, they marked him out with great freedom of speech.
> (1.4.3–5)

At 1.3.103, the verb *notare* is used in its sense of "articulate, give sense to," while here it denotes censure and stigmatization.[34] The sense of the term evolves along with its contexts, from primitive community to democratic *polis*. But the account of that evolution still illuminates the crude beginnings of law and social criticism. Read in sequence, the passages hint that satire's method of marking out offenders derives from raw violence.[35]

In subsequent poems, Horace continues to scramble the abstract linear narrative in which aggression gives way to order and civilization. Violence has certainly had a large role in shaping Horace's own world, the backdrop of the later poems in book 1. The poet himself has had a risky personal history fighting for the Republican cause, and has now been socially integrated with the victors, Octavian and his supporters.[36] In the *Sermones*, he is silent about the dangers in his own past, and presents several ostensibly trivial poems that look like substitutes for accounts of more grave conflict.[37] Yet the violence of the civil wars seems to fascinate him, infecting his stories in curious, muted ways. Tagging along on an embassy aimed at reconciling the political heirs of Julius Caesar, Horace and his friends enjoy an invective battle between jesters as dinner entertainment (1.5.51–70). The exchange of verbal abuse in the courtroom of the conspirator Brutus, which takes place shortly after the assassination of Caesar, ends with one litigant's blunt joke about regicide (1.7.33–35). The tree trunk that is made into a statue of the god Priapus (1.8.1) starts out resembling a headless victim of proscription—a fate that caught up with many opponents of Caesar's heirs.[38] These "entertainment" pieces have sharp edges.

The poet stands at a distance from each of these scenes of conflict: observing in the first, relating the second as a piece of gossip, and clearly donning an alien persona in the third.[39] But each of these roles also turns him into a participant in subtle ways, revealing the enduring current of violence that influences Horace's new role as satiric poet. The account of the battle of buffoons in *Sermones* 1.5 highlights this problem especially well. Sarmentus and Messius Cicirrus seem to engage in a form of reciprocal violence, the kind that is guaranteed only to assimilate the participants to one another and continue without resolution. The poet hints that this is the very source of entertainment for his group. His mock-epic introduction to the vignette conjures a martial atmosphere while also figuring the pair as characters from farce.[40] Sarmentus strikes out at Messius with two animal comparisons: his opponent resembles a wild horse and, with the ugly scar on his forehead, a dehorned bull (56–61). Messius responds by calling Sarmentus a slave at heart and mocking his thinness (66–69). Roman orators may use physical traits as grounds for mockery and criticism of character, but these two combatants are more like symmetrical targets than performers in control. The briskness of their exchange conveys this sense of symmetry, as does Horace's closing remark that the group of spectators prolonged their dinner just to see it continue (70).

Horace's ability to identify with his social group is influenced by this performance, a perpetual battle of lowly equals that makes the group more aware of its own higher status and internal bond. To show on which side he stands, Horace shares his friends' laughter (*ridemus*, 57). Among friends, deformity calls for euphemism (1.3.43–48); in this entertainment context, it is cause for open amusement. This is so even though one performer resembles a dehorned bull, a perfect description of the satiric Horace outside of his iambic context, and when the other is a scribe (66), just as Horace himself used to be.[41] The performers on view subtly represent Horace's multifaceted self, acting out its composite complexity even as the "present" Horace looks on as if from a distance. Not all of these associations are negative, but they are all foils for the persona of the satirist on this occasion. The scar on Messius' forehead that attracts such attention (Sarmentus makes "numerous jokes about his face," *in faciem permulta iocatus*, 62) is a fitting metaphor for this effect. It is a permanent reminder of past injury;[42] similarly, the performance conjures the whole realm of the poet's experience, including aspects that are suppressed in his current identity.

In 1.7, too, Horace appears at first to be telling a story from a distance, relating a matter of common gossip (1–3). But the verbal conflict between the litigants Persius and Rupilius Rex becomes entwined with satiric violence. The two men square off in a manner that Horace describes with the vocabulary of iambic poetry: their weapons are "pus and venom" (*pus atque venenum*, 1), "spite" (*odio*, 6), and "bitter exchange" (*sermonis amari*, 7); the two men "fiercely sally forth" (*acres procurrunt*, 21).[43] Horace's language in recounting the assaults recalls not only the aggressive persona of his *Epodes*, but his critical assessment of Lucilian satire as harsh and muddy (1.4.8–11). Persius in particular, like Lucilius in 1.4, is "harsh" (*durus*, 6), and his tumid style of invective, "like a river in winter" (*tumidus*, 7; *ruebat / flumen ut hibernum*, 26–27), is a variation on Lucilius' allegedly muddy stream of satire.[44] Yet this account does not simply represent invective from a critical distance; as he does with mock-epic language in 1.5, Horace finds a way to participate vicariously in this conflict. He constructs his dramatic retelling with a vocabulary of violence that would not have been present at the event itself; the poet recognizes the "ambivalent pleasures" of verbal violence.[45] As narrator, he plays an active role in rendering the litigants' muted verbal aggression as more concrete images (*pus atque venenum, sermonis amari, acres procurrunt*; cf. the description of Rupilius Rex as a "tough vine harvester," *durus / vindemiator*, 29–30). His function here inverts the image of his genre as a means of muting violence (as in the theories of Freud, Elliott, and Kernan); the observing satirist simulates physical attack where previously there had only been words.

The idea that verbal violence replaces physical aggression is also undermined when Persius delivers his final, punning blow to Rex ("King"). The judge knows how to kill kings; "why don't you cut the throat of this King, too?" (*cur non / hunc Regem iugulas?*" 34–35) Brutus, until now an invisible observer, is revealed as a participant in real, recent violence, still stained with blood and anticipating the final struggle with Caesar's avengers. Persius' verbal abuse of Rex, in retrospect, looks like a prelude to this startling moment, in which the trivial courtroom conflict falls away to reveal a volatile political struggle still in process. Judge becomes participant, much as Horace inserts himself in the story to embellish it with his own brand of satiric aggression.

Violence is a method of marking enemies, a process that the buffoons in 1.5 simulate with no costs or benefits to themselves. When it is practiced off the stage and in earnest, this method may actually backfire on its user. This idea is illustrated in *Sermones* 1.8. Horace speaks in the persona of a wooden statue of Priapus, the god who attacks—or to use the model of Bogel, identifies—transgressors and sexual deviants. When witches invade the garden of Maecenas aiming to practice necromancy, the guardian god scares them away with a fart so violent that it splits his wooden buttocks apart (*pepedi / diffissa nate*, 46–47). While the strategy of Priapus is an attempt to repel Others, it is also ironic (in that the god does not use his traditional and more effective weapon, his phallus) and self-disfiguring.[46] The semi-potent god experiences real injury in the face of the very Others whom he drives away. This paradox becomes attached to the satirist figure via his affiliation with Priapus.[47] The poem brings together the elements of boundary making, self-destruction, and humor, thereby acting out all the complications of satiric violence that are signaled in programmatic contexts.

In 1.8, rather than being a witness or an audience to a story, Horace merges with the poem's speaker and actor. On one level, this experiment in impersonation protects the poet from the ridiculous image that Priapus earns in the poem. But considered in light of the analogous scenarios in 1.5 and 1.7, in which Horace observes or narrates, the mask of Priapus is also the device that finally delivers Horace directly into the arena of regulatory violence. Moreover, when we consider the poem's play with the themes of change, assimilation, and boundaries, the associations between Horace and Priapus point to an even more significant conclusion: the experience of the statue dramatizes the precarious position of Horace himself. For transition and accompanying uncertainty color the entire tale, beginning with the creation of both the statue and the garden. The original block of wood might have become a bench instead of a god, but for the carpenter's whim (2–3). Maecenas' garden used to be a plebeian cemetery (8–13), which explains the witches' interest in the place. Priapus is charged with protecting the boundary between this enclosed space and the outside world, and, by association, with maintaining his culture's traditional prejudice against witches.[48] The witches themselves embody problems with boundaries, for they assume the pale appearance of the corpses that they hope to raise (25–26).

Priapus' body, however, becomes the major site of ambiguity in the poem when it accomplishes a greater division than anticipated. The one act that the poet/god manages to perform in order to separate himself from Others (and to prevent the witches' own boundary-blurring behavior) ends up rupturing his own body (*diffissa nate*). Permanently marked, Horace's Priapus is a monument to the idea that regulatory violence performed on Others may actually produce cracks (so to speak) in the groups and individuals who are attempting to dominate. Moreover, this most overt act of authorial impersonation in *Sermones* 1 is colored by the ultimate failure of boundaries in the poem. When Priapus' self-protection is compromised, we are reminded of Horace's own presence in this not so solid disguise. Positioned in his patron's private garden, the satirist is only partially successful at concealing himself in this persona.

Horace's evolution into the satirist of *Sermones* 2 delivers him into similarly ambiguous positions, as the next two chapters will show. Horace begins book 2 on his guard, gesturing with his metaphorical sword at "thugs" (*latrones*, 2.1.42), who recall the social problems tackled by law in 1.3. The marginal status in which the poet continues to find himself—as recipient of lectures, as ignored would-be dinner companion—governs this series of self-incriminating poems. While violence is largely absent from the scene, the book's penultimate poem reintroduces the theme of corrective violence and the threats that it poses to its perpetrator. *Sermones* 2.7, in which Horace is lectured by his slave Davus in accordance with the rules of the Saturnalia (4–5), is of particular interest because it dramatizes a temporary reversal of the normal social hierarchy—if not dissolving boundaries, at least reversing their effects. Davus becomes the satirist; his master, according to the lecture delivered, is a slave in his soul—to his social connections, to his passions, to the very vices that he condemns. Horace eventually attempts to silence his interlocutor and regain his normal position with a threat of violence. He must borrow from his iambic side, calling for stones and arrows (*unde mihi lapidem? . . . unde sagittas?* 116).[49] The accusations that Davus launches toward the end of the poem continue to emphasize Horace's vulnerability in the Saturnalian scenario. The discontented poet avoids his own self like a fugitive slave (112–113), and his writing is a compulsive activity, a sign of addiction (in Davus' cheeky last words, "the man's either mad, or he's versifying," *aut insanit homo, aut versus facit*, 117).[50] Horace comes close to merging with his slave even as he moves to regain power in the poem's abrupt close.

This conclusion serves to reenact on a personal and domestic level the violence-tinged social evolution that Horace portrays in *Sermones* 1.3. In 2.7, the satirist tries to reorganize the unstable Saturnalian world in order to reclaim his higher position. Horace may be entitled to regain his authority over Davus, but his response to the slave's lecture undercuts the victory that is implied by its abrupt end. Not only do the poet's actions and Davus' criticisms liken Horace to a slave, but by silencing the author of a sermon with violence, Horace also enacts—this time in a different role—the retaliatory violence that he describes in programmatic poems as a hazard of the satiric trade. Satiric targets have always been a threat: reprobates "fear verses and hate poets" (1.4.33), and Horace must protect himself with his swordlike pen (2.1.39–42). Now, their revenge is fulfilled through the satirist himself, who has moved into their position. This comes at double expense to Horace, for he both displays his own insecurity in the face of another's criticism, and validates a violent response to critical *sermo*.

In the *Sermones*, satiric attack masquerades as a mode of handling conflict, but it is revealed to be reciprocal and self-regenerating. Horace dramatizes the satirist figure's movement between the roles of aggressor, victim, and spectator to violence. His experience in these roles highlights their instability, and so the instability of a system of definition and correction that relies on them. This introduces into satire the theme of the satirist's own vulnerability, manifested both in the dangers to himself as a generic symbol and in the varying success of his work. While this development has an especially pronounced influence on the *Satires* of Juvenal, the poet who comes between them also probes the activity of violent boundary making, with unique consequences.

ATTACKING WORDS

The satirist who half claims to heal (*radere vero / auriculas*, 1.107–108; *pallentis radere mores . . . culpam defigere*, 5.15–16) is also skilled at graphic representation of deformity and bodily degeneration. Persius styles vice as a physical condition and so employs a kind of verbal violence in depicting it. More provocatively, he exposes the misguided ways in which individuals in society attempt to protect and define themselves. The satirist's method of marking always wins out, but through comparison with others it is also exposed as a more complex and playful process than mere healing.

Persius' poems revolve around metaphors, and his corporal images in particular are associated with moral themes.[51] Many human characters in the *Satires* are depicted as suffering not just from moral illnesses but from physical deterioration that mirrors their internal condition. Persius proposes to counter this phenomenon with the aggression of his own work, using the metaphor of the satirist as physician. By displaying and diagnosing faults, he pretends to take a step toward healing them. But Persius also augments this basic metaphor when he lingers on images of self-inflicted violence in his model of the world. His procedure of exposure, particularly in the first four *Satires*, reveals this pattern: the satiric subjects who carry about damaged bodies seem to have initially begun a process of self-healing, self-instruction, or self-definition, at least in their own minds.[52] These processes have been derailed and transformed into self-inflicted violence. Persius' own healing approach, which employs a strategy of exposure and probing on both bodies and minds, reveals that there is a fine line between the construction of boundaries and the process of self-destruction.

The world described in *Satire* 1 is the contemporary literary climate, in which neo-Alexandrian epyllion, elegy, and tragedy captivate many listeners while the satirist carves out his own niche with a small, enlightened audience. Persius holds a literary-critical debate with a proponent of the popular poetry, which evolves into a defense of satire. The satirist's opponent and his kind clearly wish to be seen as discriminating critics, as evidenced by their effusive praise at recitals ("bravo and well done," *'euge' . . . et 'belle,'* 49) and technical literary-critical language in debate (e.g., 63–66, 92). But in the satirist's eyes, their project of self-definition through discrimination only opens them up to violation by the very poetry that they praise. At recitals, even "huge Tituses" (*ingentis . . . Titos*, 20) let themselves be penetrated and titillated: "The poems enter their loins and their secret places are scraped with quavering verses" (*carmina lumbum / intrant et tremulo scalpuntur . . . intima versu*, 20–21).[53] In search of self-defining boundaries, the devotees of fashionable poetry become penetrable.

Persius' description of audience titillation draws extensively on contemporary discourse on the "effeminate style" of poetry and oratory. Pleasure-bringing verses are suspiciously smooth and liquid (63–65, 104–105), characteristics that are proverbially associated with unnatural effeminacy and that assimilate the poetry to the metaphorically orgasmic reader and his listeners.[54] The satirist is able to expose the critics' failed procedure of boundary making by creatively imagining the physical dimension of their critical activity. But he also represents his own satire as having a physical effect: namely, the astringent scraping of truthful words (1.107–108).[55] Although each type of poetry targets a different area of the body and offers different content, the actions performed by satire (*radere*, 107) and by the neo-Alexandrian recitals (*scalpuntur*, 21) are very similar. Persius thus appears to meld his metaphorically violent and corrective genre with an existing function of poetry that is potentially insidious and damaging. The boundary between the work of Persius and that of his targets seems very fine; the poet appears to be playing with boundaries while his targets have trouble with their own.

In *Satire* 2, Persius' subjects are similarly concerned with self-definition and control, and similarly unsuccessful, at least as the satirist represents them. The poem examines prayers that are either disingenuous (8–30) or absurdly unrealistic (31–51). Human beings seek to control their fates by bargaining with the gods: an old nurse anoints a baby's face with saliva in a superstitious protective gesture (32–34), while a man desperate for additional wealth heaps animal sacrifices on pyres (44–47). Both prayers are absurd: the old nurse's charge will never attract royal suitors or cause roses to spring up, and the man who expends his assets in sacrificing will only impoverish himself. In this light, the petitioners' gestures take on a sinister, damaging quality, as conveyed in Persius' arresting description of the wasted sacrifices: "The bowels of so many heifers melt in the flames" (*tot . . . in flamma iunicum omenta liquescant*, 47). This cynical, demystifying picture of sacrifice undermines the bargaining process in which the poem's characters are engaged. While they think they are making an exchange to control their futures, they are ruining their lives in the present.

The sacrifice theme remains Persius' focus up until the poem's conclusion, which condemns the human belief that the gods desire extravagant gifts. The criticism blurs the line between those who sacrifice and their animal offerings in referring to the "corrupted flesh" of the former (*scelerata . . . pulpa*, 63; cf. *peccat et haec [pulpa]*, 68). As Dessen paraphrases, "the demands of the flesh force man to spoil the world around him."[56] But the futile practice of sacrifice has still become institutionalized ("there is still utility in this sin," *vitio tamen utitur*, 68). The advice of the satirist is to present pure hearts and humble offerings instead of ostentatious sacrifices (71–75), a Horatian sentiment that Juvenal too will echo.[57] Nevertheless, the earlier image of melting animal flesh, and the warning that human flesh has a corrupting influence, combine to make a jarring proposition: that humans are like the animals that they destroy. This goes against the logic of sacrifice, according to which humans use animals to bargain with the gods for a degree of control over their lives.[58] Persius shows the vital boundary between human and offering collapsing; his exposing satire undoes the cultural work of sacrifice. This relates to the theme of satiric violence in two ways: sacrifice itself is an act of boundary-defining violence, and satire conducts a process of purposeful demarcation that mimics sacrifice. Persius uses his satire to undermine the ritual process that provides a theoretical model for the genre.

In the third and fourth *Satires*, characters continue to be misled by their own knowledge and their attempts to control their bodies and environment. In both poems the central character and target is educated: the internal addressee in 3 writes and has studied philosophy, while 4 features Socrates' pupil Alcibiades. But both characters are still morally—and so in Persius' version of the world, physically—diseased, and the satirist duly exposes their condition. The snoring scholar of *Satire* 3, a poem that is much concerned with the consequences of metaphorical porousness and breakage,[59] is apathetic and sluggish from wine. His interlocutor warns him that he risks becoming like a man who is "numb with vice . . . thick fat has grown on his vitals . . . and he is deeply submerged" (*stupet hic vitio et fibris increvit opimum / pingue . . . et alto / demersus*, 32–34), or like another who fatally combines rich food, wine, and bathing against doctor's orders (88–106).[60]

The latter anecdote is reminiscent of an analogy in Horace's first apologia poem, in which the doomed man also serves as an exemplum. As a boy, Horace was affected by the examples of vice pointed out by his father "just as a neighbor's funeral terrifies sick men who overeat and forces them, through fear of death, to take better care of themselves" (*avidos vicinum funus ut aegros / exanimat mortisque metu sibi parcere cogit*, *Sermones* 1.4.126–127). But the event that Horace sketches quickly is treated with much more lavish attention by Persius. The gourmand's physical condition combines symptoms of spiritual sickness seen elsewhere in the *Satires*: his heart quakes just as the avaricious man's does at the sight of precious objects in *Satire* 2 (53–54), and he gradually transforms into a dissolute collection of failing body parts—a swollen belly, shaking hands, dribbling lips—that recall the pompous poet-critics of *Satire* 1. The sickness addressed in *Satire* 3, however, is no metaphor. The gourmand obviously lacks wisdom, but it is his attempt at physical self-care—his badly timed bath—that is especially destructive. His doctor, consulted too late and then ignored, emerges as the alter ego for the satirist in this poem. The lecturing interlocutor also arrives late, as indicated by the mid-morning sun at which he points disapprovingly (1–7). He, too, meets with protest from his charge: the scholar denies having physical symptoms like those of the gourmand, although he will be proved wrong (107–118).

The condition of Alcibiades in *Satire* 4 can be similarly described as ill-advised self-care. The politician's self-image as an adept administrator is misguided, as Socrates' opening question implies: "Are you managing the people's business?" (*rem populi tractas?* 1) This flaw is summed up in his attempts to control his own body's appearance. He has feminized his body as much as possible, as if presenting it for the people's pleasure.[61] He pampers his skin (14, 18,

33), eats dainty foods (15–16), and depilates his private parts with a particularly aggressive procedure (38–40). The corporal image complements the poem's moral argument about self-presentation in society. At the same time, there is a suggestion that Alcibiades has a sense of more positive versions of self-correction, and is perhaps incorrectly applying the principle. Even the constructive practice of mutual criticism involves some risk, as Persius acknowledges in a metaphor that evokes an agonistic context: "We strike in turn, and in turn expose our legs to the arrows. This is how life is lived, this is how we learn" (*caedimus inque vicem praebemus crura sagittis. / vivitur hoc pacto, sic novimus*, 42–43).[62] This certainly contrasts with the feminizing grooming practices that Alcibiades is actually engaging in. But the graphic quality of the *sententia* adds to the overall emphasis on the body as site of both failing and learning. If the principle has some value, Alcibiades has not quite grasped how to use it.

The purpose of the lecture is not so much the enlightenment of the internal audience as the reading audience's recognition of what is wrong with him. When Socrates describes his pupil's body, he lets us see even through its manipulated exterior to the "hidden wound" underneath (*caecum vulnus*, 44). He predicts that Alcibiades will also get a glimpse of his condition with his advice in the final, graphic line: "Live with yourself; you'll come to see how damaged your equipment is" (*tecum habita: noris quam sit tibi curta supellex*, 52). The adjective *curtus* can mean "cut short" or "mutilated," but also "castrated" (cf. *Sermones* 1.6.104). Alcibiades' emasculated and sterile body merits the last sense, while his metaphorical *supellex* ("furniture") can also refer to his mental and psychological faculties. His physical self-styling veils, but also mimics, his own self-destruction.

On one level, the characters described in *Satires* 3 and 4 are guilty of inadequate and catastrophic practices of self-definition. On another level, however (and in a way analogous to Horace's method in *Sermones* 1.7), the narrating satirist plays the dominant role in the production of physical defects. The recurrent metaphor of moral health as physical health requires lavish representations of disease, deterioration, and wounding. If Persius may be likened to the ignored doctor in *Satire* 3, he also remains as a narrative voice to relate the patient's demise and death; the healer becomes the witness and judge of self-destruction. And in *Satire* 4, the end of the lecture enacts a verbal assault on Alcibiades that leaves him alone (*tecum habita*) and self-aware, and perhaps recognizing an allusion to his physical self-multilation in *curta supellex*. Via the lecturer Socrates, the satirist has worked his way into his student's wounded interior (*caecum vulnus*), recalling Persius' description of his immediate satiric predecessor. Horace "touches on every fault in his laughing friend, and is allowed in to play around his heart-strings," (*omne . . . vitium . . . tangit et admissus circum praecordia ludit*, 1.116–117). Persius as Socrates uses his privileged position to expose vice—and perhaps to play—but in an invasive manner hardly foreshadowed by the description of the innocuous Horace. The corporal images in *Satires* 1–4 remind us that satiric description of physical defects or suffering is also a kind of assault, a branch of "mirroring-punishment." Persius' programmatic representations of his poetry enable the reader to make this connection: this kind of satire scrapes, nails, fouls (1.112–114).

As his ancient biography suggests, Persius also pleases, even prompting a reciprocal metaphorical violence in his excited readers—the first of whom "set about tearing his book to pieces" in their enthusiasm (*librum . . . diripere coeperunt*).[63] Persius' images of sick bodies bring us back to the theoretical question about the relation of violence to the pleasures of satire. Persius may be a dedicated healer of illness, or he may conjure suffering only to mock it. If we return to the programmatic *Satire* that featured the poet's ambiguous claim to "scrape ears with the truth," we find another allusion to this theoretical issue. At the close of *Satire* 1, Persius characterizes the people who would and would not like his poetry. The former group is represented by the reader of Old Comedy; into the latter falls the sort of man "who could say to a one-eyed man, 'One-eye!'" (*lusco qui possit dicere 'lusce,'* 128). The poet's gesture of discrimination, specifically exclusion, judges another such gesture, namely mockery that responds to deformity. Like Horace and his friends laughing at the exchange of the buffoons, Persius frames one act of boundary making with another. The joker's low style of mockery makes him unfit to understand Persius' subtle poetry.

But the essence of this style of mockery is unclear. The targeted *luscus* has a wound that represents a past injury, something like the scar on Messius' forehead in *Sermones* 1.5. This line is typically taken to mean that Persius morally disapproves of those who mock the deformed, and expects the same of his audience.[64] But the pointed repetition of *luscus* and the verb *possit* suggest an alternative, amoral interpretation. Might the man in question have poor taste only in that he cannot come up with anything better than *luscus* to describe a *luscus*? Could a one-eyed man be funny after all, if the joker makes more of an effort? Roman rhetorical theory certainly allowed for such jokes in and out of court, with certain exceptions. A passage in Cicero's *De oratore* criticizes a speaker for mocking a one-eyed man's disfigurement, in part because the attack was unprovoked, but also because the joke was too generic ("it could apply to all one-eyed men," *quod in omnis luscos conveniret*, 2.246).[65] The latter criticism gives more weight to wit than to ethics; Persius, judging by his wording, may be doing the same at 1.128. Alternatively, the dative *lusco* with *dicere* might be the operative word: Persius could be criticizing the joker for using his target as an audience, when (as Freud sees it) a third party would be the appropriate audience for mockery of a physical deformity.[66] As Sarmentus needs his audience when he mocks the scar of Messius, this joker should be performing for a party other than the *luscus*. Whatever the intended sense of the line is, it seems difficult to argue that it aims only to criticize mockery based on deformity. It conveys a more subtle set of rules for humor, and the images of afflicted bodies throughout the *Satires* seem to respond to the implicit challenge. Persius brings out the element of intrusion that is latent in gentle Horatian "touching." His cultivation of verbal violence expands satiric theory and has a significant influence on Juvenal.

AMBIGUOUS PLEASURES

Persius excludes from his audience the sort of person who would mock Greek sandals or call a one-eyed man *lusce* (1.127–128). His successor in satire finds room for both of these subjects in his own work, as if he saw an irresistible challenge in Persius' quickly sketched theory of mockery. Juvenal has Umbricius complain about native Romans wearing Greek "dinner-runners" (*trechedipna*, 3.67), and he seems to find missing eyes particularly amusing—the more incongruous and gratuitous the reference the better. To name a few cases, the satirist remarks that a woman would sooner choose to have one eye than just one lover (6.53–54); a struggling gigolo has only one slave, as solitary as the Cyclops' eye (9.64–65); and a blind old man envies his one-eyed neighbor (10.227–228). Other images are more elaborately drawn, such as that of a crumbling statue of a nobleman's warlike ancestor, described as *lusca* (7.128). Here, as in Persius, the actual word *luscus* appears surprisingly and humorously at the end of the line. Similarly, Juvenal's portrait of the ambitious Hannibal riding his elephant toward Rome adds the incongruous detail of the general's ruined eye (*luscum*, 10.158). Such deflating climaxes at the ends of lines or lists are typical of Juvenal.[67] Perhaps the most pathetic image is that of the civilian in *Satire* 16 who has been beaten by a soldier, and now along with his bruises and missing teeth possesses just one eye "with the doctor making no promises" about it (*oculum medico nil promittente relictum*, 12). These examples provide a useful entry point into an examination of Juvenal's brand of satiric violence. In a more engaging manner than that of Persius' inept joker, Juvenal draws attention to his subjects' disfigurement—even tricking the reader into laughing at pathetic characters. Elsewhere, with his abundant images of mockery laced with violence, the satirist brings physical and verbal abuse closer and closer together, and implicates his own audience in their theoretical association.

Juvenal first illustrates his relationship to violence in the programmatic image of the satirist's punishment (1.155–157, discussed in chapter 1). That image adapts the metaphor of violence in two ways. It moves the setting of satiric violence from more private spheres to public view, and it envisions a cycle of satiric attack that ends with very literal violence perpetrated in revenge on the practicing satirist. In performing these transformations, Juvenal likens the experiences of the satirist figure to the violence of public, orchestrated spectacles. His programmatic gesture thus connects satire with a key Roman institution. For their Roman audience, violent spectacles were not merely distracting entertainment; they worked on a grand scale to create community identity and to stage conflict-dispelling violence in a controlled setting. Spectators were directed to view the combatants as liminal figures, Others who were at the same time capable of absorbing and quashing any political turmoil that threatened the Roman state.[68] The shows thus functioned to set up boundaries between Romans and Others, while confirming that those Others helped the Roman community to remain united. As discussed in chapter 1, spectacle also had the tangential but important effect of socially stratifying the audience by way of seating arrangements and the dynamic between audience and attending sponsors and leaders. The performance of violence in the Roman world, especially in the early Imperial period, was designed to keep the world in order on the human level, while also answering to divine demands.

Juvenal's most arresting programmatic images of satiric violence emphasize judgment in a public sphere. Lucilius brandishes his sword, a move so effective that it makes the guilty sweat inside; the satirist who goes too far ends up burning in the arena, making his mark both in flames and in the sand. The spectators of each of these events are meant to identify with and interpret what they see so as to monitor their own behavior. Both types of satiric violence have visceral effects on the viewer, but they also engage and reinforce values. Correspondingly, in Juvenal's narrative scenes, the act of perpetrating or viewing violence or disfigurement is always loaded with cultural prejudice. Pain experienced by some characters becomes a source of pleasure and self-satisfaction for others. In some cases, this act is institutionalized, parlayed into enduring cultural practices. Such a process ensures both the stability of the social system and the continuation of the useful violence itself. Because these self-perpetuating institutions mirror the process of satire, Juvenal, in the tradition of his predecessors, ends up exposing the workings of his own violence-infused, boundary-making genre.

In *Satire* 2 Juvenal attacks pathics, including a subgroup that hides its true nature with affected masculinity and moralistic ranting. Juvenal is the principal agent of exposure, but he first creates an accomplice, who provides a vivid metaphor for the satiric process:

> hispida membra quidem et durae per bracchia saetae
> promittunt atrocem animum, sed podice levi
> caeduntur tumidae medico ridente mariscae.
>
> Shaggy limbs and rough bristles along your arms certainly
> advertise a fierce nature, but the doctor laughs as he carves
> the swollen piles from your smooth-shaven anus.
> (2.11–13)

This doctor is a perfect alter ego for the satirist figure, combining Lucilian exposure, Horatian laughter, and the medical approach of Persius. The scalpel that he wields is the source of his power and knowledge.[69] His access to secrets is made more threatening to the hypocrites because it is manifested in a doubly physical way: he both sees hidden deformity and, in a way, physically attacks it. It is still more significant that the doctor laughs while performing his operation. The scene links one person's physical discomfort with another's knowledge and consequent laughter. Like Persius with his deluded targets in *Satires* 2 and 4, the doctor thwarts the pathics' attempt to redefine themselves with a revealing gesture of his own. But in contrast to the surgeon-satirist, who causes pain in the effort to enlighten his audience (Persius 1.107–108), this doctor takes pleasure in the discovery of secrets.

In *Satire* 3, abuse and violence take place in a more public setting: the streets of Rome. The entire urban landscape, as Umbricius draws it, is filled with physical dangers—poets whose recitals torture nearby statues and trees, collapsing wagons and buildings, chamber pots falling from windows, stampeding crowds. But Umbricius' pauper protagonist also faces some less random threats. His very appearance makes him susceptible to mockery by his social betters. The cruelty of this scenario lies in the idea that such amusement is caused by suffering:

> quid quod materiam praebet causasque iocorum
> omnibus hic idem, si foeda et scissa lacerna,
> si toga sordidula est et rupta calceus alter
> pelle patet, vel si consuto volnere crassum
> atque recens linum ostendit non una cicatrix?

> What about the fact that [the pauper] furnishes everyone with material
> and occasions for jokes, if his cloak is ugly and ripped,
> if his toga is a little grubby and one shoe gapes open
> with its hide torn, or if multiple scars display thick new
> thread where the wounds have been sewn up?
> (3.147–151)

The pauper's clothes and shoes are torn from wear, of course, not from a beating, but they are drawn to resemble an afflicted human body. The cloak is split (*scissa*), the leather hide of the shoe is torn (*rupta . . . pelle*), and, in a true metaphor, the holes in the shoe leather are described as wounds with scars (*volnere, cicatrix*).[70] While Umbricius may be exaggerating the cruelty of those who would mock the pauper by coloring his description with the language of violence, at the same time he implies that the pauper might be funny precisely because he looks wounded. Physical abuse is an actual catalyst for jokes (*materiam . . . causasque iocorum*).

This joker's work is the transformation of the poor man's damaged clothes into wounded flesh, a process that Umbricius subtly incorporates into his account. But Umbricius' own narrative ends up connecting metaphorical with real violence by drawing the pauper into situations that are increasingly physically threatening, as well as degrading, in that they allow the protagonist no *dignitas* or revenge.[71] This is the same stock character who inhabits the upper floor of an apartment building and loses his few possessions when it burns (199–211). Back on the street, the pauper must navigate a rough crowd, all the while being battered by objects, elbows, and soldiers' hobnailed boots (243–248). When a loaded wagon collapses, his body disappears in the rubble (254–261). As if resurrected only to undergo more torments, he soon reappears to pick his way through the dangerous night, and encounters a drunken bully who terrorizes and then beats him

(278–301). Like the civilian beaten by the soldier in *Satire* 16, this pauper limps home with his few remaining teeth at the end of the fight—"if it can be called a fight, when you [the bully] punch, and I just get clobbered" (*si rixa est, ubi tu pulsas, ego vapulo tantum*, 289). Umbricius identifies himself with the victim at this most pitiful point of the story, reinforcing his criticism of those who would abuse the unfortunate. But this rhetorical move thinly masks Umbricius' own part as controlling narrator—his role in enacting the violence against the pauper.

The satirist himself plays a similar role in the final poem of the first book, in which Virro stages his homemade dinner theater. The *cena inaequalis* involves not only humiliation, but violence, and therefore approximates the kind of ritualized making of difference simulated by Horace's buffoons and practiced by Juvenal's bullies in *Satire* 3. Early in the dinner, Trebius and his fellow guests are served such cheap, harsh wine that they end up in a brawl: "Quarrels are the preliminaries, but eventually you'll hurl your cups as well; and, once hurt, you'll wipe your wounds with a reddened napkin" (*iurgia proludunt, sed mox et pocula torques / saucius et rubra deterges vulnera mappa*, 26–27). The adjective *saucius* can mean "drunk" as well as "wounded,"[72] and it seems possible at first that the napkins are red from the cheap wine. With the word *vulnera*, however, the ambiguity ends. The entire sequence is a creation of Virro's, who has devised a way to generate real violence with an amusing edge of mock violence. Verbal quarrels (*iurgia proludunt*; the root *ludo* evokes performance) progress to physical conflict. Aggressive language whets the appetite of participants and host alike for performed physical violence. Cups become epic weapons ("hurled" like javelins); wine becomes blood.

As I argued in the previous chapter, the absence of any reference to Virro's pleasure puts the poem's readers into the role of spectacle audience; at the same time, the host's intentions in designing the *cena* are made clear. While Juvenal criticizes Virro's manners, at the end of the poem he expresses a degree of admiration for his strategy ("he who uses you [Trebius] this way, knows what he's doing," *ille sapit, qui te sic utitur*, 170). The submissive client, for his part, deserves what he gets ("[you are] worthy of such a feast, and such a friend," *his epulis et tali dignus amico*, 173). The last word of the poem—*amico*, "friend"—refers not, of course, to an affection between Trebius and Virro, but to the Roman patron-client relationship known euphemistically as *amicitia*.[73] With this pointed reference to the institutional structure behind the *cena*, Juvenal implies that such dinners are routines, not isolated incidents. He even peers into the future, predicting that Trebius will gradually adopt the appearance and behavior of a slave awaiting his regular beating (171–173). The *cena* just described will be performed over and over, as long as Trebius is willing to endure it. The real significance of the dinner, then, lies in the ingenious way in which Virro has worked it into a long-term, institutionalized relationship that is already structured to emphasize socioeconomic difference. Juvenal's account of the role-defining *cena* illuminates (admittedly with much exaggeration) one way in which Rome's social hierarchy maintains itself.

In a book that treats Rome as a perverse spectacle capable of eliciting a range of emotions from anger to amusement to despair, *Satire* 5 makes an appropriate conclusion. The poem's poor protagonist is more sympathetic than the criminals of *Satire* 1, the pathics of 2, or the monsters of 4, recalling instead the urban pauper with whom Umbricius identifies in 3. But Juvenal draws the reader away from sympathy and toward derision by putting Trebius on display as a spectacle and using his pain to generate pleasure. When the satirist expresses explicit admiration for Virro's skill, the balance tilts for good. The reader who laughs at the final appearance of Trebius as a submissive slave has abandoned all feeling of identification with the client. *Satire* 5 both enacts and exposes the process by which a viewer's sympathy is converted into mockery, the pleasure that satire offers at the expense of the consolation or glimpses of justice that it might also offer.

Patronage, in standard practice or in Virro's twisted version, accentuates socioeconomic difference between Romans. But other kinds of difference may allow entire communities to feel superior to others. Juvenal puts these difference-making mechanisms on display as well. The broad narrative scope of his fifth book, matched only by that of book 1, is an appropriate context for the satirist's ambivalent examination of the boundaries between Romans and Others. *Satire* 13 is broadly concerned with the origins and consequences of crime, but it also offers an interesting digression on the topic of cultural differences. Crime is Rome's own age-old plague, the satirist explains, analogous to the physical peculiarities of different races or marvels in foreign lands. The legendary battle of the pygmies and cranes is his most extended example:

ad subitas Thracum volucres nubemque sonoram
Pygmaeus parvis currit bellator in armis
mox inpar hosti raptusque per aera curvis
unguibus a saeva fertur grue. si videas hoc
gentibus in nostris, risu quatiare; sed illic,
quamquam eadem adsidue spectentur proelia, ridet
nemo, ubi tota cohors pede non est altior uno.

The pygmy warrior in his tiny armor runs toward the
sudden rushing and clamorous cloud of Thracian birds,
and ill-matched to his enemy he is soon snatched through
the air in curved talons, borne by the savage crane. If you
should see this happen in our own land, you'd shake with
laughter, but over there, where the whole company is no
higher than a foot, although such battles are seen constantly, no one laughs.
(13.167–173)

The bizarre story of the battles between pygmies and cranes is as old as Homer (*Il.* 3.3–6). Juvenal, however, gives it a Roman and a satiric twist that both turns conflict into entertainment and delivers an unexpected lesson about sympathy and laughter. The vignette of the faraway event takes on the quality of a spectacle: *gentibus in nostris* could be paraphrased as "in a controlled setting with a Roman audience present to make the spectacular context clear." Such a spectacle would cater to the Roman fascination with deformity, especially that which occurs in conjunction with arena violence.[74] This context is necessary to provoke the response of laughter. While sympathy derives from identification and proximity, amusement and pleasure are achieved through incongruity (the mismatched battle of equally odd-looking combatants) and a distance imposed by context even more than by geography. On the surface Juvenal endorses the amused, Roman response with the matter-of-fact prediction "you'd shake with laughter" (*risu quatiare*). But he goes on to explain the pygmies' very different perspective with a shade more effort (*ubi tota cohors pede non est altior uno*). This aside serves two purposes at once. It explains the motivation for their sympathetic response, but it belittles those sympathizers with one last mocking description of their physique, enhanced by the rush of dactyls. The existence of a different audience that feels fear and pity may actually enhance sanctioned "Roman laughter." It is their freedom from fear that allows the Roman audience to use this imagined spectacle as a difference-making ritual.

Juvenal's alignment with the Roman perspective is balanced by his exposure of its underpinnings. This is especially true of the narrative *tour de force* in book 5, the fifteenth *Satire*. Juvenal's most savage and extended attack on a group of Others is also the poem that best exposes the anxieties and mechanisms behind the project of making difference. *Satire* 15 concentrates entirely on an act of violence that takes place far from Rome, which the poet uses to argue his own culture's moral superiority. Juvenal turns an incident of cannibalism in Egypt into a prolonged narrative spectacle, designed to shock civilized readers. There is ample reason to suspect disingenuousness in the satirist's moral claims; scholars have noted the irony in Juvenal's praise of Rome in a poem that provides plenty of evidence that the imperial machine practices its own version of barbarism.[75] But the most interesting aspect of the poem's self-consciousness is the fact that it features two levels of difference-making activities: the spectacular physical violence of the Egyptians and, framing that, the verbal attack of the satirist. *Satire* 15 illustrates the dependence of verbal violence on its literal counterpart by meshing together the agendas of two seemingly different parties. It also represents the speaker's attempt to claim for himself and his culture the very right to make difference, a right that the Egyptians have apparently appropriated.

The exordium tellingly walks through the process of establishing culture-based alliances and differences. Juvenal addresses a fellow Roman by his family name and *cognomen* (*Volusi Bithynice*, 1), inviting him to share in the condemnation of Egypt. He mocks the land's religious practices: Egyptians worship animals rather than proper—that is, Roman—gods (2–8). True, different rules apply in different regions of Egypt: "one place" favors the crocodile, "another place" the ibis (*pars haec, [pars] illa*, 3), still others worship the ape, the cat, the fish, or the dog ("in one place . . . in another . . . in another," *illic . . . hic*

... *illic*, 7). These regional variations betray the fact that Egypt has cultural divisions of its own, but Juvenal lumps them into a single category of perversion that explains the occurrence of cannibalism (13).[76] This contradiction is maintained at the beginning of the actual tale, when the satirist acknowledges that the fatal conflict stemmed from a religious disagreement between two villages:

... summus utrimque
inde furor volgo, quod numina vicinorum
odit uterque locus, cum solos credat habendos
esse deos quos ipse colit.

... On both sides there is intense anger
among the people, from the fact that each place loathes the deities
of its neighbors, since it believes that the only gods meant to be recognized
are those whom it worships.
(15.35–38)

Again, differences between Egyptians become grounds for lumping all of them together. Although religious differences prompt the satirist's attack, he trivializes this rationale when it sparks a quarrel among people he views as Others.

Juvenal collapses the two rival villages together in the battle narrative as well. Though he names the villages, Ombi and Tentyra, he does not indicate which side began the fighting. When one village (*alterius populi*, 39) held a feast, the other took advantage of the relaxed atmosphere to invade. Here the violence begins. As with the pauper's encounters with bullies in Rome in *Satire* 3, and the staged brawls at the *cena* in *Satire* 5, "verbal abuse is the prelude, and this becomes the battle call for raging tempers" (*iurgia prima sonare / incipiunt; animis ardentibus haec tuba rixae*, 51–52). But the play between clothing and flesh, between wine and blood, which gave those earlier scenes their audience-pleasing ambiguity, is now gone. The Egyptians disfigure one another's jaws, noses, cheeks, and eyes (54–58); eventually, the villagers from Ombi pursue and overtake a straggler from Tentyra, tearing him apart and eating him bones and all (78–83). One member of the mob, deprived of a piece of the body, scrapes the dirt so as to get a taste of the blood (90–92).

The battle between Ombi and Tentyra is the kind of symmetrical, reciprocal aggression that corrective, sacrificial violence aims to curtail.[77] The entire narrative serves as a difference-making violent spectacle, and the fact that the victors in the battle consume the straggler is the crowning piece of symbolic evidence for the satirist's surface argument. It conveys the idea that the combatants have failed in their attempt to assert difference, and instead have collapsed into one undifferentiated mass. Like the petitioners in Persius' second *Satire* who merge with their own excessive, fruitless sacrifices, the Egyptian villagers cause their most personal, physical boundaries to dissolve. This guarantees both visceral pleasure and a sense of superiority for Juvenal's imagined audience. To make this purpose more clear, the poet conjures a prescriptive internal scene of spectatorship. He imagines that the savagery exhibited at the event, combined with the unheroic puniness of the participants, elicited "laughter and hate" from any god who might have been surveying the scene (*deus, quicumque aspexit, ridet et odit*, 71).

On its rhetorical surface the poem styles the Egyptians as savages and the Romans as enlightened conquerors, introducing classical education and philosophy to their new subjects (110–112). But if we probe beneath that surface, we find that Juvenal also supplies clues indicating that the boundary between the two is fragile. His exordium indicates that Romans and Egyptians resemble one another in their susceptibility to religious prejudice. They also share an appetite for luxury, as a careful reader may deduce from Juvenal's reference to Canopus (46), a resort town for crowds of well-off Greeks and Romans.[78] And while they may be barbaric, Juvenal's Egyptians are also resourceful, as they undergo a process of evolution in weaponry that resembles the progress of Horace's cave-people. The violence begins with the parties "raging with bare hands" (*saevit nuda manus*, 54); they gradually acquire stones from the ground (*saxa . . . per humum quaesita*, 63), and complete their work with blades and arrows (*ferrum . . . et infestis . . . sagittis*, 73–74).[79] The accelerated progress of the Egyptian combatants represents humanity's development in warfare, though without its hoped-for result of civilization and order.

This sameness implicates satire, a verbal descendent of such violence. Like the stones that the villagers pick up, the genre has its roots *per humum*, as Horace puts it when he modestly refers to "my *sermones* that creep along the ground" (*sermones repentis per humum*, *Epist.* 2.1.250–251).[80] The villagers intensify their combat when they decide that their scuffling is mere play (*ludere se credunt*, 59), just as satire must augment its play with a sharp edge. Though it means accelerating toward the self-defeating violence with which satire also flirts, the Egyptians take the risk. Their impression on spectators also brings them closer to the satirist. Juvenal joins the imaginary god watching the scene in "laughing and hating" (71). But satire, too, is capable of eliciting strong and mixed feelings from its audience with such shocking subject matter. This is suggested when Juvenal draws an analogy between himself and Odysseus, relating tales of man-eating monsters at the Phaeacian court. The storytelling hero, the satirist concedes, met with "bile or laughter" (*bilem aut risum*, 15), and one bystander even threatened to toss him back into the sea for his lies (16–18). Juvenal firmly defends his own story by referring to historical specifics (27–28). But he has set up an analogy between himself and the beleaguered storyteller of fragile status, who attracts the outrage of listeners instead of directing it toward his subject matter. Satire's picture of the world, like angry violence, is capable of eliciting ridicule and contempt instead of awe.

One group's difference making can certainly be another group's object of derision. But in this case, the satirist's prolonged inspection of Others reflects a fascination with the origins and possibilities of his own genre. This includes aspects of his own development as a satirist, for the Egyptians' emotions evoke Juvenal's authorial past. The villagers are driven by an "ancient quarrel, undying hate and an incurable wound" (*antiqua simultas / immortale odium et numquam sanabile vulnus*, 33–34), "madness" (*furor*, 36), "burning passions" (*animis ardentibus*, 52), and the rest of the narrative continues in this vein. In this they are not so distant from the early Juvenal, the angry observer of Rome motivated by a "blazing heart" (*animo flagrante*, 1.152), and fighting back against tedious recitations and rampant vice with his writing. The poems of book 5, especially *Satire* 13, counsel against self-destructive appetites and emotions, and *Satire* 15 provides a colorful illustration of the dire consequences of anger—albeit in a remote, un-Roman place. A reader of *Satire* 15 is being given the opportunity to look closely at anger and violence being practiced by a far-off community of Others, and to join satirist and hypothetical god in expressing scorn. But the same reader cannot help but be reminded of the centrality of anger in early Juvenal, and of satire's associations with violence and conflict. The genre acts out the desire to separate one's own group from Others, including those who are "dangerously like" oneself, in Bogel's words. This climax of Juvenal's oeuvre presents the satirist engaging in such a process and, along the way, exposing himself with his own version of Priapus' crack.

Of all the satirists, Juvenal comes the closest to articulating a theory of mockery's relation to violence, stressing the importance of context and pointing to the fine line between violent words and acts. But his theoretical suggestions only complicate the situation for the reader of his satire, who is at once shown examples that invite a mocking response, and encouraged to see the artificiality of the divisions between groups. This predicament is illustrated in the final poem of book 5, *Satire* 16, in which Juvenal criticizes the behavior and unfair legal rights of soldiers. The group that serves as the vital physical boundary between Romans and barbarians seems to be failing at that function, or at least is proving dangerous to Romans themselves.[81] This collapse mirrors the problem of identification attached to the reading of the poem.

Juvenal begins by describing a civilian who has been beaten by a soldier. The victim sports gaps where his teeth were, black and blue lumps on his face, and one remaining eye—at least for now ("with the doctor making no promises," *medico nil promittente*, 12). This image bears traces of some rather different victim characters in the *Satires*—certainly the downtrodden pauper in *Satire* 3 and the humiliated Trebius in 5, but also the helpless pygmy facing his larger assailants in 13 and the brawling Egyptians in 15. In each of those earlier cases Juvenal has given his reader permission to laugh, even as he acknowledges the alternative response of sympathy. In this new case, if we mock the victim, we experience satire's pleasures—but we also reject the opportunity to ally with the honest Roman. Satiric violence can put the reader in the position of choosing between pleasure and order. Juvenal embraces the problem originally raised by Horace's invented critics.

When *Satire* 16 breaks off, we have long since been led away to examine the enviable legal rights of soldiers and have left the beaten civilian behind still searching for redress. Juvenal does not help us decide how to respond to the civilian, but he weaves an important thematic connection nonetheless. As the next chapter will show, this poem integrates violence closely (and disturbingly) with its civilized counterpart, legal process. Horace, in the evolution narrative in *Sermones* 1.3, also subtly indicates that violence lurks in more civilized methods of social organization such as law. Chapter 3 will examine the satirists' self-identification with players in the legal scene, and the theoretical issues that they illuminate when they address legal matters. This method of judgment, like those featured in the theaters and streets of the Roman world, makes an appealing model for satire because it employs quasi-theatrical exposure and criticism, invoking what may seem to be enduring standards of right and wrong. Legal process also aims at producing satisfaction for wounded parties and society as a whole by punishing offenders. But legal programmatic statements and anecdotes in satire indicate that the law operates on theoretical propositions and perceptions as complicated as those seen in the arenas of performance and violence.

3

Satire and the Law

Satire's fundamental connection with violence lurks even in the evolved literary state of the genre, as manifested both in programmatic statements and in violent subject matter. Horace's self-reflexive narrative of human social evolution in *Sermones* 1.3 describes physical aggression as an adaptable means of organization that remains as an influence on social life. At the same time, the primitive experimental violence in that account has a more civilized *telos*, the birth of laws (105–106). It is a key contention of this study that the satirists recognize persistent connections between crude and civilized versions of the same basic behavior, and that in reading the genre we cannot see one version as completely separate from the other. This tension is especially visible in the satiric portrayal of legal process, which Horace represents as the evolved form of punitive and difference-making violence. The present chapter will examine how the satirists both borrow from and portray the world of law and its theoretical construction. Like physical violence, the law both offers a model for satire's agenda of correction and social organization, and introduces unique theoretical and moral problems into the genre's image.

The genre's name *satura* is of ambiguous origin, but one of the etymologies proposed by the grammarian Diomedes points to a link with law. Diomedes mentions a type of bill called a *lex per saturam* in which various provisions are grouped together (reflecting the essential meaning of *satura*, "stuffed").[1] While classical scholars generally discount the legal etymology as the least likely of the group, Knight makes a case for its metaphorical relevance to satire's forms and topics. He stresses two ideas that are fundamental to the present study: the connection between content and form, and the mutability of the satirist's identity within a particular arena. First of all, satire's connection to law in Diomedes "indicates both a characteristic topic of satire and a basic satiric method."[2] A number of the satirists' poems explore the legal ramifications or contexts of base behavior (e.g., Horace *Sermones* 1.2, 1.3, and 2.5; Juvenal 8 and 13), and Juvenal styles many *Satires* after declamations, the mock-legal exercises that were so prominent in early Imperial education.[3] This connection is made more rich by the fact that the satirists do not consistently play the same legal role: "The satirist is a prosecutor, but he is also a defendant against the attacks of those he has offended."[4] In prompting this alternation of roles, the legal model for satire resembles the models of theater and violence, although in the legal case such instability has special implications. In criticizing criminals or fools, the poet may be appropriating the authority and function of the law, but he also risks transgressing societal norms or even laws against libel.

Each of the Roman satirists wrote in a different legal context that presented special challenges to the poet himself and to his conception of the genre.[5] But all of their satire engages deeply with the broad concepts of law and regulation as products of an evolved society and as reflections of that society's moral and political concerns. In this regard, Roman satire constitutes an early phase of a venerable tradition. Law is a long-standing literary topic that appears in a range of contexts, from "revenge literature" to works "indicting legal injustice."[6] An author who writes favorably or critically about the law appropriates the moral authority, if not the technical expertise, of a jurist. Literary representation can also bring out the literary character of legal discourse. Legal practice is a form of play derived from humanity's competitive instincts; legal language, especially as fiction, drama, and poetry represent it, has inherent literary qualities that can undermine surface impressions of clarity, objectivity, and immutability.[7] In literature, law can be made to appear tricky and arbitrary at best, or dangerous at worst, in its influence on social life and history.

Roman satire is among the earliest literature to exhibit both of these types of engagement with law. The legal analogy for satire functions in the same manner as the analogies of theater and violence, providing both a programmatic language and rich subject matter. In programmatic discussions, each poet situates satire in the realm of legal or mock-legal process and discourse. That realm also serves as a recurrent narrative backdrop and topic. The satirists construct their peculiar authority in part by employing legal terminology and allusions (although that authority is also colored by their occasional distortion of legal details[8]). But the key strategy in the poets' legal self-presentation is the mutability of their perspective: they assume on different occasions the roles of prosecutor, defendant, vigilante, and observer of legal process, often with the purpose of critiquing the theory and operation of the law. As with other models, satire's range of perspectives fleshes out the basic programmatic analogy in interesting ways, and leads the reader to more insights than a single perspective would allow. Most notably, when the poets depict the workings of law, they tend to illuminate its origins in cruder methods of regulation. Satire's version of the law partakes of violence, implicating the satirist and his characters alike in the scheme of attacker and victim. Rather than offsetting the genre's associations with violence, the legal analogy imports some of the same complications that violence does into the satirist's image.

In addition to surveying the legal world from a shifting point of view, the satirists question the language and the theoretical framework of that world itself. Legal discourse, because it attempts to define human beings' moral obligations to one another and their relationship to the system of law, is an irresistible tool for poets who are in their own way constructing an account of human moral character and social relations. But this same discourse is easily dismantled: the poets manipulate legal language to bring out the slippery aspects of the concept of justice, and they also acknowledge that several conflicting "legal" frameworks—societal, philosophical, poetic—influence their subjects and themselves. This has important implications for the construction of satire as a quasi-legal process. The poets' evolving definitions of their own relationship to law reveals a paradox of their legal identity. While the restrictions of societal, moral, and poetic systems lead the satirists to contemplate carving out a privileged, extralegal space for themselves, such a move only constructs yet another relationship to the law, so confirming the inescapability of the system. Some of satire's most interesting dramatic scenarios and vignettes explore the benefits, the dangers, and the very possibility of a world unrestrained by law.

THE SATIRIST'S LEGAL PREDICAMENT

Satirists find themselves interacting with law, or rather with many kinds of law: state law, moral law, poetic law, and the composite and dynamic law of the satiric genre itself. The critical, censorial, and punitive function of satire aligns the genre with the state and constructs the satirist figure as a champion of common justice. This chapter will focus mainly on this primary sense of law as a social practice and on its representation in satire. But the satirist's moral criticisms do not always adduce state law; the poet may be guided by moral and philosophical principles that function separately from or even in opposition to the public justice system. Satires that draw heavily on philosophical precepts and discourse (e.g., the Epicurean *Sermones* 1.3 and the Stoic-themed lectures in Persius 2–5) situate the genre in the more metaphorical legal system of moral philosophy. As poetic artists, the satirists also acknowledge technical and stylistic laws of poetry, which sometimes bleed into the idea of a *lex operis* (generic law) peculiar to satire. This term may be used to indicate special license for poetry: Martial, for example, claims such a *lex* for himself (1.35.10). But a *lex operis* usually imports generic guidelines of its own (cf. Plin. *Ep.* 4.14.5, Cic. *De or.* 1.256, *Leg.* 1.5). This becomes apparent in satire's case when the poets suggest that they have been accused of breaking a generic *lex* with their tone or material (Juvenal's transgressive tragic style at 6.635; cf. Horace's ferocity at *Sermones* 2.1.1–2, an ambiguous case that will be discussed below).

Allegations of transgressions against poetic or generic law allow us to see the satirists as potential lawbreakers as well, although there is of course a more strictly legal sense in which the poets risk being branded as criminals. The series of Roman laws directed against *nominatim* slander and mockery, beginning with the fifth-century BCE Twelve Tables statute (cited to Horace by the jurist Trebatius Testa at 2.1.82–83) and taking on revised forms in the late second and early first centuries were all meant to put writers of lampoons and criticism on guard.[9] The nature of the late Republican revisions is evidence of a continuing debate over whether such attacks harmed individuals only (hence the charge of personal injury, *iniuria*) or the state itself (inviting the charge of treason, *maiestas*). The visibility and impact of these laws on the literary culture of Lucilius' time is attested by the story that the satirist himself brought a charge of *iniuria* against a mime writer (*Rhet. Her.* 2.19). While the effect of the laws on Lucilius' own satiric self-presentation is not clearly known, Horace certainly integrates the issue of libel into his own legally flavored programmatic poems, *Sermones* 1.4 and 2.1. After Horace, in the first century CE, charges of *maiestas* focusing on libelous or ideologically challenging publications threatened exile for the authors and/or the burning of their works.[10] The punishment that Juvenal imagines himself receiving for satirizing Tigillinus, death by burning in the arena (1.155–157), exaggerates the traditional image of the satirist's legal problems just as it amplifies his traditional association with punitive violence. As noted in the previous chapter, this image bears more resemblance to the fate of low-status criminals accused of serious crimes than to that of satirical or critical authors, even in the Neronian period to which Juvenal's scene alludes. But Juvenal may be playfully conflating satirist with text here, and alluding to the fate prescribed for certain *libelli* or controversial histories.

Before all of these programmatic formulations appeared, Lucilius played up the idea that the satirist figure may draw himself into conflict by speaking out. In the fragments of books 26 and 30, there are references to the poet's mixed audience and literary reputation (632–636 W) and descriptions of his slanderous verse (especially 1075, 1078, and 1083–1089 W, cited in chapter 2 for their metaphors of satiric violence). The latter group of fragments may represent a dialogue between Lucilius and an angry victim of his satire, in which the victim accuses Lucilius of slander but the poet then "invite[s] him to do his worst" as if to point out that each party is capable of harming the other.[11] If this reconstruction is correct, Lucilius is making it clear that he himself is as vulnerable to attack as his victims are; as we saw with satiric violence, there is a fine line between the satirist's stances as attacker and victim.

As they assume alternately the roles of censor, jurist, philosopher, literary author and critic, and defendant, the satirists appear to be legally bound in multiple and even conflicting ways. But the presence of so many legal contexts and risks, far from being a hindrance to satire's construction or definition, creates a fertile poetic environment. It provides an incentive for the poets to shift legal roles and perspectives, thereby conducting a more illuminating analysis of law and its effects on society than a single, fixed role would allow. Like theater and violence, the law as a satiric subject invites examination from all sides. Even more important, the presence of multiple legal systems and discourses becomes part of the genre's programmatic fabric, so that we are encouraged to see the satirists as writing the laws that bind them rather than reacting to external legal systems.[12] Satire's generic law is equivalent to this process of writing, examining, and even undoing laws, and to the authorial self-positioning that facilitates this task.

Chapters 1 and 2 showed that the programmatic *apologiae* situate the satirists within the contexts of theater and violent behavior, assuming an essentially defensive stance opposite critics or advisors. Understanding the poets' complete control over the type and order of charges uttered by these characters allows us to see the satiric apologia for what it is: a calculated articulation of satiric theory that incorporates and explores both defensive arguments and potential criticisms. The same apologiae reveal how the poets construct and reconstruct their complex legal world. In their defensive postures, the satirists are assuming a legal role, and in their responses they employ the traditional tools of rhetoric. The imagined *adversarii* identified as dramatic characters in chapter 1 are also rhetorical devices (*Rhet. Her.* 4.52, Quint. *Inst.* 6.4.14; cf. *Sermones* 1.10.12, which notes that the satirist must sometimes be a *rhetor*). The individual satiric apologiae are pieces of a history of "satiric law," which depict the genre's evolution as intertwined with the evolution of law itself.

Sermones 1.4 demonstrates that satire's legal status and its literary status are both indeterminate and reactive. In the poem, Horace pretends to provide a defense of satire based on literary-critical and moral standards, as if the book's first three poems have elicited a negative public response. The defense begins with the rather skewed account of the tradition of social criticism in Athenian Old Comedy and Lucilian satire (1–5), attributing to these early satirist figures the function of "marking out" vices and crimes in society (*notabant*).[13] Later in the poem, Horace constructs his biological father as a literary father figure as well, in another naturalizing description of the censor's function (*notando*, 106).[14] The function of marking out thieves, murderers, and adulterers aligns these critic figures with their state laws. Nevertheless, Horace finds himself on the defensive from the beginning: first simply as a poet, called to a contest in versifying (13–21), and then as a satirist.

As with other programmatic formulations of satire's social models, functions, and effects, the legally flavored complaints that Horace's *adversarius* proceeds to make—however much they may reflect historical reality—are shaped by the poet himself.[15] In *Sermones* 1.4, Horace's first method of defense is to represent his work's literary form as "more like conversation" (*sermoni propiora*, 42). This claim is both facetious and tangential to the question of satire's moral and legal propriety; Horace's machinations in "proving" satire's nonliterary status are meaningful articulations of poetic theory in themselves.[16] Horace's abrupt conclusion to this section of this poem employs an evocative term: "Enough for now; on another occasion, I'll investigate whether or not this type of writing is proper poetry" (*hactenus haec: alias iustum sit necne poema . . . quaeram*, 63–64). The adjective *iustum* has a nonlegal valence here, meaning "[poetry] as it is strictly defined." But the latent legal sense of the term allows us to see satire's literary and legal legitimacy as interwoven.

The comment at 1.4.63–64 carries two important implications. First, it implies that elsewhere in his work, Horace will examine his genre's status. He does assume the role of literary critic again in *Sermones* 1.10,[17] but we may also infer that his nonprogrammatic poems will explore satire's poetic affiliations indirectly just as *Sermones* 1.4 does. Second, the application of the term *iustum* here recalls a point made in the previous poem, where Horace argues that sensible laws are not born from nature but from experience and practice: "You must admit . . . that justice was discovered through fear of injustice" (*iura inventa metu iniusti fateare necesse est,* 1.3.111). If we entertain the idea that poetic *iura* or *iustitia* might follow such a reactive process in its development, we see (and *Sermones* 1.4 supports this idea) that satire is being defined there through reference to its foils and near relatives. Satire itself is feared in society (1.4.33, 70); the satirist must address his critics, as this poem pretends to do, by examining and responding to their fears. Mutable, discursive, reactive satiric law cannot be separated from the process of its construction.

It is interesting to note that in a literary-critical work written two decades later, Horace describes the first phase of Roman literary practice as an almost symbiotic interaction between the *licentia* of mockery and the state law that evolved to curb it.[18] The abusive Fescennine verses prompted a law curtailing poetic mockery, an event that Horace uses essentially as an occasion to explain the origin of law itself:

> . . . doluere cruento
> dente lacessiti; fuit intactis quoque cura
> condicione super communi; quin etiam lex
> poenaque lata . . .
>
> . . . those harmed by that bloody tooth
> were upset; among those untouched, too, there was concern
> for the common cause; so that at last a law and a punishment
> were introduced . . .
> (*Epist.* 2.1.150–153)

Horace's account envisions Roman literature being born into a ready-made environment of state regulation.[19] But the converse of this is equally true: as Horace relates it, the development of mocking verse becomes a turning point for the rustic community, which applies the principle of the common cause (*condicione . . . communi*) even when some members are themselves unhurt (*fuit intactis quoque cura*). This literary history suggests that law needs transgression to occur—here transgression in verse—to help it define its own purpose. The Fescennines, in turn, grow tamer (154–155); law and literature develop in response to one another.[20]

Satiric writing may be defined and shaped by the law that reacts to it, and by extension, by the array of more unsavory quasi-legal activities with which satire seems to share functions or contexts. In the *Sermones*, the existence of such analogues for Horatian satire constitutes another system within which the poet must define and defend his work. In *Sermones* 1.4, in order to build his authorial image, Horace must circle closely around potential alter egos for himself who operate in or near the legal arena. The boundary that separates them from himself begins to weaken at points. One accusation against the satirist that Horace raises, through his imaginary interlocutor, is that he resembles the opportunistic informers who stalk Rome with notebooks (*libellis*, 66) in hand, identifying potential victims. Not so, Horace responds to the charge: his own little books (*libellos*, 71) do not reach a broad audience, so that although his critic may well be a criminal, he himself is no informer (69–70). The two appearances of the term *libelli* so close together in two different senses ("libelous books"/"little books") seems a provocation, the sort of coincidence that a real informer might use as evidence of the satirist's malice.[21] Nor does Horace do much to erase his resemblance to informers when he half accuses his interlocutor of criminal behavior; the retort lacks proof and relies on possibility ("although you may be . . . ," *ut sis tu*). At this moment, the satirist actually resembles someone less open and more insidious than the informers, who inspire fear with their visibility and notoriety. Horace keeps his own *libelli* invisible, and composes them in private (138–139; cf. 1.6.123).

Creating another ostensible foil for himself, Horace accuses his interlocutor of a tendency to slander, suggesting that he would express open surprise at a friend's acquittal in court (93–100). To make his point, the satirist acts the part of the malicious speaker, who gives his friend's full name, confirms their long acquaintance, and concludes, "I'm baffled as to how he got off at that trial" (*admiror quo pacto iudicium illud / fugerit*, 99–100). Horace's act of ventriloquism aims to show the malice of one who would betray a friend, yet by conjuring a scenario in which a real criminal has been acquitted, he undermines his own criticism to a degree. For the imaginary speaker to keep silent may also be a reprehensible choice; as it is, his commentary on the faulty justice system is not so alien to satire's mission. Even Horace's description of the man's comment as "pure black ink, unadulterated poison" (*hic nigrae sucus lolliginis, haec est / aerugo mera*, 100–101) recalls the metaphors of violence associated with the iambic poet's pose and their role in the construction of the satirist of book 1.[22] The slanderer subtly partakes of satiric discourse; by the same token, the satirist who mimics him vicariously performs his role, experimenting with a new legal position.

Sermones 1.4 constructs a legal atmosphere for satire's work, a setting filled with various standards (poetic, philosophical, social) and characters who play legal or auxiliary roles (censor figures, informers, indiscreet friends, wits). The poem recalls Hutcheon's illustrated spectrum of responses to irony in the way that it animates a range of legal and critical players, many of them unsavory, against which Horace positions himself in defending his own genre.[23] It demonstrates that satire cannot escape its legal contexts, even when the satirist pretends to take a purely defensive and reactive position. Rather, the poet's reactions to accusations define satire and import the associations of its potential foils and relations, elements that will resurface throughout book 1.

In *Sermones* 2.1, the dialogue with the jurist Trebatius Testa, Horace pretends to be taking criticisms into account as he prepares to style his new book.

He first complains that readers either think that his verses are too harsh ("I seem to be too fierce and to stretch my work past the law," *videar nimis acer et ultra / legem tendere opus*, 1–2) or too weak ("[others think I'm] without vigor," *sine nervis*, 2). The multiple significations of this group of terms have generated much commentary, a central question being whether by *lex* Horace means the state law against libel, or the conventions of the genre established by Lucilius (as in *lex operis*; cf. Horace *Ars P.* 135).[24] The consultation also ends with a gesture to the ambiguity of a particular phrase, *mala carmina*. Trebatius employs the label in its technical legal sense when he cites the law against "slanderous poems" (82), but Horace interprets it aesthetically ("[then I won't write] bad poems," 83). This framing of the poem through play on legal terminology is a cue that Horace is incorporating into his genre's construction not only satire's potential interaction with state law, but the potential for that relationship to be reinterpreted or rendered ambiguous.

Between the first and the last legal references comes a series of recommendations from Trebatius and responses from a resourceful Horace, in which poetic, personal, moral, and legal considerations are entertained. Borrowing the conventional Callimachean *recusatio*, the poet rejects Trebatius' initial proposals that he cease writing entirely or attempt panegyric poetry (5–20). This intransigence prompts the jurist to condemn satire in stronger terms as offensive and dangerous to the poet, who risks incurring chilly relations with powerful members of society (21–23; cf. 60–62). Horace responds with several different lines of argumentation. He writes for fun (24–29) and when necessary, in self-defense (39–53). Furthermore, the precedent of Lucilius, whose powerful friends protected him against possible social and legal repercussions, encourages him (62–74). The picture of satire that emerges is of a genre that draws on the poetic, legal, natural, personal, and moral spheres for inspiration and justification.

The poem acknowledges that satire must adapt to changing political circumstances.[25] But besides representing a dynamic generic history, the programmatic dialogue in the poem is itself dynamic. Horace shifts from one type of appeal to the next,[26] hanging his work on one system after another and even letting one blur into the next. The attempt at *recusatio* invokes a "law" from a particular category of poetic genres, and the protest that he writes only for pleasure employs a similarly conventional priamel (24–29).[27] The priamel takes on a more specific purpose when Horace invokes the freedom that Lucilius enjoyed to entrust his feelings to his books (30–34), as if lumping satire with all other private, innocuous hobbies. But the mention of the Republican satirist also seems to bring Horace back around to the genre's specifically critical function. The poet claims that he will only attack when provoked, and appeals to the law of nature that each individual fights with the tools available (*imperet hoc Natura potens*, 51). Horace sandwiches examples from the natural world (the wolf, the bull) between references to characters involved in crime or legal process (the informer Cervius, the witch Canidia, and the judge Turius, 47–49; cf. the poisoner Scaeva, 53–56). This variety of examples blurs the appeal to nature into the legal defense being conducted in the poem, and even associates Horace with criminals, as well as those on the right side of the law.[28] The remainder of the poem, beginning with the return to the Lucilian precedent, appeals to patronage (*amicitia*) and the freedoms it may afford, whether that be a safe country retreat where satire may be produced (71–74), or a dismissal of a lawsuit by a sympathetic judge (Caesar in 83–86).

The first of the final two scenarios that Horace imagines, a Lucilian country retreat offering simple food and camaraderie, reinforces the country's symbolic function in *Sermones* 2 as a place of relaxation and social equality.[29] The latter and more formidable trump card, the aid of Caesar, might put an end to a case against Horace, or as Freudenburg reads in the phrase *solventur . . . tabulae* (86), perhaps to the authority of the Twelve Tables themselves—an arresting political comment.[30] But the poem's abrupt, decisive conclusion does not undo the discursive process that precedes it. *Sermones* 2.1 acts out a legal defense by appealing to a series of systems or precedents on which satire might be hung. Horace's legal identity is not only that of defendant, but of an individual looking for the system that will allow him the freedom to be a satirist. Because Trebatius continues to offer new challenges, Horace may not anchor satire firmly in the field of Callimachean verse (which would allow him to pose as a poet with a "slender" aesthetic), or in moral-philosophical terms (which would grant him his pleasure-giving hobby just as others have theirs), or in strategic *amicitia* (which would provide him with a safe performance context and possibly with legal defense). Yet while all but the last of the defenses offered are legally unsuccessful in the consultation scenario, they are programmatically "successful." The purpose of the poem is for Horace to survey and try on all of these contexts for satire, escaping each in turn as they prove inadequate to solve his reception problem. While *Sermones* 1.4 posits a literary, social, and legal atmosphere for satire in which the poet scrutinizes and mimics potential models for his work, 2.1 constructs possible worlds in which satire may function, but which each repel the poet as he approaches.

The poems of *Sermones* 2 will respond to this atmosphere of limitation, and they especially pick up on Horace's most optimistic declaration in 2.1. After listing the analogues for satiric self-defense, the poet announces that he is determined to continue writing under any circumstances.[31] In a healthy, untroubled life or in death's shadow, "whether rich, poor, at Rome or (if chance so decrees it) an exile, whatever the shade of my life, I will write" (*dives, inops, Romae, seu fors ita iusserit, exsul / quisquis erit vitae, scribam, color*, 59–60).[32] The prophecy carries an interesting implication: what looks superficially like a gesture of defiance indicates that Horace's new program will be styled around possible limitations. In *Sermones* 2, the poet does indeed execute his announced plan by taking on more marginal dramatic roles, scripting diatribe-style lectures from the mouths of characters both rich and poor, and moving his own perspective back and forth between Rome and the country. As the next section in this chapter will show, these maneuvers merely dramatize the continuing evolution of satiric law.

Book 2 reveals how many legal or quasi-legal entanglements the poet and his genre may be understood to have.

This paradoxical status of satire is captured by a Latin term, *exlex*, which itself has two senses. Meaning literally "outside the law," *exlex* is used to define both criminals, who disobey the law (cf. Varro *Sat. Men.* 507, Livy 9.34.8), and exiles, who have been condemned by law and thrust out of the community (cf. Lucilius 64–65 W). In another fragment, Lucilius seems to recognize the inherent contradiction in the term, its simultaneous exclusive and inclusive functions: "They agree to laws by which the people become outlaws" (*accipiunt leges populus quibus legibus exlex*, 1017 W).[33] This fragment's source, Nonius, explains rather opaquely that "*inlex* or *exlex* means someone who lives without law" (*inlex et exlex est qui sine lege vivat*, 10.10). Lucilius' pointed repetition of the root *lex* in the fragment seems to make a joke of the idea that one can be made "outside law" by means of a law—even "outlaws" and exiles are so defined by their relationship to the state.[34] This paradox is important to keep in mind as we consider the legal status of satire, which might be seen as borrowing the freedom or *licentia* allowed in festival contexts and to bawdy dramatic genres. Such a privilege, Horace notes at *Ars P.* 224, is attached to the *exlex* genre of satyr play. Whether or not Horace is implying there that the same license applies to Roman *satura*,[35] in the *Sermones* his gestures toward legal self-definition do conjure the same paradox contained in the term *exlex*. An individual labeled as living outside the law—such as Horace if he indeed becomes an *exsul* after 2.1—continues to be defined by the law, for he merely enters into a new relationship with it.

The problems raised in Horace's legal dialogues are echoed both in other poems of the *Sermones*, where as we will see the satirist probes the role of law in society, and in the programmatic discussions of Horace's successors in satire. The social and personal issues that Horace and Trebatius raise are important in the first *Satire* of Persius as well. Persius' interlocutor begins by contending that few will be interested in reading the present work; this does not bother Persius (2–7), whose response recalls the similar comments of Horace (*Sermones* 1.4.71, 1.10.74) and Lucilius (635 W) on the benefits of a small readership. Despite this disclaimer, as he begins his own explanation of his motives Persius recognizes that what he has to say may offend society: "Who at Rome does not—ah, if only it were right to say it—but it *is* right, when [I look at Roman mores . . .]" (*a, si fas dicere—sed fas / tunc cum* . . . , 8–9). Here, although Persius first pretends to avoid flouting a universally recognized concept of "right" (*fas*), he leads into a claim that speaking out in the form of satire actually promotes what is right (*sed fas, tunc cum* . . .). As Horace submits in his legal question at *Sermones* 2.1.85, if the satirist himself is just (*integer ipse*), his work may be perceived more favorably. Similarly, Persius' later appeal to the precedent of Lucilius (114–115) conjures satiric violence (*secuit urbem*), but leaves open the possibility that this violence works on the side of traditional morality.

As Persius represents it, however, his critical project is essentially a private matter. Besides expressing contentment with two readers or even none (2–3, 120), Persius downplays the public and legal entanglements of satire that Horace weaves into his programmatic dialogues. Like Horace in *Sermones* 2.1, Persius is told by his interlocutor that he risks meeting with a cold reception at the doors of the powerful (107–110). But the legal dangers thematized in Horace's poem are ignored or suppressed. Even the topic of moral criticism and its effect on social relations is given a muted treatment; much of Persius' discussion of the practice of criticism itself is concentrated on the literary realm. The theme here owes less to Horace's satiric apologiae than to his literary-critical poetry, especially the recommendation of candor between friends at *Ars P.* 450–452.[36] As if to confirm that he has taken a selective approach to Horace as model for the apologia, Persius portrays his predecessor engaging not in a dangerous social and moral mission, but in a pleasant session of criticism with a friend ("Flaccus touches on every fault in his laughing friend, and is allowed in to play around his heart-strings," *omne . . . vitium ridenti Flaccus amico / tangit et admissus circum praecordia ludit*, 116–117). This private sphere is a retroactively constructed model for Persius' own extralegal space—in fact, Persius adapts it to be even more private. This satirist need not even coax a friend to laugh at his criticisms, for he aims to entertain himself alone (*cachinno*, 12; *hoc ridere meum*, 122).

Juvenal also uses the device of the cautious interlocutor in his first *Satire*, thereby appropriating both legal and literary authority for himself in the allusion to Horace's dialogue with Trebatius.[37] But Juvenal has a narrower view of motives for writing: "Indignation [i.e. not pleasure] makes my verse" (*facit indignatio versum*, 1.79). Although Juvenal immediately conjures an image of satire as retaliation, his intended victims are not the criminals of his day, but the irritating poets who dominate the landscape ("Will I always be only a listener? Will I never strike back?" *semper ego auditor tantum? numquamne reponam?* 1.1). As Juvenal's indignation is greater, so is the threat against his offensive work: the retaliation that looms is a gruesome execution, also the culmination of satire's tradition of violence (155–157). In this section of the poem, Juvenal revives the Horatian legal issues that Persius had disguised as problems of social acceptance.[38] Although he writes because he deplores vice and crime, the satirist risks being punished as a criminal, not merely snubbed in private relations. His interlocutor warns him that he might be branded an informer: "He will be [seen as] an accuser who says "that's the man" (*accusator erit qui verbum dixerit 'hic est,'* 161). The line adapts Persius 1.28, where the satirist's interlocutor uses the quote *'hic est'* to refer to coveted literary fame ("But it's nice to be pointed at and hear people say 'that's the man,'" *at pulchrum est digito monstrari et dicier 'hic est'*). Juvenal's reworking of the line in a programmatic and legal context succinctly illustrates his redirection of the genre to legal issues of the sort raised by Horace.[39] But Juvenal's response to possible retaliation will not resemble Horace's: he resolves to avoid the issue by attacking only the dead (170–171).[40] Juvenal's legalistic evasion of punishment here only underscores—in dramatized form—satire's programmatic interest in the workings of the law, rather than signaling the birth of a form of satire that is detached from the law. Instead of devising a programmatic definition of satire that emphasizes other functions, Juvenal situates his satire directly in the path of his potential punishers.

In the conventional apologiae, the satirist figure moves between the roles of jurist, vigilante, and criminal, bringing out both the tensions between these roles and their potential to blend. The indeterminacy of the satirist's legal role is enhanced by other factors, too, including his attachment of his work to other quasi-legal systems, and his exposure of theoretical problems in society's methods of discriminating between right and wrong. As with the practices of theater and violence, the stakes of the poets' self-definition in a legal context are high. The legal world in which the satirist works also provides a model for his own acts of exposure, judgment, and punishment. Satire draws on both the appealing aspects of law—the gratification that can come from passing judgment, the organization of society that law makes possible—and the pitfalls of those effects.

By identifying with different players in the legal system and by perceiving law's artificial construction, the satirists claim special liberty to explore the workings of law in their portrayals of human experience. Law in the satiric version of the world reflects the same problems that are seen in programmatic poems. As dramatized especially effectively by Horace and Juvenal, it is subjective, mutable, and prone to reverse its evolutionary direction, rediscovering and reviving its cruder ingredients. It is also inescapable, catching up to define the subject who attempts to flee it—a theme that shapes Horace's second book and Persius' *Satires*. These reminders of law's reach reflect its continued role in the narrative landscape and critical agenda of satire. In Juvenal, law's functions and limitations are merged with satire's in the most concrete manner, as if the genre's entire evolution has been a process of legal definition.

LIVING WITH LAW

A number of Lucilian fragments show that the law holds interest as a satiric subject from the beginning of the tradition. The *Satires* staged courtroom disputes, and even irreverently recounted real trials of Lucilius' time.[41] Book 1 apparently depicted a posthumous trial of Lentulus Lupus, a political opponent of Lucilius' patron Scipio, before the assembly of gods (called the *Concilium Deorum*, frs. 5–47 W). Book 2 contained another, earthly trial scene, in which Scipio's enemy Mucius Scaevola is prosecuted for extortion (53–93 W). Lucilius also refers to sumptuary legislation passed during his lifetime, the Licinian law (599 W).[42] Other scenes of legal dispute and activity are scattered throughout the Lucilian corpus; some memorable ones are a cuckolded husband threatening to castrate himself as punishment for his wife (303–307 W) and the vivid description of the "rat-race" that highlights people's artifice and greed in legal contexts (1145–1151 W). Although it is difficult to reconstruct Lucilius' subtler commentary about the law, such scenes attest his interest in legal process as a narrative context and a source of language and ideas concerning wrongdoing and punishment. Particularly striking is the case of legal wordplay noted earlier, the *exlex* fragment (1017 W). The satirist's joke on the paradox of *exlex* status conveys two key ideas: first, that legal status and legality are conferred on individuals and actions by external, artificial means; second, that there is no way to escape being defined in some way by the law, even if one is labeled an outlaw.

Law is an appropriate topic, and the court an appropriate dramatic setting, for a genre that concerns itself with social conflict. But satire's own relationship to the law, established as slippery, volatile, and at the same time definitive and fertile, provides extra motivation for the poets' discussions of the law in society. The same legal world that defines the satirists by alternately justifying and thwarting their work is also an important backdrop for characters in satiric vignettes. This begins in the first poems of *Sermones* 1. Horace introduces 1.1 with the diatribe theme of discontent (*mempsimoiria*), observing people's tendency to envy one another's ways of life. The first pair of lifestyles that Horace contrasts are those of the soldier and the merchant (4–8), and the second are those of "one skilled in the law" (*iuris legumque peritus*) and the farmer (9–12). These generic characters will appear in more concrete forms later in the *Sermones*, such as the rustic Ofellus and the juriconsults Trebatius and Teiresias in book 2. Here they appear to represent the perspectives of their respective trades: the jurisconsult praises the country when his clients are pestering him at daybreak, while the farmer, forced to travel to the city for a civil case, longs for the convenience of an urban home. Horace's construction of this *mempsimoiria* passage is noticeably inept, as he contrasts professions that involve rather similar lifestyles and challenges.[43] Also curious is the portrait of the farmer entangled in a legal matter, "dragged into the city, having pledged sureties" (*datis vadibus qui rure extractus in urbem est,* 11). While this is a realistic enough detail, in this significant position in the book it serves as a paradigm for the legal world constructed in the *Sermones*. Legal activity becomes symbolically associated with the city, while law also proves an inescapable force for both city and country dwellers.

The diatribe poems, 1.1–1.3, continue to sketch a theory of law, weaving together traditional ethical topics to illustrate the origins of wrongdoing and the responses that it elicits from society.[44] While the three poems are connected thematically, they also have a broad subplot: they act out human progress toward definition by law. The first poem probes human desires, surely the catalyst for most crimes; the second observes how people stumble into behavior that is either illegal or reputation-destroying; the third examines systems of punishment for crime and misbehavior. Thus the three poems anticipate the discussion of satire's function in 1.4 with their generalizations about human behavior and their piece-by-piece construction of ethical recommendations.[45] The characteristics and problems of this legal world merit a closer look.

In 1.2, Horace advises moderation in sexual behavior, complaining of two prevalent extremes among his contemporaries—dalliance with married women, and devotion to prostitutes and actresses. These equally blameworthy paths are almost indistinguishable in terms of the damage they do to a man's reputation, despite the fact that the latter type is deliberately attempting to avoid the stigma of adultery (47–63). This point follows a warning about the legal and personal risks of adulterous affairs: scourgings, fines, assault by the cuckolded husband's slaves, even castration (37–46). Such risks motivate those who seek lower-class mistresses. In other words, even these two opposite types are equally defined by the law: the adulterer at the moment of his capture, the lover of a *mima* by his reactive flight from the perils of adultery. As Horace puts it, "fools, in avoiding one fault, rush into the opposite one" (*dum vitant stulti vitia, in contraria currunt*, 24).

As the methods of retaliation for adultery are a grab bag of violent and nonviolent penalties, society's response to the lawbreakers in the poem, the adulterers, is also mixed. In the most violent vignette of the cuckold's revenge, we are told that the community approves of the castration, while a certain Galba dissents ('*iure' omnes, Galba negabat*, 46).[46] This humorous climax to the accounts of revenge makes the point that legal principles do not necessarily reflect universal opinion.[47] While Horace has thus far been aligning himself with the law against adultery, his recognition of multiple perspectives at this point nuances his legal position as social critic. This is more colorfully dramatized in the last section of the poem, where Horace drives home the difference between uncomplicated sexual liaisons and risky adulterous affairs. The satirist begins to use the first person, first describing his safer "available love" (*parabilem Venerem*, 119) with a freedwoman, and then assuming a comic role as he imagines the alternative scenario of adultery. Horace-as-adulterer barely escapes when his lover's husband arrives home, and luckily so, for "it's a wretched thing to be caught" (*deprendi miserum est*, 134).

Sermones 1.2 ends, surprisingly, from the perspective of the adulterer—specifically the caught (*deprensus*) adulterer. This second comic description of the adulterer's mad dash, unlike the first, does not end with reference to punishment or judgment but simply to the misery of capture. Instead of witnessing consequences, we are invited for a moment to commiserate, a response that Horace asserts would be universal ("I could prove that even with Fabius [the Stoic] judging," *Fabio vel iudice vincam*).[48] The consequences are left up to Horace's readers, who have seen once before that the community's hunger for justice (*omnes*, 46) can still be diluted by the protest of one (*Galba negabat*). The poem ends on a note of sympathy (even if that sympathetic perspective is forced upon the reader) that foreshadows a new investigation of the serious ethical issues connected to legal revenge.

Horace shoulders the responsibility for crime at the end of 1.2. As if taking under consideration the appropriate response to "his" misdeed, in 1.3 he advises moderation in judgment of wrongdoing, and condemns the Stoic teaching that all crimes are equal (one that the Fabius of 1.2.134 would presumably espouse). A foundational text for all three satirists' treatment of legal and ethical issues, this poem especially anticipates the discussion of satiric criticism in *Sermones*

1.4 (cf. chapter 2); it also represents the satirist himself in a critical function (condemning hypocrisy as "worthy of being marked out," *dignus . . . notari*, 24; cf. 1.4.5). Horace's concern over the zealous application of harsh standards prompts him to redraw humankind's moral priorities.[49] This occasions theorizing about the origin and purpose of the legal system. Horace anchors his recommendations in the poem's narrative centerpiece, the account of law's evolution (99–106) that also cryptically locates the violence of satire in early human social practice. This passage also stresses, in Epicurean fashion, that use and experience constructed the first laws.[50] Nails, fists, clubs and arms gave way to speech, boundary-making, and law codes: in sum, "justice was discovered through fear of injustice" (*iura inventa metu iniusti*, 111). This formulation is an etymological conundrum not unlike that in Lucilius' *exlex* fragment: Horace proposes, paradoxically, that it was the experience of the *iniustum* that gave rise to a definition of *ius*. While supporting the argument that *utilitas* created law, the claim also brings out the idea that law must be perpetually under construction, often subjective, and always human-made. The chicken-and-egg relationship of *ius* and *iniustum* illustrates law's slipperiness and detachment from absolutes. Justice depends for its meaning on the existence of its opposite. This is shown to apply to satiric law as well, when Horace proceeds to write that law in 1.4 as a pretended response to criticism of the first three poems and with frequent reference to his work's literary and social foils.

The connection of *ius* to *metus iniusti* also makes an appropriate climax to the first three poems of *Sermones* 1, which rewrite first the origins of vice and crime, and then the origin of law. Horace will shortly write satire, the genre that feeds on all of these elements, into that landscape. It is in this sense that the poet does begin to explain satire's status as a *iustum poema* even before he stages the discussion of its "just/proper" literary status. Like the human subjects of the diatribes, satire is itself defined by rules and systems; it constructs its own law from the experiences related in that series of poems. As a quasi-legal system itself, it builds up its agenda based on its observation of injustice and folly (*iura inventa metu iniusti*). This is not an exclusive agenda of correction, however: Horatian satire will also continue to observe and comment on law's evolution, as well as its own.

While the diatribe poems put law in a human social context and illuminate its potential instability, constructing the system in which satire exists, the middle group of poems in book 1 centers on the poet himself as a human subject— poet and son (1.4), friend and client (1.5, 1.6). The satirist figure emerges from this set of poems with a more complexly drawn social role, and engages in a new narrative experiment. In the third trio of *Sermones* 1, satire takes on a new legal identity, in that the three poems act out individual conflicts with unique modes of resolution.[51] Satire moves from being the medium of criticism itself (*notare*) to a narrative medium, the rhetorical structure that frames, explores, and relates conflict to its readers. *Sermones* 1.7–1.9 also draw out some of the suggestions made about law in the earlier poems: namely, that it is primarily associated with the urban landscape while having a certain reach into more distant parts (cf. the jurist and the farmer, 1.1.9–12), and that it has a historical connection to more violent methods of regulation (cf. the evolution narrative, 1.3.99–106) that may also be represented in alternative strategies for revenge in the present (cf. the adulterer's fate, 1.2.37–46).

Physical setting and the nature of the conflict in each poem help to shape the presentation of the dispute and its settlement. The story of Persius and Rex has been spread in doctors' offices and barbershops (1.7.3), presumably in Rome, but the event took place in Brutus' province of Asia. The fierce verbal confrontation in the provincial court, removed from the gossip venues that process it, ends with a violence-evoking joke rather than a resolution to the trial. The next poem, 1.8, is set in the vicinity of Rome, but in a former cemetery outside the Servian Wall (now Maecenas' private garden). The transgression of the witches, which combines invasion of the protected space with sinister *carmina* (19), is not punished until they have achieved considerable success—their activity comprises the poem's principal narrative section (23–45). Priapus must administer his own crude and muted form of justice with his threatening pose and, finally, his terrifying fart. The witches disappear *in urbem* (47), finally leading us into the city proper for the final poem of the group. Here, Horace's walk through Rome with the pest in pursuit ends with a mixed victory for the satirist, as he is dragged into a court procedure.[52]

These three poems dramatize a movement from the city to the provinces and back into the city again, providing different settings for its series of conflicts. The series represents the range of primitive and civilized metaphors for satire: crude verbal abuse and wit, sexual or quasi-sexual violence, and formal legal procedure. It also points to appropriate physical contexts for each of these activities: outside the city for cruder forms of revenge, and inside for formal process. At the same time, Horace blurs the distinctions between these versions of satiric prosecution. As humankind's evolving methods of social control are fundamentally related, if different in style, the grouping of these three poems suggests an underlying link between the regulatory methods that they depict. We may even note a small reversal of the simple scheme of rustic crudeness versus urban formality. The confrontation between Persius and Rex is a proper trial, however crude its execution, while the court case of the pest in the city has nothing to do with Horace's animosity for him, but is tacked onto the poem as a sort of *deus ex machina*.[53] While law provides a framework for the poems, its intended purpose seems irrelevant; its historical variations and hidden surprises prove to be more vital ingredients in the creation of satire. The role of Brutus in 1.7 well illustrates the hidden potential of law to harm and disrupt. At first a silent, observing presence with a mission of judging, Brutus is revealed by Persius' concluding pun to have a violent and partisan past. The past that this figure carries with him resembles that of the law itself, an idea that will generate interesting narrative experiments in Juvenal.

During *Sermones* 1, law's original evolution is captured and unraveled; satirist and characters experience the birth and development of law, but they also watch it lapse into weaker or more primitive forms. At the opening of book 2, law's force in the poet's world is a given. As Horace's legal consultation is positioned as an introduction, the book is framed as a response to the problems outlined there. The indirect satire of *Sermones* 2, in which the satirist himself either stands on the sidelines or takes the position of target, strategically offsets the real Horace's recent social ascent while also showing awareness of the new world order after Octavian's final defeat of Antony.[54] Although the book portrays ordinary *sermo*, "chat," as a mode that arises organically from relaxed conditions (among friends at the poet's Sabine estate, 2.6.71), these conditions themselves are created in response to the external changes announced in 2.1. The book's satiric *lex* acknowledges the *leges* that surround the poet; it is even more reactive than the societal *ius* that Horace imagines deriving from *metus iniusti* at 1.3.111.

The book presents a series of escape scenarios that allow the satirist to deflect the criticisms raised in 2.1. Horace's approach is to substitute and metaphorize: culinary principles symbolize ethical or poetic ones (2.2, 2.4, 2.6, 2.8), country replaces city as a setting (2.3, 2.6), mythological figures stand in for contemporary characters (2.5), and a holiday atmosphere, that of the Saturnalia, prompts the complete didactic role reversal of 2.3 and 2.7. These thematic substitutions and reversals are complemented by a rhetorical and dramatic overhaul, in that in book 2 Horace becomes a principal actor whose experiences tie this new satiric project together. To put it more accurately, while Horace retains ultimate rhetorical control, he constructs a second self, entering the book's world as a dramatic character who is passive, marginalized, and criticized. This new rhetorical structure of Horatian satire, while its elements still derive from Roman traditions and moral discourse, bears little resemblance to the direct Lucilian mode of attack and mockery to which Horace and Trebatius refer in shorthand as the satirist's work (2.1.21–23, 62–70).

Horace's new methods of participation in the world of his satire allow him to act out the problems of law's reach heralded in 2.1. The experiment in different perspectives and levels of authority especially recalls the poet's confident-sounding prediction at 2.1.59–60: "Whether rich or poor, at Rome or—if chance so decrees it—an exile, whatever shade my life has, I will write" (*dives, inops, Romae, seu fors ita iusserit, exsul / quisquis erit vitae, scribam, color*). The statement has elicited little scholarly comment, perhaps because it seems such a generic announcement of literary inclination; yet as Oliensis points out, it gets at the heart of Horace's ultimate legal position in the poem, for line 59 "could be paraphrased as 'whether in Caesar's favor or out of it.'"[55] Moreover, the entire claim may be said to be the only firm prediction (in the fiction of the dialogue) that Horace will actually produce the rest of book 2. This is so because the declaration is broad enough to encompass many hypothetical outcomes, including one in which the advice of Trebatius fails to help the poet to practice satire just as he likes; thus it nods at the ambiguous ending of the consultation.

The allusion to possible exile, the climax of the list and line in 59, seems especially significant even though it is suppressed in the subsequent discussion. The mention of exile hints that Horace's satire may bring him trouble after all, and offers a particularly stark alternative to being at Rome (*Romae*)—one might have reasonably expected the opposite of *Romae* to be "in the country," something like *ruri*. In fact, the condition of exile makes an appropriate metaphor for what we may construe as Horace's preemptive solution to the legal troubles presented in 2.1: his withdrawal, occasionally from the urban scene (2.3 and part of 2.6), but more consistently from the position of traditional satirist. Instead of staying for trial (*ius iudiciumque*), as it were, Horace imitates the common practice of voluntary exile, with loss of citizen status, before or after conviction.[56] By abandoning his expected role, he can remain secure from harm.

But exile, as we know, does not equal freedom from the law; and like all exiles, Horace ends up being bound by law all the same. The escape scenarios of book 2—whether the poet is escaping from a place (Rome), a subject (ethics), or a position of authority—still conjure worlds that are defined by law. The casual atmosphere in which Horace imagines Lucilius and friends joking (2.1.71–74) suggests a new rule: namely, satiric freedom is best exercised over a pot of simple greens. Accordingly, 2.2, 4, 6, and 8 explain *ad nauseam* that gastronomic culture recognizes a rigid dichotomy of simple and elaborate, each mode with its own *iura*.[57] The Saturnalia holiday, while associated with free speech and relaxation of everyday hierarchies, is itself a quasi-legal framework in which players take on prescribed roles.[58] The law of the land at Horace's Sabine estate is to ignore "crazy" drinking laws (*[quisque] solutus / legibus insanis*, 2.6.68–69). His use of the negative construction *solutus legibus* to express his freedom is another expression of the paradox of lawlessness; the group's behavior has meaning by virtue of its deviation from the more typical procedure. And the estate itself, whose atmosphere produces natural *sermo*, was a gift from Maecenas, bestowed within the framework of *amicitia*. Just prior to this disclosure comes 2.5, in which we learn about the most calculated and corrupt version of "friendship," legacy hunting. If we are not unsettled by the juxtaposition, 2.6 still makes us aware of Horace's relationship of exchange with his patron.[59] Horace is bound by this new set of laws, experiencing the paradox of being *exlex*.

The term that sums up Horace's circumstances also has criminal connotations, as we are reminded when the poet makes occasional gestures of resistance. The two Saturnalia poems represent the most complete reversal of the poet's position, but in neither case does Horace completely relax into his new role. At the opening of 2.3, Damasippus observes that Horace has fled Rome in a state of sobriety for the duration of the holiday (*ipsis / Saturnalibus huc fugisti [sobrius]*, 4–5). This detail makes it seem as though Horace's initial plan was to avoid the holiday's consequences, and so clashes with the metaphorically Saturnalian dramatic structure of the poem. A mathematical problem springs up when we attempt to interpret the "double negative" setting of 2.3: what kind of legal environment do reversal *and* escape add up to create? Nor have the original legal worries of 2.1 disappeared yet. Damasippus charges Horace with attempting (unsuccessfully) to "pacify envy" (*invidiam placare*, 13) by abandoning his literary work. In 2.1, Horace had imagined *Invidia* personified as his foe, but defied her with bluster (78). By conjuring envy, Damasippus implies that Horace has neither conquered nor escaped that problem; he will simply be criticized for shirking the art at which he excels (*virtute relicta . . . contemnere miser*, 13–14).

The second Saturnalia poem, 2.7, entangles Horace in law in a different way. Like 2.3, it begins with a change in the normal order; this time, the traditional holiday arrangement in which slave dominates master is authentically replicated. This is not a holiday for Davus alone: free Romans viewed the Saturnalia as an occasion for their own temporary liberation, as if the burdens of ordinary life (including slave ownership) were the free person's version of slavery.[60] Horace approaches his interlocutor with indulgence and anticipation of this infectious *libertas*: "Come then, since our ancestors willed it, enjoy the freedom of speech that December grants" (*age, libertate Decembri / quando ita maiores voluerunt, utere*, 4–5).[61] But Davus' lecture, elaborating the Stoic paradox that all fools are slaves, appears to push the premise of the Saturnalia too far—perhaps, as Bernstein suggests, because the poem recognizes the equally compelling proposition that a slave cannot really know what freedom is.[62] Driven to exasperation by his slave's criticisms, Horace enters self-defensive mode, requesting rocks and arrows as if he intends to cut short the slave's lecture with violence (116). The next and final exchange pushes Horace into a comic master's role as he threatens Davus with relegation to the farm (117–118).[63]

All of this adds up to convey the poet's reintegration into a legal framework and its concomitant problems. It is worth recalling that in the book's introductory poem, Horace envisions himself responding in self-defense to external attacks with his satiric "sword" (2.1.44–46). Without denying the comic feeling of the end of 2.7, we may still appreciate the way in which it echoes the prediction of 2.1. Ironically, it is the speech of a slave that drives Horace to self-defense, and that furthermore prompts him to write himself back into the normal, hierarchical social order. His first threat, to attack Davus physically, is reinforced and also refined by his second, to validate the usual hierarchy by demoting him. The poet essentially reenacts the regulatory process that built society after humans crawled from the earth: first violence in the name of order, then linguistic and legal structures (1.3.99–106).

By the end of 2.7, Horace's ambivalence about his ability to escape the legal world has been revealed. The satirist figure's experiment in withdrawal has proved only to tie him back up in multiple "legal" systems, as should be expected even of one who is *exlex*. Horace even finds himself ascending to the top of the system again, and into the role of the earliest humans who worked to create social order. Law's long evolution turns out to be a never-ending and cyclical process. The proposition that hangs over *Sermones* 2.1, that satire might evade legal limitation, is proved unrealistic. This discovery is only possible, however, because Horace handles the question by inventing a new form of satire, writing a new generic code. His second self, a dramatic character visiting misleadingly low-pressure environments, is instrumental in drawing satire's new limits and identity. As the next chapter will show, the experience of this character plays a major role in the project of generic construction.

BOUND BY METAPHOR

In lecturing Horace, Davus aims to attack the master-slave hierarchy by means of the Stoic paradox "all fools are slaves"—his allegedly fickle and lecherous master being the perfect example. This attempt to reconfigure moral authority appears to end without complete success. Persius enters the arena of satire at this very place where Horace and Davus have left it, each reminded of his own vulnerability. The first *Satire* of Persius attempts to carve out a place for the genre that augments his claim to moral authority while keeping him safe. This means separating his own critical standards from those that dominate the environment of the poem. The scene of *Satire* 1 is a world in which criticism—and most tellingly, self-criticism—has died.[64] Although the poem's misguided *literati* marshal an array of metaphorical tools—the scale, the critical nail, the straight-edge, the razor[65]—they are incompetent (because fundamentally unwilling) judges both of poetry and of morals. The satirist's remedy, though modeled on the more tactile satire of Lucilius and Horace (Lucilius "cut into the city," *secuit . . . urbem*, 114; Horace "touched vice," *vitium . . . tangit*, 116–117), appears to be hands-off: a quiet whisper directed discreetly at a hole in the ground (119–120). But again, appearances deceive. That hole is dug right where Persius' imaginary critic has denied him access: *hic* (120) is the sacred ground that the satirist has been forbidden to mark ("'I forbid anyone,' you say, 'from making a stink here,'" '*hic,*' *inquis, 'veto quisquam faxit oletum,'* 112).[66] By digging into the earth, Persius illustrates his satire's prescription for self-scrutiny; at the same time, he circumvents his critic's order and achieves access to the audience that is trying to avoid him, those whose tender ears his satire will scrape.

This metaphorical architecture of Persius' new version of satire seems to avoid one important piece of Horace's self-presentation: the poet's relationship to the law. As I noted earlier, while Persius echoes the dialogue with Trebatius in referring to his potential rejection at the doors of the great (108–109), he does not evoke the "law and trial" that hang over Horace's head in *Sermones* 2.1 (*ius iudiciumque*, 82–83). Correspondingly, Persius makes no claim to attack vice on behalf of the laws of the state. On the surface, then, Persius aims to construct for his satire a personal set of regulations while being unconcerned with external legal threats.[67] This poet, by avoiding programmatic reference to the law, may have found a way to operate *exlex*.

Like Horace, however, Persius cannot live without law. Several rhetorical and thematic features of the *Satires* suggest this. First, Persius clearly alludes throughout *Satire* 1 to Horace's consultation with Trebatius; although he omits reference to the legal points made in his source text, this strategy of suppression still forges a relationship between "extralegal" satirist and the law. Second, Persius constructs his satire in part around a set of laws that, although separate from the laws of the state, are notoriously rigid—the moral precepts of Stoicism. While Persius' deployment of Stoic principles is interrogative and complex, he clearly distances himself from Horace's more Epicurean attitude to crime and punishment; his satire is like the harsh "knotted thong" that Horace criticizes (*horribili . . . flagello*, 1.3.119).[68] Where Horace is subtle, polished, and mild (morally, as stylistically), Persius aggressively and creatively advocates the idea that a small sin may be as destructive as a serious one.

Third, via another allusion to Horace, Persius does weave the law into a discussion of moral authority. In *Satire* 5, following a series of poems that emphasize internal standards of justice, the mechanical world of society's laws intrudes when Persius interrogates the artificial, institutionalized procedure of manumission (described at 73–90) as compared with true freedom. In this, the "only sustained engagement with the law" in Persius,[69] numerous and telling adjustments are made to the Horatian scenario. While Davus the slave had given the Stoic lecture on fools-as-slaves and then been silenced by his master, Persius restores authority to the Stoic principle by delivering the lecture himself, uninterrupted by competing authority figures. The centurions who appear at the end of the poem to laugh at the sermon (189–191) do not undermine its validity but reinforce it by proving their ignorant self-satisfaction. Judging by these features, it might seem that Persius lets the sermonizing slave win in this case.

At the same time, the reversals effected on the Horatian scenario do not restore Davus himself to his Saturnalian position of moralist; the addressee that Persius conjures up to be his target is a manumitted slave. Ironically, Persius ridicules the false sense of freedom possessed not by the ordinary citizen or self-styled sage (as we might expect from one who is trying to level the field) but of the slave who has managed to escape the condition imposed on him at birth. By criticizing the slave's assumption that manumission gives him freedom (88–90), Persius locates freedom not in personal integrity or enlightenment, but in the cultural law that calls some people slaves and others free. Undermining the institution of manumission without also questioning the existing structure only reinforces the unspoken assumption that a slave is naturally suited to his position. Yet Persius adduces natural law here to warn the new freedman away from error:

> stat contra ratio et secretam garrit in aurem,
> ne liceat facere id quod quis vitiabit agendo.
> publica lex hominum naturaque continet hoc fas,
> ut teneat vetitos inscitia debilis actus.
>
> Reason stands before you and whispers privately into your ear,
> that no one may do what he'll spoil in the doing.
> The common law of humankind and Nature hold this rule,
> that weak ignorance should regard action as forbidden.
> (5.96–99)

Ignorance of a different kind ("of our inviolable laws," *sanctarum inscitia legum*) is the condition about which Trebatius warns Horace at the close of their consultation (*Sermones* 2.1.81). Ignorance in a deeper sense may be the cause of the faults that Persius surveys in his book, in the cases of misguided literary critics (*Satire* 1), people who pray for wealth and status (2), reluctant students (3), vain politicians (4), and misers and anxious heirs (6). But on the heels of the description of the freed slave—and one who has been bold enough to ask the satirist about the meaning of freedom, at that—this pronouncement upholds the system of state law as much as the Stoic idea of reason (*ratio*). Thus when Persius goes on to invoke institutional slavery as a metaphor for mental and emotional weaknesses (126–131), he has already laid the groundwork for his listener to fear the accusation.

Persius does not seem unaware of the potential artificiality of his terms, however. The image of natural law itself in the same passage seems on the surface to rebut Horace's account of law based on *utilitas* in *Sermones* 1.3, but may be understood to convey a more complex message. Persius uses not one but three terms to denote the authority that should be followed in lieu of state law: *ratio*, the "common law of humans" (*publica lex hominum*), and nature (*natura*).[70] These terms are used almost interchangeably here, yet Persius piles them together here as if to shore up his argument. This calls attention to their constructedness and even suggests their fundamental inadequacy to the present discussion. At the same time, these evocative terms seem to relate closely to Persius' own satire: like his own poetry, *ratio* directly addresses its target's ear (cf. *mordaci radere vero / auriculas*, 1.107–108); like satire, *publica lex hominum* and *natura* employ physical coercion ("holds [in]," *continet*).[71] This collective force even claims a quasi-religious privilege by holding out its rules as *fas*. This recalls the satirist's (exaggerated) claim that his work is restricted by a commonly recognized sense of "right," followed by his sudden conclusion that his satire actually upholds what is *fas* ("ah, if only it were right to say it—but it *is* right, when . . . " *a, si fas dicere—sed fas / tunc cum* . . ., 1.8–9). *Fas* is the notion of right that is associated with the will of the gods rather than that of the state (as implied in the phrase "justice and right," *ius ac fas*[72]). While the aposiopesis in that passage may give the impression that Persius decides to seek a more subtle way of expressing himself,[73] the first words he does deliver locate his satire in the sphere of religious law.

This scene of an interaction between state law, natural law, and a human subject is of interest to an investigation of satire's metaphorical connection to law because it alternately assumes and deconstructs the authority of the law. While the threat of legal retaliation does not concern Persius in *Satire* 1, this does not preclude his satire from intersecting with the law in other ways, such as appropriating its function or noting instances of its neglect. Persius gives his satire special privileges by aligning it with *ratio*, *publica lex hominum*, and *natura*, all of which he crowds together in his audience's ear in that grave, confidential recommendation of *Satire* 5. But he simultaneously demonstrates that these "natural" concepts can be (and, perhaps unjustly, are) deployed in culturally determined contexts. Attacking a poem of his satiric predecessor's that destabilizes and confuses satire's legal affiliations, Persius attaches his satire to legal concepts that his very treatment calls into question. The achievement of a perspective removed from society—celebrated in the epistolary sixth *Satire*—is compromised by the poems' entanglements with the real world. Metaphor is the vehicle of these entanglements—the metaphors of law and of slavery, on which Persius depends.

SELECTIVE JUSTICE AND LEGAL QUICKSAND

The law of Nature is also cited in Juvenal's *Satires*, but only for its failure to hamper the progress of vice. Nature prevents men from having children together, but it is no barrier to sex and marriage between them (2.137–142); it induces people to feel pity when appropriate, but is no match for barbarian religious zeal (15.131–174); it is even responsible for human weakness, as it makes children vulnerable to bad example (14.31–37). The failure of Nature's laws is mirrored in the legal landscape of the *Satires*, which bear witness to frequent failures of the legal system. A recurrent complaint in Juvenal 1 is that Rome abounds with known criminals who nevertheless have not paid for their deeds.[74] The man who has debauched and defrauded his ward continues to parade through the city with his retainers (46–47); another man receives an "empty conviction . . . for what's infamy, when one's riches are still intact?" (*hic damnatus inani / iudicio . . . quid enim salvis infamia nummis?* 47–48), while the governor convicted of extortion lives a pleasant life in exile, leaving his province to mourn despite its victory (*at tu victrix provincia ploras*, 50).[75] Rather than punishing, the laws provide standards for success in this warped world: "Dare to do something that merits banishment and prison, if you want to be something" (*aude aliquid brevibus Gyaris et carcere dignum / si vis esse aliquid*, 73–74). The law, or more precisely behavior designated illegal, defines and elevates people—makes them *aliquid*. Thus satire's targets are *exlex*, in all the paradoxical sense of the word. Meanwhile, the satirist figure risks facing the most extreme form of retaliation possible, execution (155–157). Besides innovatively combining the metaphors of satiric performance and satiric violence, this image illustrates Juvenal's dramatic extension of the legal analogy.

Appropriately, the theme of impunity extends to Juvenal's own poetic stance as well; the satirist sees droning poets as offenders and wants a chance to be heard himself ("will I never strike back?" *numquamne reponam?* 1). As we know, Juvenal achieves his poetic revenge beginning with the first line of *Satire* 1, for he is now being allowed to say his piece. His articulation of *indignatio* coincides with his discovery of a venue for expressing it: his satire. Moreover, despite his complaints that real crimes constantly go unpunished, Juvenal also dramatizes the punishment of his own targets. Freudenburg reads the "big-fish" poem, *Satire* 4, as a figurative *apomullosis* (rape with a mullet, the adulterer's poetic punishment; cf. 10.317) of Crispinus and Domitian. This method of vengeance, while creative, is also carefully encoded and belated; this play between direct and subtle methods is one characteristic of Juvenalian satiric justice.[76] We may note that *Satire* 4 offers one more equally indirect mode of punishment, in that it ends with an abrupt allusion to Domitian's eventual assassination (153–154). Appended to the main narrative's metaphorical and retroactive punishment is a viscerally gratifying gesture to the real, and ultimate, retaliation to which the emperor was subjected.

Even this harsh conclusion, however, falls short of accomplishing proper revenge: Domitian was murdered by his lower-class victims, not by the oppressed noblemen whose suffering is highlighted throughout *Satire* 4.[77] The poem's criticisms and the story of Domitian's real fate do not quite cross paths. We can describe *Satire* 13 in the same way. In that poem, Juvenal presses the point that legal revenge for wrongs is unlikely to succeed; the lecture seems designed to whet its addressee's anger, not to gratify it with exposure and retribution.[78] But in the final fifty lines, Juvenal helps Calvinus to envision his enemy suffering later in his life, first from his guilty conscience, then at the hands of his inevitable future victims. *Satire* 13 expresses the same uncertainty about satire's punitive power as does *Satire* 4. Calvinus has two less than ideal options: he may either refrain from revenge while feeding on his anger, or take satisfaction in an envisioned future punishment that is unconnected to his own suffering.

The comparison of *Satires* 4 and 13 makes a useful introduction to Juvenal's portrayal and metaphorical execution of justice. In both cases, the satirist encourages indignation in his audience (the first external, the second internal), but then shows justice being achieved in indirect, unexpected ways. The two parts of this process are equally important in creating the legal world of the *Satires*. Legal transactions are a part of everyday life in Juvenal: his characters testify in court and know the law (5.5, 7.13–14, 8.49–50 and 80–84), and both the streets of Rome and the more remote parts of the empire teem with opportunistic informers and lawyers (1.32–36, 4.47–48, 7.148–149).[79] It is the noisy presence of this system and all its parts—all ultimately ineffective in stopping criminal activity—that makes the indignation of victims so intense. Juvenal compensates for this by revealing the operation of other methods of punishment in society, recalling the different phases of the law's evolution as imagined by Horace in *Sermones* 1.3. In Horace, law evolves from violence and occasionally has recourse to its cruder earlier methods. In Juvenal, this association between regulation and violence is even more pronounced, and law's ambiguous evolution more illuminated. If the response of Persius to *Sermones* 1.3 is to restore the validity of the extreme response to vice, Juvenal's is to take up Horace's suggestion to "unroll the annals and records of the world" in the investigation of justice (1.3.112)—and to keep them unrolled, opportunistically miming now primitive, now muted, now evolved forms of punishment. In this palimpsest version of law's history, satire's legal place is as both observer and parasite.

A scenario of justice that comes late and unofficially, but comes all the same, occurs already in *Satire* 1—deviating from that poem's dominant theme of impunity. Significantly, Juvenal frames in quasi-legal terms a vignette that he has borrowed from Persius, as if to mark his satire's revived interest in the legal world. The drawn-out story of the rich man who takes a fatal bath after dining (135–146) is an adaptation of Persius 3.88–106.[80] While Persius' tale serves as an illustration of madness, Juvenal puts a moralistic and essentially legal twist on the story with the declaration "your punishment awaits you" (*poena tamen praesens*, 142). Juvenal deems his rich man worthy of his untimely death not just because he unwisely bathed after eating, but because he has been neglecting his poor clients (132–141). Even this metaphorically legal mentality—by which the poet calls the man's death his *poena* despite its accidental nature—is a signal that Juvenal will sometimes portray external consequences of vice and crime, not just the moral weakness that generates them.

But Juvenal's story, and the rich man's punishment, do not end with the death itself. The news of the miser's death spreads, and his funeral procession draws cheering crowds ("the new tale, not a sad one, travels through all the dinner tables; your corpse is carried out amid the applause of angry 'friends'," *it nova nec tristis per cunctas fabula cenas; / ducitur iratis plaudendum funus amicis*, 145–146). These *amici* are of course the man's ex-clients, who unlike Trebius in *Satire* 5 manage to see their cruel patron suffer for his behavior. The response of the angry crowd, whose indignation we have been made to feel in the preceding account of their frustrated hopes, now stands in neatly for the voice of the satirist. The punishment that the *amici* give is public and meant to strip the man of his *dignitas* in death; it is prompted by emotion and yet ironic in tone; and it turns pain into humor. Juvenal's own satiric procedure is dramatized in the vignette.

As narrator in control, Juvenal may also withhold justice, as he does for Trebius. The story of miserly cruelty avenged in *Satire* 1 turns out to be a cruel joke on the likes of that long-suffering client, who we may imagine taking heart at the vision offered in the programmatic poem. Trebius himself finds no gratifying climax awaiting him at the end of his own drama. The satirist's model of the world does not always provide justice to wronged parties, though it may tempt them to hope for it, as later examples will show.

When justice comes in satiric narrative, it comes from outside the courts, with Juvenal unrolling the history of law to find means that prove more effective. We learn in *Satire* 1 that a governor convicted of extortion feels no pain as a result; Juvenal makes this observation again when he returns to the theme of criminal behavior in *Satire* 8. In this instance, however, his addressee is a potential wrongdoer, and so the idea has a different impact. A governor-to-be might be encouraged by the satirist's remark "what difference does a conviction make?" (*quid damnatio confert?* 94) even in the context of a sermon about the numerous motivations for noble behavior. After all, a long-awaited post as provincial governor (*expectata diu . . . provincia*, 87) represents a climax in the aristocrat's own evolutionary path. Juvenal seems to lure his addressee toward that point: his long lament about the historical phenomenon of extortion (98–112) is moralistic, but it also stresses the ineffectiveness of the law even in famous cases of corruption exposed (Dolabella, Antonius, Verres). The satirist continues to dangle enticements before the prospective governor as he catalogues the now-lost riches of Asia and Greece. But this proves to be a sly prelude to a vision of retaliation from an unexpected source, the victimized provincials themselves. Juvenal gives the advice to avoid a post in a warlike province:

> . . . tollas licet omne quod usquam est
> auri atque argenti, scutum gladiumque relinques
> et iaculum et galeam; spoliatis arma supersunt.
>
> . . . You can take away all the gold and silver
> they have, but you'll still leave shield, sword,
> javelin, helmet—plundered people still have their armor.
> (8.122–124)

In *Satire* 1, the plundered province is left to weep (50); here, having suggested at first that his addressee will enjoy similar impunity, Juvenal gives the provincials back the power to satisfy themselves. The post of governor is a trap that can send the greedy man tumbling back down the evolutionary ladder into a more primitive context of justice, where arms stand waiting in catalogue-like formation (*scutum gladiumque . . . et iaculum et galeam*).[81] Convictions in the courts have no influence, but weapons do.

Violent justice lurks in the future of Juvenal's wellborn addressee; as the conclusion of *Satire* 8 dramatically shows, the phenomenon also has precedent in Rome's earliest history. The establishment of the Republic was quickly followed by an instance of paradigmatic violent punishment, when the sons of Brutus were thwarted in their attempt to restore the Tarquins to power (266–268; cf. Livy 2.5). Juvenal gives the conspirators their due all over again in narrative form, relating the two parts of their punishment: a status-stripping scourging (*verbera*, 267), then execution by "the first axe [to act on behalf] of the laws" (*legum prima securis*, 268; cf. Verg. *Aen.* 6.819). Each weapon used has symbolic power that makes this story paradigmatic for Rome's legal and political history: the whip humiliates sons of a noble father, while the axe declares victory for the new political order. But this paradigm also memorializes the role of violence in regulation and political evolution.

Like Juvenal's first poem, *Satire* 8 deals with human social behavior and misbehavior, including the consequences of crime and vice, in a broad sense. A similarly expansive survey is found in *Satire* 10, although here the satirist's moral theme is ambition rather than general depravity (or hypocrisy, a major theme of the poem's Persian model[82]). Juvenal's choice of subject allows him to enact a parade of narrative punishments, as each of his examples of foolish prayer carries its own disadvantages. The external, tangible nature of these consequences means that Juvenal's narrated punishments line up with a whole spectrum of legal and extralegal forces, from the laws against adultery (311–317) to the paranoid actions taken by tyrants. The latter subject in particular brings out the ambiguous association between violence and law, as well as the third element of civilization highlighted in *Sermones* 1.3, language. Juvenal selects famous and dramatic cases that revolve around the role of powerful speech in crime and punishment. In the case of Sejanus' conspiracy against Tiberius, the prefect met with a swift and unconventional trial, as the bystanders in Juvenal's account point out: "What was the charge? What informer, with what evidence, what witness, proved him guilty?" (*quo . . . sub crimine? quisnam / delator quibus indicibus, quo teste probavit?* 69–70). These civilizing elements were in fact absent, replaced by another linguistic weapon: a "wordy and weighty" letter to the senate from Tiberius (*verbosa et grandis epistula venit / a Capreis*, 71–72). The succinct account of Juvenal mimes the abruptness of Sejanus' downfall (contrast the full account of Dio Cassius at 58.9–10). It also rewrites the Horatian story in which language aids the construction of laws (*Sermones* 1.3.103–106). In this world, the potential of language to function as a weapon analogous to nails, fists, and sticks is realized. Caesar's language is not even a screen for violence, to use Fish's phrase;[83] it is tantamount to violence. In a variation on this theme, other regimes have famously punished oppositional speech with violence, as in the cases of Cicero and Demosthenes. The former doomed himself in speaking against Antony, as Juvenal puts it: "His talent is what cut his hands and head off" (*ingenio manus est et cervix caesa*, 120). The latter made a particularly ironic exchange in his childhood that shows the uncomfortable intersection of speech with violence. Demosthenes escaped the humble, noisy, and dirty work of sword-making to receive an education that led him to his death—although not literally a death by the sword, certainly one that ironically thwarted his father's good intentions (129–132).

In these diatribe-style poems, Juvenal warns the ambitious to beware of punishment from extralegal sources, and his cautionary tales pack together the powers of violence, words, and law in a single blow. But when the satirist addresses victims looking for satisfaction, such visions are more elusive. As Trebius in *Satire* 5 fails to benefit from the imagined punishment of the rich patron in *Satire* 1, so other injured parties in Juvenal are tempted without gratification. Book 5, which mirrors book 1 in its broad chronological, geographical, and moral scope, also mimics the way in which the first book torments the vulnerable victims of crime and cruelty. *Satire* 13 plays on the desires of its addressee Calvinus, who has been robbed of a loan and longs for legal reparations. The satirist's advice to avoid anger has a self-conscious dimension, in that Calvinus greatly resembles the angry persona that characterized Juvenal's early books. Now more cynical, the satirist mocks his friend's desire for revenge; he sheds an unflattering light on the burning guts, moral intolerance, and quaint singlemindedness that characterize both his old self and his current addressee.[84] In *Satire* 1 Juvenal is a would-be Lucilius, born too late; now, Calvinus earns ridicule by trying to play the same role.

But *Satire* 13 is not simply a programmatic update on Juvenal's perspective on immorality. The poem presents what we may describe as an inverted legal dramatic scenario. Juvenal counsels against seeking revenge in court while also making his addressee relive the crime, its causes in human nature, and its effects on himself. By describing Calvinus' longing for revenge so colorfully, and by dwelling on the cause of his anger while denying him the legal satisfaction that he wants, the satirist turns his friend into an actor in a drama of frustration. To maintain this theme, Juvenal allows Calvinus one brief glimpse into the legal system for which he yearns. After listing numerous crimes that are far more damaging than default on a loan (143–156), the satirist imagines the misery contained even in the everyday docket of a single judge:

> haec quota pars scelerum, quae custos Gallicus urbis
> usque a lucifero donec lux occidat audit?
> humani generis mores tibi nosse volenti
> sufficit una domus: paucos consume dies et
> dicere te miserum, postquam illinc veneris, aude.
>
> How long a list of crimes does Gallicus the city prefect
> hear all day from sunrise right till sunset?
> If you want to learn the ways of the human race,
> one courthouse will be enough: spend a few days there
> and, when you emerge, dare to call yourself wretched.
> (13.157–161)

The glimpse of this generic courtroom is only a tease; Juvenal uses it to scold his friend's self-pity and to assure him that to bring his own case there would be futile. But the brief description is powerful: to observe a day of legal activity is to know humanity (*humani generis mores . . . nosse*). The courtroom, depicted in such expansive terms, resembles the world of Juvenal's satire, as described programmatically in *Satire* 1 ("whatever people do—their prayers, their fears, their anger, their pleasures, their joys and goings-on," *quidquid agunt homines, votum, timor, ira, voluptas, / gaudia, discursus*, 85–86) and now more deeply examined in *Satire* 13.

The poem's rhetorical agenda is full of telling contradictions. Juvenal engages a version of his old persona, giving that persona a voice while denying the validity of its claims. He discourages Calvinus from his desire for revenge while offering him images of his enemy suffering from guilt and fear—to the point of starvation, illness, and despair (210–235), and ultimately prosecution for future crimes (just not this one; 237–249). Most intriguingly, Juvenal waves in front of Calvinus—and us—a tableau that resembles his own satire, broadly conceived, but he undermines that irresistible comparison by keeping Calvinus—and us— out of the courtroom. Law is a half-effective presence in the poem in several ways, suggesting still more ways of construing the ambiguous term *exlex*. The law has failed to deter crime; it is an object of Calvinus' fruitless desire; yet in its elusiveness, it serves the satirist as both a suitable narrative framework and an analogy. Juvenal simultaneously invents a new connection between satire and the law, and delivers us a kind of satire that denies us access to legal methods or analogies.

To be more precise, *Satire* 13 in particular denies its addressee access to the law. In book 5, Juvenal proceeds to seek moral satisfaction elsewhere: in an analysis of the patterns and lessons of human psychology (as *Satire* 14 attributes crime to bad examples within the family) and in the satisfyingly horrific tale of crime among barbarians (*Satire* 15). But at the end of the book, Juvenal offers a new addressee a chance to do what Calvinus could not: to take a grievance to court. Of all Juvenal's poems, in fact, *Satire* 16 is the one most thoroughly concerned with law. The poem, of which we have a truncated portion, is broken into three sections: one on assault cases (7–34), one on boundary and financial disputes (35–50), and one on testamentary law (51–57).[85] Juvenal even mentions the procedure for suing a debtor (40–41), as if to resume the issue that he dismissed in *Satire* 13.

This is not, however, the legal system from which Calvinus sought satisfaction. *Satire* 16 treats not the legal system familiar to the ordinary Roman citizen, but the particular legal benefits of military service, including access to a judge and jury of one's peers. The lucky man in *Satire* 16, whom the satirist himself claims to envy (1–6),[86] is himself a soldier. This man can not only feel immune to physical assault himself, but may attack a civilian secure in the knowledge that he will be able to deflect all charges. The rare civilian who would dare to take his attacker to court will find himself in a nightmare:

> Bardaicus iudex datur haec punire volenti
> calceus et grandes magna ad subsellia surae
> legibus antiquis castrorum et more Camilli
> servato, miles ne vallum litiget extra
> et procul a signis.
>
> When he wants reparations, he'll get Illyrian boots for a judge,
> and a row of huge calves as jurors before the great bench,
> since according to ancient laws of the camp and the honored
> Camillan custom, a soldier does not litigate outside the rampart
> or far from the standards.
> (16.13–17)

Earlier *Satires* convey law's connection with violence by conjuring the tools of summary punishment: fire, swords, whips, axes. This poem goes further, filling the entire courtroom with reminders of that relationship. This menacing military judge and jury, represented by their large boots and brawny calves (as well as their hobnailed boots, armor, and belts; 24–25 and 48), bring instruments of warfare into a legal setting.[87] The civilian seems to run the risk of experiencing his earlier assault again in his search for justice.

As the poem goes on to relate, the military court threatens the civilian plaintiff in more than just a physical sense. This unlucky character is faced with a homogeneous jury and a sudden lack of sympathetic witnesses or even listeners (20–34). Military trials are speedier than those conducted in civilian courts (48–50), which means greater stress and a smaller window of opportunity for this civilian in hostile territory. In the most frightening reversal of all, the soldier is likely to turn the charges against him around and accuse the plaintiff (32–34). Meanwhile, in the one scene of a civilian court in the poem, trial dates are delayed, and even at the moment of commencement, the lawyers take their time getting seated (42–47). While the military trials proceed instantly, we must wait in the civilian court for one lawyer to take off his cloak, and another to relieve himself (45–47). In this poem, the civilian trial never even takes place.[88] Juvenal, identifying with the underdog, laments that "we fight our battle stuck in the unmoving sand of the court" (*lenta . . . fori pugnamus harena*, 47). His account makes an analogy between everyday legal struggles and gladiatorial combat, which heightens the sense that civilians are humiliated victims of an ineffective system. Like the satirist who imagines himself being punished in the *harena* at 1.157, civilians who visit the court are drawn unwilling into performances of abjection. Rather than dwell there in uncomfortable sympathy, Juvenal returns to the military court ("but back among them . . . ," *ast illis*, 48).

Juvenal's last poem plays out scenarios of two very different types of justice: one effective but biased, the other theoretically fair but ineffectual. *Satire* 16 justifies the argument of 13 by offering at best an uncooperative, and at worst an insidious, legal system into which the wronged addressee may bring his complaint. Frustration is the theme of the day both in Calvinus' imagined court appearance and in the civilian's in 16. Should we miss the general parallel, *Satire* 16 repeats almost exactly a line from 13 that imagines the futility of legal process: the prediction "they [will] declare the signatures meaningless, the tablet [confirming the debt] useless" (*vana supervacui dicunt chirographa ligni*, 13.137) reappears at 16.41 (with *dicens* replacing *dicunt*). Juvenal rarely repeats himself thus in the same book; if both lines are authentic, as Courtney believes they are,[89] the repetition underscores the two poems' thematic correspondence. In 16, the satirist's choice of an extreme example with which to make his case allows him to display a trap-filled "real world" that denies satisfaction to anyone but members of the military—whom we might describe as enviably *exlex*, removed from the aggravations of the civil legal world.

Obedient only to their own legal system, the soldiers crush the aspirations of the ordinary civilian. The poem does not accomplish justice for its civilian addressee. Ironically, however, it is in this legal scenario that Juvenal finds a place for satire. He comes to it late (and unintentionally makes an early departure), but he has finally created a satiric narrative that hangs on the structure of legal proceedings. The distorted legal setting in which Juvenal's satire chooses to do its work illustrates, dramatically and absurdly, the genre's persistent failure to operate in harmony with the law. The dissatisfaction with which he leaves the addressee of *Satire* 16, as with 13, symbolizes the fundamental inability of his genre to fit neatly into a legal model. Satire does not take the side of justice against injustice, or hold a consistently oppositional position, or even simulate legal satisfaction for its readers.[90]

At the same time, satire still appears defined and energized by a legal setting and legal subject matter. The same ambiguous features that make the law treacherous or disappointing for those who crave its benefits the most are also what make it appealing both as a satiric topic and a model for the satiric process. In considering vice from a legal framework in the poems that frame his last book, Juvenal tempts wronged parties (and their sympathizers) with the promise of moral and visceral satisfaction. To Calvinus, Juvenal denies legal process, instead walking him through alternative courses of action and granting him visions of substitute punishments. While these visions uncover the cruder roots and the less seemly analogues of legal process, appearing to give the wronged party a full gamut of opportunities for reparations, this process is also undermined by Juvenal's pointed refusal to allow his addressee the more civilized brand of justice. The satirist dangles legal process before Calvinus as a temptation, as if reminding him that society developed its practice of judging and punishing for a good reason. In *Satire* 16, Juvenal inverts this process, leading the victim into court only to draw him into potential reenactment of the original crime or, perhaps even worse, into a static legal world where justice is indefinitely delayed.

The problems that the legal model imports into satire recall those connected to drama and violence. Satire shows its own models functioning not neatly and effectively, but in a complex and challenging environment that targets and exposes all their weak spots. The option of putting targets on theatrical display offers the satirist an opportunity for public vindication, but it may also drag him into an unstable theatrical world, undercutting his ostensible moral program. The model of physical violence, even the supposedly constructive model of ritualized public violence, actually reflects the anxiety of its orchestrators enough to undermine its constructive purpose. Legal process shares the dangerous attributes of theater and violence, in that it is conducted publicly, and so any revelations of inherent problems can be especially damaging to participants. Law also has a special appeal as a model for satire in that it may be conceived as not-violence and even not-theater (at least, as having a more direct regulatory purpose than that of theater). Because of the expectation that the complications of those practices will be avoided in court, law's tendency to fail or to show its violent roots is all the more startling.

As usual, however, what seems to be a failure of the real-world model for satire translates into a richer definition of the genre. As a representative of the law, the satirist compounds his power by carrying the baggage of law's early, violent forms. As opponent of the law, he becomes a living illustration both of law's reach and of its conflicts with equally legitimate systems of regulation and values. What might cause damage to the image of law itself is programmatic and narrative fuel for the adaptable, parasitic satirist figure. Any publicity is good publicity for the poet who aims to entrench his work in society's existing institutions and their histories.

The recommendations to look inside oneself for fair evaluation and moral guidance (e.g., in Persius and in Juvenal 13) raise the possibility that satiric criticism is as much a manifestation of individual morality as a public, institutionalized practice like law or theater. The next and final chapter will consider the relevance of the satirists' individual voices, as represented in fictional autobiographies, to the metaphorical construction of the genre. The satirists build their work on several contemporary models, but they also look to a model that takes into account generic changes over time. The poets construct a satirist figure that expresses not only the genre's social functions, but its dynamics of literary succession. The preceding chapters have attempted to reveal the depth of satire's metaphorical self-presentation as a means of approaching the genre's most tendentious fiction—the presentation of its author figures as authentic, autobiographizing subjects.

4

Teaching Satire

The satirist figure's associations with theater, violence, and law put him in precarious positions again and again. When employed for the purposes of exposing and punishing vice, these practices tend to draw their agents as participants into the arenas (literal or metaphorical) that they are trying to control. But the fragile boundary between agent and victim is exactly what makes satire a uniquely thorough critical endeavor instead of a simple replication of any entertaining or punitive practice. The mobility of the satirist figure allows him access to multiple perspectives on the functions and consequences of his work. By undergoing some of the same procedures of exposure and punishment that his targets do, he secures his position as the hero of his text.

Besides moving from one perspective to another in each arena, the satirist also sheds light on the ways in which these arenas blur into one another. Punitive violence can resemble exposing theater; legal process can overlap with both of these, as it employs both performance and punishment. Although it may seem paradoxical, these relations are suggested in compound definitions of the genre, such as Rudd's "[balanced blend of] attack, entertainment, and preaching."[1] Definitions like this one really depend not on the clear distinctions between the functions named, but on their ambiguous relationships with one another. They are both different and defined by their shared boundaries, both separate and related. As the preceding chapters show, the functions of attack and entertainment are intertwined in Roman satire; similarly, the third practice in the list, "preaching," has its agonistic and its performative elements.

Satire's didactic function is highlighted as early as *Sermones* 1.1, even before its other agendas are discussed in programmatic poems. Horace, beginning his first diatribe, compares his strategy of "laughing while telling the truth" (*ridentem dicere verum*) to that of indulgent teachers who give their young students cookies (24–26). There is a double allusion to didactic literature here. The reference to bribery with sweets recalls the simile of the honeyed cup of medicine, a motif in Lucretius' self-presentation as didactic poet (1.936–950, 4.11–25).[2] The same remark also justifies Horace's mixing of laughter and seriousness; this strategy, called *spoudaiogeloion* in Greek, is associated with the diatribe tradition that informs so many of the *Sermones*.[3] The early placement of Horace's analogy ensures its impact on readers. The later satirists, too, seem to uphold the connection with teaching and diatribe. Persius' discussion and demonstration of Stoic precepts have earned him such labels as "doctrinaire poet" and "Stoic satirist," although this "preacher's" arsenal includes as much empathy and irony as it does rigid doctrine.[4] While Juvenal does not explicitly claim the role of teacher, his grand style evokes prophetic and didactic discourse.[5]

The didactic agenda—even the programmatic fiction of a didactic agenda—personalizes satire in a way that the functions of performance, attack, and prosecution do not. It would seem to derive just as much from the individual qualifications and impulses of the author and his audiences as from a generic legacy. Satire's typical rhetorical structure helps to create this impression. Even if we understand the satirist figure to be a fictional *ego*, he comes across as an *ego* nonetheless, recording his thoughts "as if on a votive tablet" (Horace's description of Lucilian satire, *Sermones* 2.1.30–34). This basic idea is the glue that holds a satirist's oeuvre together, programmatic, discursive, and narrative portions alike.[6] This is not grounds for a biographical approach to satire, but an indication that we have another option for interpretation. Recent studies have helped us to understand how a satirist may employ personal commentary to shape his genre as something both identifiable with, and bigger than, himself. Horace has a "face" and a *natura* that correspond to the genre as it takes shape in his hands.[7] The satirist's *ego* is defined as much by metaphorical associations between author, genre, and society as it is by the rhetorical performance of the persona.

The teaching satirist figure in particular is also a construction of the satiric genre, and depends to a great extent on the authors' individual self-portraits. Education is the central theme of the conventional "programmatic autobiography," a metaliterary device that projects aspects of the genre onto the satirist figure.[8] Horace, Persius, and Juvenal each recount episodes from their days as students that can be read together as constructing a generic posture. The young satirists-to-be experience trials similar to those faced by their adult counterparts. Horace as a child endures the precarious position of freedman's son among noble peers (1.6.71–88); throughout the *Sermones* we are made to see that the poet has retained the physical and moral vulnerability of his younger self, while developing his own didactic agenda. Persius adapts the educational autobiography to illuminate both the vulnerability and the transgressive impulses of the satirist figure. His former self, the student of Cornutus who solemnly absorbed the Stoic's lessons (5.30–51), is associated with more ambiguous figures such as the rebellious child and the impressionable adolescent. Finally, Juvenal's child figure appears at a younger age; we glimpse him practicing declamation and suffering corporal punishment (1.15–17). Both of these activities are associated with the satirist figure in Juvenal, although after *Satire* 1 this figure is more a disembodied voice than a fleshed-out character.

First-person statements by the satirists also have the effect of putting the satiric tradition into historical perspective, simultaneously highlighting convention and revealing how conditions change from author to author. This in turn evokes the agonistic scenario of literary succession (an inevitability whether or not Bloom's familial metaphor adequately explains its motivations and workings[9]). In the tradition of Roman verse satire, the agonistic dynamic certainly has much to do with changing political circumstances. The most recent study of the tradition highlights the struggle of the post-Lucilian satirists to revive the genre that, as they suggest, truly belongs in a now-lost Republican context. While Lucilius' successors valorize him as the patron saint of *libertas*, they also become his competitors, ultimately outdoing him by writing creative satire in the more repressive circumstances of a totalitarian state.[10] This reading supports the idea that satiric programmatic discourse builds narratives about the tradition that are often cryptic and metaphorical. The present chapter will identify one such narrative that deals with literary rather than political concerns and is constructed around the didactic analogy. Like the models of drama, violence, and law, the model of teaching allows the satirists to build a diachronic account of satire that does not hinge on external changes.

Satiric social criticism has moral content, which is both embedded in and makes a special contribution to Greco-Roman moral discourse. The focus of my examination, however, will not be the content—the "what"—of satiric teaching, but the rhetorical and social didactic framework onto which it is projected—the "how." Diatribe, a genre whose influence on satire is made clear in *Sermones* 1, offers a didactic model in which authority is equivalent to the right to speak, and students learn by absorbing the content and significance of lectures. Actual educational practice in antiquity certainly worked on a more nuanced model, in which the goal was not just instillation of knowledge, but the properly controlled social performance of the student.[11] The didactic dynamic that I will uncover involves a similar process, which has as its starting point the simpler diatribe model. The students who populate satire's narratives do not remain passive listeners. Horace's initial pose as the teacher imparting lessons sets in motion a more realistic process of active participation by his internal audience. The power with which his students are armed is the ability to replicate and extend their teachers' work, to make their own *sermo*. This is how the practice of teaching intersects with the production of satire.

When Horace first proposes a model for satiric teaching, he shows as much interest in the complexities and the consequences of the didactic process as in the communication of moral content. From this starting point, he constructs a satiric didactic plot in which his students evolve and begin to objectify and displace their teacher. The satire of Persius and Juvenal continues this plot, taking into account and responding to the aspects of teaching that Horace illuminates. This does not just create the effect of a recurrent and evolving theme, but adds up to a story of succession in the satiric tradition. Teaching and learning symbolize literary production and generic evolution, and the teaching analogy enables each poet to advertise his work as different from what has been seen before.

FROM *PRIMA ELEMENTA* TO SATURNALIA

The opening of Horace's first book of *Sermones* promotes an association between satiric discourse and teaching. As noted above, Horace likens his strategy of gentle criticism to the approach of indulgent schoolteachers:

> . . . ridentem dicere verum
> quid vetat? ut pueris olim dant crustula blandi
> doctores, elementa velint ut discere prima.
>
> . . . what's to prevent one from telling the truth
> with a laugh? So too at an early stage, wheedling teachers give cookies
> to children, so that they'll be willing to learn their ABCs.
> (1.1.24–26)

Although in this passage Horace is actually preparing to adopt a more earnest tone ("still, let's address serious matters, joking aside," *sed tamen amoto quaeramus seria ludo*, 27) the tag *ridentem dicere verum* has stuck, as it seems an accurate enough characterization of Horatian satire. The element of humor reappears in Horace's rhetorical formula for satire at 1.10.14–15 ("humor is more forceful than harshness, and is generally more effective at cutting through big issues," *ridiculum acri / fortius et melius magnas plerumque secat res*). The allusion to teaching has also been taken as a programmatic declaration of didactic aims, and it certainly fits the diatribe style of *Sermones* 1.1–1.3.[12]

But Horace's comparison of satirist to cookie-distributing teacher, and of addressee-reader to child learning *prima elementa*, says too little, too early, about his work. This simple picture leaves open a significant gap in which more complex effects of satiric teaching can spring up. The small pupils are bribed to "consent to learn";[13] the treats induce them not simply to absorb lessons, but to enter into a transaction with their teacher. In Horace's wording, the act of bribery recognizes the independent will of the new student. We may thus understand that the teacher-satirist, once he has caught the ear (or the reading eye) of his audience, becomes a participant in a relationship, not a monologist. The fact that Horace does not claim a didactic role at any later point lends support to this interpretation. Horace *qua* teacher does not guide passive students; he brings them into the didactic scene as players in their own right. He also subjects himself to their newly cultivated critical powers, particularly after his *Sermones* abandon the diatribe mode and venture into dialogue and drama. The *Sermones* become wide-open territory in which the teacher is vulnerable to evaluation, competition, and even retaliation.

In *Sermones* 1, the satirist figure subjects himself to this process by taking a central position, both literally speaking (in the central cluster 1.4, 1.5, and 1.6) and in a broader sense (the poet is certainly present from the first poem of the book, and especially visible in the last). Horace's satire anticipates and makes a narrative of the "[critical] descent into oneself," the *in sese descendere*, that his successor Persius recommends to his own ailing audience (4.23). This self-examination translates the *natura* of the poet into generic elements of satire.[14] Book 1 presents scenes from the poet's life that display his educational credentials, as if supporting the early gesture to a didactic agenda. Both narratives involve Horace's father and consequently describe a quasi-didactic relationship in which the satirist poses as student rather than as teacher. The first lesson that we learn from this didactic satirist is that a teacher of morals must inevitably turn back to examine his own moral—and his concomitant social—progress.

Sermones 1.4 and 1.6 integrate the figure of Horace's father into the poet's present, in which the figures of his satiric predecessor Lucilius and his patron Maecenas are also dominant influences. In 1.4, Horace begins his self-defense by citing the precedent of Lucilius (1–7), but then anchors his own satire in a more personal "tradition," his father's censorious identification of the faults of others as a means of teaching morality. The elder Horace's rather indiscreet method is the precursor to the scribbling that his son practices as an adult, with a view to his own self-improvement (103–139).[15] In 1.4, then, the art of criticism that Horace claims to follow has the aim of self-criticism, and is best practiced by one ready to look critically at himself and his own origins. The poet seems concerned to deflect public resentment of his satire by turning his own critical and didactic discourse toward himself.[16]

A similar tale of succession and self-monitoring appears in 1.6. While describing his entry into the company of Maecenas, Horace turns to the story of his own formal education (71–88). In this case, the young Horace experiences not a change of tactics, but a change of location: his father, despite his allegedly small means ("a pauper with a meager little farm," *macro pauper agello*, 71), steered his son away from the local school at Venusia in favor of an education in Rome. Instead of giving details of his schooling in *artes* in the city, Horace remembers this period as a significant socializing experience, in which he was encouraged to emulate the sons of senators and knights and to dress as if he were well-off (76–80). This emphasis on the broader social context of education helps to cast Horace senior as a teacher-figure himself and not merely as a facilitator. The young Horace recalls being vulnerable to moral corruption, a threat from which his father protected him ("he kept me chaste, the primary mark of virtue," *pudicum / qui primus virtutis honos, servavit*, 82–83). Out of his league in terms of birth and wealth, the young Horace learned to play the part of a better-off man, as well as to cultivate the homespun morality of his freedman father. This is the inheritance that he claims to have brought to his *amicitia* with Maecenas (62–70).

Horace's memories—of listening to his father's sermons (1.4), of timidly entering school, and even of being reduced to childlike awkwardness upon his first meeting with Maecenas (1.6)—are tied to his authority as poet and satirist. The image of the young Horace also exhibits ambiguous characteristics of the satirist figure such as physical and moral vulnerability.[17] Lucilius, Maecenas, and the elder Horace each play a special role in this metapoetic narrative. As Schlegel argues, both Lucilius and Maecenas are foils to the elder Horace, presenting models that the poet recognizes as significant but that he cannot or will not imitate exclusively. At the same time, these two figures serve as surrogate fathers, absorbing through Horace's subtle criticism the inherent tensions of the Roman father-son relationship; this leaves the poet free to praise his biological father without betraying any feelings of tension or competition.[18]

As surrogate predecessor and patron, however, the elder Horace is not a figure without tensions. The two poems delicately convey the sensitive issues associated with this kind of generational change: namely, that the son is likely both to modify the lessons he learned, and to outperform his father. *Sermones* 1.4 ends with the poet's claim that he has toned down the blunt critical procedure of his father just enough to be able to characterize his work as a "minor vice" (*mediocribus illis / ex vitiis unum*, 139–140). Similarly, the end of the education story in 1.6 points up the gap that opened between father and son once schooling and socialization had their intended effect:

> nec timuit, sibi ne vitio quis verteret, olim
> si praeco parvas aut, ut fuit ipse, coactor
> mercedes sequerer: neque ego essem questus: at hoc nunc
> laus illi debetur et a me gratia maior.
> nil me paeniteat sanum patris huius . . .
>
> Nor was [my father] afraid that someone would fault him if one day
> I were to pursue small wages as an auctioneer or, like himself,
> a tax collector; nor would I have complained myself; but as it is now,
> on this point he deserves all the more praise and gratitude.
> In my right mind I could not be ashamed of such a father . . .
> (1.6.85–89)

After he recalls the unconditional support that he received, Horace needs to reiterate that he has indeed achieved a higher position than his father's (*ut fuit ipse . . . at hoc nunc . . .*). This clarification is also an opportunity for him to assert that his education—as intended—led to a change in his social status.[19]

Horace's own accounts of moral, formal, and social education emphasize both the benefits and the potential tensions of the teacher-student relationship. The ultimate and most immediately visible benefit, of course, is Horace's production of his satire, made possible by the influence of his father. The tensions are the gap that opens up between teacher and student, in terms of both methods and status, once education begins to have its effect. These gaps are also discernible in the dynamics of satiric "teaching." Because Horace plays both student (in his memories) and satiric teacher (in the present), he experiences the consequences of teaching from both sides. As we continue to unroll book 1, we see that Horace, as adult and client of Maecenas, is beginning to act out these experiences from the point of view of the teacher.

Following *Sermones* 1.6, Horace explores some of satire's extraliterary origins as if probing the differences and similarities between his own art and more primitive practices. As the previous chapters have argued, the seventh and eighth poems in the book highlight and link different models for the satiric procedure: invective, legal process, attack, and magic.[20] In 1.9, back in his own skin, Horace tries out another form of self-scrutiny when he faces a social climber who wants to follow in his footsteps. The so-called pest is not simply a ridiculous outsider, as scholars used to regard him, but an uncomfortably close alter ego for Horace, engaging the satirist's anxieties about his own newly won access to Maecenas from the moment that he first uses the insinuating first-person plural ("You ought to know me/us . . . I'm/We're educated," *noris nos . . . docti sumus*, 7).[21] From the start, his shadow is relentless, claiming that he is just the right type for the learned group that congregates at Maecenas' home. Horace responds to the appearance of his potential duplicate with an attempt to continue excluding him. Although less evolved than Horace, the pest is much closer to him than are the quasi-satiric actors in the previous two poems. The pest also has an autonomy, in a dramatic sense, that Horace's narrative subjects in 1.7 and his alter ego in 1.8 do not. It is as if, following this experiment in new authorial positions (gossiping in doctors' offices and hiding in the wooden body of Priapus), Horace turns around to find that someone is hoping to move into his temporarily abandoned "authentic" role, that of poet and associate of Maecenas. The conclusion of the poem gives Horace a way out: someone else takes on the role of the pest's challenger (*adversarius*, 75) and the poet, though drawn into court, can take a more distant position as witness.

In *Sermones* 1.10, Horace responds to the threat of replacement posed by the pest in a different way, addressing the issues attached to poetic *Nachleben*.[22] The last poem of book 1 secures Horace's position as satirist and client of Maecenas by reviving the critique of Lucilius begun in 1.4, excluding the Republican satirist's uncritical admirers from Horace's ideal audience, and naming the individuals whom Horace does desire as fellow poets and as readers. This procedure of inclusion and exclusion makes a significant climax to the book, especially because it moves to redefine the process of writing satire as one that poses no threat of competition or duplication. The first of the poem's two lists of names expresses this point succinctly. Horace catalogues his fellow poets, specifically the top poets in each genre (Fundanius in comedy, Pollio in tragedy, Varius in epic, Vergil in bucolic; 40–45) and then offers himself as their proud counterpart in satire (46–49). His declaration of poetic aims pointedly and even unexpectedly reverses a Callimachean principle that poets need not confine themselves to one genre.[23] This need not be read as mere modesty on the poet's part; in the context of the close of *Sermones* 1, it emphasizes the lack of competition in Horace's own circle—an equality that depends on the one-poet-one-genre rule and thus is an artificially created condition. Horace's representation of his literary circle indicates that writing in any genre is a competitive endeavor, but satire-writing is made to appear especially risky. For at this point Horace does run through satire's literary history, mentioning Varro of Atax and other less than successful satirists (46–47), and then pointing, once again, to the genre's undisputed laureate and founder, Lucilius (48–49). Horace's digression into a diachronic history of satire here reveals that while his present social circumstances may be carefully designed to eliminate poetic competition, he is at this moment entering the competition of generations that is part of satire's literary history.

This is appropriate in *Sermones* 1.10, which figures the current satirist as critic of his predecessor, in the manner of all past poets:

> tu nihil in magno doctus reprehendis Homero?
> nil comis tragici mutat Lucilius Acci?
> non ridet versus Enni gravitate minores,
> cum de se loquitur non ut maiore reprensis?
> quid vetat et nosmet, Lucili scripta legentis,
> quaerere . . .
>
> Do you, learned one, criticize nothing in the great Homer?
> Does Lucilius, genial though he is, emend nothing in Accius' tragedies?
> Doesn't he laugh at those lines of Ennius that fall short in grandeur,
> while not claiming himself to be greater than those he criticizes?
> What forbids us, similarly, as we read the writings of Lucilius,
> from investigating . . .
> (1.10.52–57)

"Genial" or not, poets act as editors of their predecessors, and readers as critics of poets. The label *doctus* here connotes literary learning rather than moral training (cf. 1.9.7); Horace has evolved into a different kind of *doctor* from the satirist of 1.1. The term is used with sarcasm in this instance as in line 19, which refers to the admirers (*fautores*) of Lucilius.[24] But the passage still drives home the idea that poetic production sends the poet into the role of subject of criticism, with his readers acting as critics. As Horace rolls out his second list, the eminent poets and patrons whom he desires as readers (81–88), he appears to drop the irony when he calls them *doctos* (87). The naming of ideal readers recalls a partially coherent Lucilian fragment, reconstructed by Warmington as:

> <ab indoctissimis>
> nec doctissimis <legi me>; Man<ium Manil>ium
> Persiumve haec legere nolo, Iunium Congum volo.
>
> . . . that I should be read by the very unlearned
> nor by the very learned; I'd rather Manius Manilius
> and Persius didn't read this, but I want Iunius Congus to
> (632–634 W; cf. 635 W).

Lucilius seems to designate a slightly less high-brow audience than Horace's,[25] but the fact that Horace reorients Lucilius' request does not diminish the impact of the *topos* (and may be compared to Horace's adoption and restyling of Lucilian "satiric theater," as discussed in chapter 1). Both authors show concern over their reception, and even attempt to assert control over it. But in Horace's case at least, the gesture is so timed as to reveal its own motivation. At the close of his first book of satire, just before he dramatically sends it into the world (92), Horace must accept the role of subject to criticism, even as he represents his present circumstances as relatively competition-free.

Horace's criticisms of Lucilius come back to haunt him, though not in the form of an aesthetic critique. Book 2, which presents the more versatile "acting" version of the satirist, shows Horace trying on the roles of satiric target and outcast. In *Sermones* 1, the poet holds a central position as diatribist, narrative subject, and critic; *Sermones* 2 places him on the margins, although the world portrayed in the book has certainly absorbed his satire. The series of poems plays with the metaphor of satire as teaching by making Horace both redundant and vulnerable while his acquaintances make forays into didacticism and satire. The problem of reception raised in 2.1 leads Horace to assert some control over his own in the remainder of the book. But the only way for him to do so is to preempt that reception by anticipating it, envisioning it as a satiric plot, and articulating at his own expense the problems that will arise in its course.

Horace acts the part of the self-aware satirist from the very opening of book 2. The opening complaint about the critical and diverse readership of the *Sermones* (*sunt quibus in satura videor* . . . , 1) sets up the question of satire's proper form and appears to explore a spectrum of recipes for the genre in its individual poems.[26] It is also evident, beginning with 2.1, that Horace's status and his social and literary world have changed since the publication of the first book. Finally, book 2 stands out in the way that it uses different voices to deliver satire-like diatribes or tales while Horace stands by or disappears. The characters who dominate the book have interesting and varied relationships to Horace in this new context, but all of them somehow evoke the precepts or the social position of the poet, and all of them render him passive or marginal. At the same time, most of these speakers themselves are marginal characters, somehow dispossessed or disenfranchised, and pursuing new philosophies of living in a changed world.[27]

This last major feature of the book—its "Saturnalian" scenarios of satiric reversal—is especially pertinent to the present discussion, since the multiple "satirists" who take over the book resemble expert readers and imitators of Horace. The poet creates a fiction that he is recording their words, and that fiction begets another: that the characters who inhabit the world of the *Sermones* can also absorb the text's lessons and satiric strategies. It is especially important that the scenarios of reversal are part of a pattern that creates a feeling of déjà vu for readers. Horace uses virtually the entire book for his Saturnalian experiment, even recycling the themes and dramatic scenarios of individual poems. An explanation for this lies both in the teaching analogy, still relevant to Horace's work, and in the book's formal structure; as with book 1, the ordering of the book's poems creates a meaningful plot. Horace's growing loss of control over his *sermo* may be understood as a function of the teaching analogy. Book 2 dramatizes the reception of Horatian satire, not simply revisiting lessons presented in the earlier *Sermones* but telling the story of their absorption by Horace's audience. In this way, the book's dominant theme of dispossession, which indeed has political resonance, pertains also to the figure of the satirist as teacher. As the end of book 1 intimated would happen, Horace has now passed into a metaphorical older generation.

The threat of exclusion, which Horace both resisted and accepted in *Sermones* 1.8, 1.9, and 1.10, overcomes the poet in book 2. The rhetorical reality of the book is that Horace continues to have full narrative authority, and our impression of this is certainly enhanced by the flawed morality and didactic skills with which Horace endows most of its primary speakers. But within this structure a different and equally important story is being related. In his role as dramatic character, Horace becomes a listener (2.3, 2.4, 2.6, 2.7, 2.8), a satiric target (2.3 and 2.7), and a figurative slave (2.7); he is even absent from the action at times (2.2, 2.5, and, as a major part of the dramatic fiction, in 2.8). Horace's exclusion has been described metaphorically as exclusion from the *convivium*, the company of dining equals which satire aims to construct. In the book's final poem, metaphor becomes reality: unsuccessful in his own search for a dinner guest, Horace must hear a secondhand account of Nasidienus' party.[28] Throughout the book, while Horace is marginalized, attacked, and excluded, other characters lecture. This plays out the effects of Horace's career as educator-satirist, activating characters who practice the *artes* and boast of the *sapientia* claimed by the satirist of book 1. If we construe satiric authority in its basic, functional sense as the primary role in the production of *sermo*, it is clear that in the dramatic fiction Horace spreads this authority to others.

The poem that follows the programmatic dialogue with Trebatius begins with a line that smacks of Horatian diatribe: "What kind and how great a virtue it is, good fellows, to live frugally . . ." (*quae virtus et quanta, boni, sit vivere parvo,* 2.2.1). Before Horace completes the indirect question with the imperative "learn" (*discite*, 4), he interrupts himself to tell us that he is not the author of this lecture: "Now this is not my *sermo*, but that which Ofellus taught" (*nec meus hic sermo est, sed quae praecepit Ofellus,* 2). Ofellus, we learn, is a poor farmer whom Horace knew in his boyhood and who lost his farm to the triumviral expropriations (112–115). Like two of his successors in book 2, Damasippus the bankrupt merchant (2.3) and Davus the slave (2.7), he uses *sapientia* to counter adversity.[29] Horace's self-erasure from the lecture in line 2 is a transparent rhetorical ploy, but as a dramatic fiction it alerts us to the idea that *sermo* can be expected to come from sources other than the poet.[30]

The setting of 2.3 develops this dramatic fiction. Horace the character is caught by surprise when Damasippus approaches him with accusations of inconsistency and a bad temper (1–16). The poet is not just marginalized, but targeted by a sermon in a reversal of the diatribe scenarios of book 1. Damasippus condemns Horace's sloth, suggesting that he might be ready to surrender his former art: the poet should either keep writing, or "whatever you've accomplished in a better time of life, give it up with equanimity" (*quidquid vita meliore parasti / ponendum aequo animo*, 15–16). With this advice, the expected scheme of reversal ("satirist becomes audience/target") begins to transform into one of diachronic change ("satirist, his career complete, retires"). This shift continues as the facts of Damasippus' background emerge. The former businessman refers to his past errors in judgment, eliciting a knowing response from Horace as if Damasippus had been a common moral exemplum: "I've heard [of your change in circumstances], and I'm surprised that you've been cured of that disease" (*novi / et miror morbi purgatum te illius*, 26–27). Although the poet teases the eager new diatribist by suggesting that "a new disease has replaced the old one" (*emovit veterem . . . novus [morbus]*, 28), Damasippus presses on with an account of his personal enlightenment by the Stoic Stertinius (33–36).

These didactic credentials inspire Damasippus' own performance, although they are not enough to guarantee his success. His three-hundred-line lecture on madness ultimately taxes Horace's patience and elicits a retaliatory accusation ("at long last, greater madman, spare a lesser one!" *o maior, tandem parcas, insane, minori*, 326). The convert's philosophical ambition compromises the effectiveness of his secondhand lecture. Neglecting his new dialogic context, Damasippus irrelevantly repeats Stertinius' address to his original audience (77–81); in addition, the heading of madness includes an unmanageably huge list of behaviors, and the subcategories are not treated in the order announced in his formal exordium.[31] But however clumsy the new Stoic's entrance into the didactic role, as the poem's primary speaker he represents what a former student can accomplish. The poem does not simply reverse the old diatribe arrangement (just as it does not quite have a real Saturnalian setting, since Horace is avoiding the festival; 4–5); rather, it depicts the advance of a student into Horace's former authorial territory. While the lecture dissolves in comedy, it succeeds in introducing a new type of threat to the poet.

Sermones 2.4 continues to marginalize the former teacher-satirist in a new dramatic scenario. Horace, still in the picture, catches Catius on his way from a lecture on cooking; pressing him to relate what he has learned, the poet is granted the content of the lecture but not the name of its brilliant source: "The author will be hidden" (*celabitur auctor*, 11). The rehashed lecture elicits what looks like sarcasm from Horace: "Learned Catius, by our friendship and by the gods, I ask you to remember to bring me to listen wherever you attend again" (*docte Cati, per amicitiam divosque rogatus / ducere me auditum, perges quocumque, memento*, 88–89). But sarcastic or not, Horace has constructed a dramatic scenario in which he receives only secondhand scraps from his interlocutor's educational experience, and may well be excluded again. He is repentant about catching Catius at the wrong time, just as he worries in 2.1 about approaching Caesar with a new work of poetry: "I admit I've done wrong, interrupting you like this at an inopportune time" (*peccatum fateor, cum te sic tempore laevo / interpellarim*, 4–5; cf. *nisi dextro tempore*, 2.1.18). These moments in the dialogue highlight Horace's marginality and reduced power. Catius' stipulation regarding his recital of the lecture, *celabitur auctor*, echoes Horace's own pretended withdrawal from the position of *auctor* in the book.

The question of the satirist's rights that is raised in *Sermones* 2.1 seems to influence the poems that follow. In *Sermones* 2.2 through 2.4, Horace plays at passivity and withdrawal, experiences a surprise attack, and is nearly hurriedly dismissed from hearing a lecture secondhand. The parenthetical *nec meus hic sermo est* (2.2.2) becomes relevant to other poems in which characters other than the poet practice *sermo* (or engage in discourse that through Horace's pen becomes the content of the *Sermones*). In the remaining four poems of the book, the same formula seems to continue operating: in 2.5 Horace is entirely absent in the conversation on legacy-hunting between Ulysses and Teiresias, in 2.6 he retreats to his Sabine farm with friends, in 2.7 he is lectured by another newly converted Stoic, and in 2.8 he hears an account of a dinner party from which he was excluded.

These continuing scenarios of exclusion and reversal point up the book's bipartite and parallel structure. Each half of book 2 progresses in the same order through a series of dramatic situations: the first poem (2.1 and 2.5) presents a legal consultation, the second (2.2 and 2.6) a discourse on country living, the third (2.3 and 2.7) a Saturnalian lecture criticizing the poet, and the fourth (2.4 and 2.8) a discourse on gastronomy.[32] Yet the book is not organized solely and predictably around thematic parallels; Muecke rightly stresses that "the differences between the satires as we encounter them are sufficient to counter the sense of predictability that could come from the strong architectural scheme."[33] More specifically, rather than merely repeating the same dramatic settings and themes with variations, the second half of the book revises and fine-tunes the poems of the first half, putting on display stand-in satirist characters who are more heavily armed than their earlier counterparts. This structural feature engages the didactic associations of satire, for in the book's internal chronology the lessons generated in the early poems are absorbed and used in their later analogues. Even after Horace takes the passive role in 2.2, his satire continues to teach—and to his disadvantage. The poet's displacement becomes more acute as his replacement satirists become more skilled.

Sermones 2.5 begins this process by returning to the scenario of legal consultation in 2.1, but using epic characters as its players. Ulysses' consultation of Teiresias, which in Homer's version concerns his plan to reclaim his home from the suitors, takes on both a materialistic and a topical flavor when the hero expresses anxiety over his lost wealth. Teiresias urges Ulysses to restore his property by becoming a legacy-hunter, flattering his way into the wills of the childless wealthy. The *artes* that Teiresias teaches are not endurance and frugality, such as Ofellus recommends, but sycophancy and dissimulation.[34] Though be balks at first, Ulysses declares that he is willing to restore his wealth at any cost (20). While the moral contrast with 2.2 enhances the comic effect of this mock-epic interlude, other comparisons bring the seedy picture of legacy-hunting closer to home for the satirist and his circle. The consultation scenario recalls 2.1, in which the satirist seeks poetic legitimacy in a new world order just as Ulysses struggles to re-establish himself through material gain. The satirist comes out of this comparison looking far more respectable than his heroic counterpart; still another pairing, however, does not shed so kind a light on Horace. Following Teiresias' advice to Ulysses, *Sermones* 2.6 opens with the poet restored to the position of *auctor*, speaking in his own voice and giving thanks to Maecenas for the gift of the Sabine farm. "This was in my prayers" (*hoc erat in votis*, 1). That this poem immediately follows Teiresias' recommendations on seeking inclusion and financial restoration is a provocative element of the book's narrative chronology: as Freudenburg bluntly puts it, "Did our hero sell out and pander his way to the top, just as Teiresias said he should?"[35] Was Horace present in the background of 2.5 after all, taking in Teiresias' instructions like a good student?

Without using these tantalizing pairings to undermine the more appealing account of Horace's career, we may still employ these observations toward a better understanding of the role of teaching in the chronology of book 2. The ordering of the poems, their possible pairings and parallels, do play with the question of Horace's authority as satirist in the book. The transition between the book's two halves is particularly dramatic. Having lost his voice and the company of even ridiculous *docti amici* such as Catius in the book's first half, Horace disappears entirely during the fifth poem and substitutes a Romanized and cynical version of the tale of Ulysses. The myth is oddly relevant. Like Ulysses, Horace in the book has lost his patrimony (his satiric *auctoritas*) and his companions (his equal *convivae*, analogous to the hero's *hetairoi*). The appearance of the Sabine farm in 1.6 promises to restore both: Horace speaks to his external audience, is able to retreat from the city and the interrogations of the invidious, and finds the company of friends at his farm in a scene that resembles his earlier description of Lucilius' circle (63–70; cf. 2.1.71–74). With a simple meal and relaxation of even the rules of drinking (67–70), Horace again achieves—or better put, constructs—a kind of social equality.

His comfort is apparently so complete that he allows the production of *sermo* to pass once again from himself to his associates. "From this [atmosphere], chat arises" (*ergo / sermo oritur*, 70–71); this shift seems as innocuous as the parenthesis at 2.2.2 in which Horace attributes the *sermo* to the irreproachable, paternal Ofellus. Once again others share the privileges of the diatribist, this time producing a kind of organic *sermo* directed at generic ethical questions (71–76) and naming no names. It is only when Horace narrates a particular item from these *sermones* that he begins to risk marginalization again, raising the possibility that this time the poet is more vulnerable than ever. His neighbor Cervius speaks up to tell the tale of the town and country mice (77–117). It has been proposed that Cervius is targeting his host with the tale, portraying Horace as the city mouse who pretends—as long as he can bear it—to enjoy his retreats to the country.[36] The visible parallels between Horace and the city mouse—for Horace resembles him at least as much as he does the truly poor Ofellus, and Davus' accusations in the next poem attest his fickleness (2.7.22–37)—make this humorous fable from Horace's *vicinus* look a bit more malicious. Cervius has used the occasion of free and equal *sermo* to launch a subtle attack on his host, the originator of *sermo*.

Perhaps *sermo* can never be a scene of equality—or perhaps the supposedly equal scenarios that Horace is able to design, such as the company of "top" poets in 1.10, are contrived and transparent. Horace's second attempt to share his poetic authority leaves his status among friends (who are also students of his satire) more ambiguous than ever. Nevertheless, the poet takes on another experiment in 2.7, seating himself for a second Stoic lecture that creates the most obvious parallel with the first half of the book. Horace situates this lecture too in the Saturnalia holiday, but observes the rules more closely this time, producing a real slave to be the poem's primary speaker.[37] Like Damasippus, Davus has recently heard a Stoic-themed lecture (45) and is ready to apply its main points in practice. This time, Horace will be exposed not merely as a madman, but as a slave to his passions and ambitions. In the end, he will react just as badly, reasserting his identity as Davus' master by threatening him with physical punishment and hard labor.

In several conspicuous ways, the lecture of Davus revises 2.3, avoiding the mistakes that Damasippus made there.[38] While Damasippus launched his lecture without introducing himself, only to be interrupted in mid-proem (2.3.1–16), Davus cautiously approaches his master and asks permission to use the license allowed by the festival (Horace responds genially with *age, libertate Decembri . . . utere; narra*, 4–5). Horace relinquishes authority more liberally than ever, but the price he pays is a more airtight and more penetrating lecture from his most liminal alter ego yet. His slave uses as his starting point his knowledge of Horace's own satire: "I have been listening for some time, and [desire] to speak to you" (*iamdudum ausculto et cupiens tibi dicere*, 1). Davus has been listening not only to Horace's diatribes and his claims of personal virtue, but apparently to his most recent *Sermones*. He is well aware, as we readers now are, of Horace's bad temper, a flaw that Damasippus had addressed just prior to being cut off for good (*horrendam rabiem*, 2.3.323), but against which Davus steels himself from the start. Horace calls him "scoundrel" at the onset of the lecture (*furcifer*, 22), but the slave holds his ground, warning his master to check his threatening looks and his angry impulses (*aufer / me vultu terrere; manum stomachumque teneto*, 43–44). And throughout, in order to press the theme of "slavery of the mind," Davus explicitly compares Horace's behavior with his own. Damasippus had had to be prompted to relate his more abstract lecture to Horace, as seen in the poet's exasperated question near the end of the poem: "Stoic, with what foolishness do you think *I* am afflicted?" (*Stoice . . . qua me stultitia . . . insanire putas?* 2.3.300–302).

Davus' superior strategy is best reflected in his accusation of hypocrisy, put in the mouths of *scurrae* who witness Horace's behavior: "You, as if you were a better man, assail [me] and cover over your vice with seemly words?" (*insectere velut melior verbisque decoris / obvolvas vitium?* 41–42). This is exactly the practice that Horace imagined Lucilius to have exposed in his own satire: "[He tore away] the hide in which everyone went about in public looking shiny and clean, though foul within" (*detrahere et pellem, nitidus qua quisque per ora / cederet, introrsum turpis*, 2.1.64–65). As if he has reviewed his master's history of satire, Davus uses the weapon of Horace's own predecessor against him. Horace's transformation from satiric *auctor* to satiric target and audience is virtually complete.

The second self that the invisible, controlling poet creates in book 2, the dramatic character who is removed from the production of *sermo*, affords both poet and readers a better look at the fate of the satiric teacher. Davus is a particularly effective vehicle of displacement and exposure, both the ideal student-reader of satire and the most threatening one possible. His closeness to Horace affords him access to the most effective satiric techniques, such as admission of one's own small vices (passion for a prostitute, 46; cf. 1.4.130–131). By the same token, his relative success in comparison to Damasippus only underscores the validity of his accusations. Significantly, Davus is channeling wisdom that he received not directly from a philosopher, but from the doorman of Crispinus (45), a poetic foil of Horace's in book 1 (1.1.120, 1.3.139, 1.4.14). Davus has manipulated his own marginal status in such a way that he doubles his victory over Horace: even a slave, using lessons from a hack philosopher's doorman, can overcome his satirist master. The poem ends with Horace making useless threats (for as a slave, Davus can fear nothing more than worse conditions of slavery) and so breaking the Saturnalian agreement, hardly making a case for his defense. Horace's student-slave brings home the threat of displacement by alleging that his master cannot even stand his own company (*non horam tecum esse potes . . . teque ipsum vitas fugitivus et erro*, 112–113). In a figurative sense, this is exactly what is happening when Horace silences his too-close other self just to avoid hearing any more charges.

The poem that ends book 2 also repeats and heightens the displacement of Horace achieved in its own earlier counterpart, 2.4. Horace had asked Catius to include him in his next outing and make him a "fortunate fellow" (*beatus*, 2.4.92; cf. *vitae . . . beatae*, 2.4.95). In 2.8, the highly didactic dinner of *Nasidieni . . . beati* (1) is over before the poem begins. While the satirist is the first speaker in 2.8, his address to Fundanius reveals that even prior to the poem's dramatic setting he had been excluded: "When I was looking for a dining companion yesterday . . ." (*mihi quaerenti convivam . . . here*, 2). Correspondingly, Horace is shown to lack satiric *auctoritas* during the account of Nasidienus' party. While he prompts Fundanius with questions and expressions of approval, the comic poet brushes away at least one detail from the dinner in a rather insensitive *praeteritio*: apples picked under a less than full moon are redder, but "why this makes a difference, you would hear better from the man himself" (*quid hoc intersit ab ipso / audieris melius*, 32–33). This comment only serves to remind us that Horace was not present at the event itself.

It is particularly appropriate that Horace's source in 2.8 is Fundanius, the comic poet who topped Horace's list of fellow authors at 1.10.40–42. First glimpsed in that scenario of carefully maintained equality, Fundanius has since crossed the line that separates the satirist from his friends. He is the final inheritor of *sermo* (an especially surprising fate for a representative of satire's ancestor, comedy) and agent of Horace's displacement.[39] His performance is the last in a series that demonstrates the effects of didacticism in the *Sermones*. Long past the stage of merely listening to lessons, the internal students of book 2 show that education can eventually destabilize the authority of the teacher. The geniality of Horace's didactic *sermo* is a tool to bring students in, but what happens next is less under the teacher-satirist's control. Even when he remains present to witness his work, to experience his reception, Horace finds himself targeted and excluded by his successors.

The satirist's double role and loss of status in book 2 invite multiple interpretations. In the sense stressed in the readings above, as he is displaced from the position of speaker and observer, the character Horace becomes an object of ridicule. In another sense, the poet Horace who orchestrates this process from behind the scenes exhibits his own authority and success as a teacher-satirist, for his students' progress gives book 2 its dramatic momentum. Put together, these interpretations point to a third: namely, that Horace has found a way to control his own reception by envisioning it himself. While *Sermones* 2 pays up on Horace's behalf for the criticism of Lucilius in book 1, it also accomplishes the considerable feat of appropriating Horace's own future as narrative material for satire. The poet is able to act out a fictional version of a process from which by definition he will be excluded. The concept of the "chronology of the unrolling book," which ordinarily allows us to appreciate the *liber* as a self-contained world, creates in this case the impression of a world outside the text.

Horace's narrative of his didactic reception draws attention to the differences between the didactic model and those examined in earlier chapters. Where the satiric genre imitates practices that expose and punish, it allows the reader to walk through the implementation of those practices and to experience their effects while also viewing them from the outside. Theater, violence, and law are institutionalized practices with essentially ritual functions in society, and as such have a kind of permanence that makes the satirist's critical role seem quite secure. But in Horace at least, viewed through the lens of the didactic model, satire's doubly mimetic nature produces a rather different effect. Because teaching prompts change in individual students, satire's didactic plot appears linear and finite, aiming ultimately toward the removal of the satirist. It is understandable that a poet would show ambivalence about how to represent this process, but the existence and shape of *Sermones* 2 constitute our best proof that Horace found his own fate—like his genre's origins—too fascinating a subject to ignore.

CHANGING THE TERMS OF TEACHING

Persius and Juvenal each respond to Horace's engagement with the teaching metaphor, revisiting and revising the associations between satire, teaching, and authorship. Their posture toward Horace is not so much critical as validating, for they confirm that teaching is a major generic theme with metaliterary resonance. As usual, however, Persius reconfigures the Horatian paradigm ingeniously. Though he was once regarded as the fervent "Stoic satirist," his teaching program clearly goes much deeper than Stoic doctrine. In Henderson's revolutionary reading, the *Satires* thematize teaching in order to challenge its traditionally perceived structure. The book pretends to present a methodical course in self-reliance, beginning with the command "do not seek outside yourself" (*nec te quaesiveris extra*, 1.7) and leading the student on to a vicarious graduation (*Satire* 5) and withdrawal from society (6). All the while, however, the dialogic satire of Persius challenges dichotomies that are traditionally imagined to govern the experience of education: "Subject and object, agency and passivity, satirist and victim, self and other, Teacher and Pupil."[40] In this compelling account, education is revealed to be neither a stably hierarchical nor a finite process.

The choliambic poem attached to the book of hexameter *Satires* makes an enigma of the poet's own status and qualifications to write. Persius denies having received inspiration of the mystical sort (1–3), shrugs off the divine associations and mundane trappings normally bestowed on bards (4–7), and calls himself a "half-countryman" (*semipaganus*, 6), an enigmatic term that seems to problematize his poetic status without explanation. The remainder of the poem describes birds who readily learn to chatter in human language (or to become "poets and poetesses," *poetas et poetridas*) in return for food (8–14). Persius' own position in this landscape of mimicry and opportunism seems meaningfully obscured, but the poem clearly introduces language and images pertaining to literary status, authenticity, and didactic dynamics.[41] This is appropriate, since as Hooley's work has shown, the key ingredient of Persius' satiric method is creative mimesis. This topic has special resonance after our reading of Horace's didactic narrative. It is through reference to Horace's commentary on teaching and reception that Persius builds his own didactic plot, thereby affirming both the relevance of teaching to the satiric agenda and the link between that function and issues of literary succession.

The first *Satire* also problematizes the poet's status, but in this case in a dramatized didactic scenario. *Satire* 1 contains a subtle play on the Horatian didactic analogy that foreshadows the treatment of teaching in the rest of the book. First, the multitude of voices that clamor for attention in the poem immediately configure Persius' satirist figure in relation to Horace's. When we first meet Persius, he is entering not the world of *Sermones* 1, in which the satiric poet takes center stage, but rather the Saturnalian world of book 2.[42] The interlocutors of Persius, his internal audience and his targets, talk back to their lecturer from the beginning. Persius sends out the inflated hexameter "oh the cares of humans, oh the emptiness of affairs!" (*o curas hominum! o quantum est in rebus inane!* 1) No sooner is the line finished than Persius is interrupted: "Who will read this?" (*quis leget haec?* 2). The poet has company: not a friend who has come to listen sympathetically, like the audiences that Lucilius and Horace request (Lucilius 632–635 W; cf. *Sermones* 1.10.76–90), but an anonymous and hostile character. In these allusive lines, Persius constructs himself simultaneously as a reader and critic, and as an author who will be read—who in fact is at this moment being "read" by his interlocutor.[43] While the poet's later address to his desired audience is tantalizing enough (1.123–134, discussed in chapter 1), this initial encounter with an audience is truly destabilizing. The secrets of Persius' Old Comedy-loving reader are kept classified, but the interlocutor who appears at line 2 almost stops Persius from maintaining his authorial role at all.

This is of course an artificially constructed drama over which Persius the author has complete control; it is also a game with a purpose. When the poet's interlocutor complains that the *Satires* are unreadable, he is contradicting himself on a very basic level by engaging immediately with their author, and helping to demonstrate the particular appeal that Persius' polyphonous work is meant to have. At the same time, however, Persius animates his unlikely fan and frames the dialogue in a way that masks his own authorial role. The interruption of a hostile listener contrasts with Horace's momentous abdication of authority at *Sermones* 2.2.2 (*nec meus hic sermo est*), in which the *meus*, ironically, serves to secure Horace's position as controlling narrator. When Persius meets a competitor for his readers' attention, it happens "live" and with no introduction; the poet feigns surprise with his response "are you talking to me?" (*min tu istud ais?* 2).

This remains true throughout the poem, where interruptions are so frequent and abrupt that editors have struggled over the correct assignment of lines. Part of the problem is that these confident respondents are not two-dimensional puppets, articulating transparently foolish ideals like those who speak in Horace's diatribes. When Persius invents direct speech for his interlocutors, he makes a point of giving them complaints just as savvy, belligerent, and colorful as his own. As Nisbet puts it, "Persius' characters talk like Persius."[44] The interlocutor of *Satire* 1 and his kind are also versed in Horatian stylistic criticism; although they use it too inflexibly, it is one of the strategies that liken them to Persius.[45] Unlike Horace, Persius does not pose as teacher only to see his authority drift into his students' hands; he enters the scene without claiming authority at all, and his satire will portray him occupying new didactic niches rather than a central, controlling role.

In *Satire* 1, Persius strategically avoids the authorial stance of somber *sapiens*. We find quite the opposite as the poet emerges as an *ego* and offers a more precise memory of Horace. Persius' first self-defining act, after the grand preamble and the exchange with his interlocutor that establishes "everything we do" as his satiric material (9–11), is to burst out in laughter (*cachinno*, 12). This onomatopoeic word evokes Horace's own ingratiating laugh (*ridentem*, 1.1.24), but it reconceptualizes satiric laughter as more intense and mocking than a *risus*.[46] The scholiast on this line writes that "a *cachinnus* is a more unruly and noisy kind of laugh" (*cachinnus est risus lascivior cum voce*). Juvenal associates this cackling laugh with the philosopher Democritus, famous for his refusal to let human folly perturb him (10.31).[47] In this light Persius' satirist figure seems perhaps less interested in communicating with others than in amusing himself. This idea is expressed again at the end of the poem, where Persius describes his work as "this [ability to] laugh of mine" (*hoc ridere meum*, 122); unlike the laughter of Horatian satire, which is part of a friendly bond between author and target (*ridenti . . . amico*, 116). Persius' laughter is more solipsistic, as well as harsher, than that of Horace in *Sermones* 1.1.

But there is another difference as well: Persian laughter lacks the other half of the Horatian formula, the "serious" part of the diatribists' *spoudaiogeloion* and the element that turns laughter into teaching: truth-telling (*dicere verum*). We may not come to *Satire* 1 expecting Persius to revive every programmatic utterance made by his predecessor, but this half-allusion to Horace's neat and clearly announced formula is striking. Its significance grows when we notice that Persius actually does complete the *spoudaiogeloion* recipe later in the poem. Only after the long debate about contemporary poetry (13–106) does Persius return to an explicit discussion of his own satire. The interlocutor has finally recognized that the satirist's complaints about poetry recitals add up to something bigger, and he changes his own response to address the larger issue of Persius' intentions. "Why this need to scrape tender ears with biting truth?" (*quid opus teneras mordaci radere vero / auriculas?* 107–108) The mention of truth as a satiric instrument with iambic bite is easily missed, for it is integrated with a more noticeable allusion to Horace (the interlocutor next issues his warning about ostracism, echoing Trebatius at *Sermones* 2.1.60–62).[48] But the image of "biting truth" marks the return to a focused discussion of satire, which occupies the rest of the poem. Thus this complaint about Persius' painful satire, which reopens the discussion of the genre's aims and relevance, bookends the discussion of poetry along with the opening twelve lines.[49]

The revision of the Horatian tag, then, has two striking aspects. First, Persius changes the nature of the constituent terms: he cranks up the satirist's laughter to make it a noisier, more cynical cackle, and correspondingly twists Horace's sober *verum* into a pain-causing instrument (*mordaci . . . vero*). Second, he changes the relationship between the ideas: he severs the neat tag *ridentem dicere verum* into its original two parts, intimating that they may not be easily synthesized at all. Persius confirms the built-in complexity of Horace's misleadingly simple formula by finding an entirely new crack to probe. Where Horace uses the formula to activate a story whose complications arise over time, his successor dismantles the formula itself, as if to make its construction part of the work that the audience of satire must perform.

In stylistic terms, the splitting of laughter from truth-telling is typical of Persius; the poet often tortures and fragments language that his source texts construct gracefully.[50] This instance may also be seen as an inversion of Persius' poetic technique of "sharp joining" (*iunctura . . . acri*, 5.14; cf. the less harsh "ingenious joining," *callida . . . iunctura*, praised by Horace at Ars P. 47–48) In the work of a poet skilled at joining words effectively, it is perhaps not surprising to find a case of ingenious severing. This stylistic trick fits well in the didactic landscape of *Satire* 1. In the poem, the aggressive *docti* deliver performances that compete with the satirist—who is now not a controlling voice but a participant in a dizzying dialogue about the use and abuse of poetic techniques. Persius drops into a scene in which his internal addressees already claim to be learned, and furthermore to be eager to hear candid evaluation of themselves. The poet mockingly quotes such a person: "'I love the truth,' you say; 'tell me the truth about me'" (*'verum' inquis 'amo, verum mihi dicite de me,'* 55). But the truth that this bad poet and critic wants is a "bravo" for his work (*'euge' . . . et 'belle,'* 49) not the rasping truth that satire has to deliver. Persius reclaims the very term, as the description of satire in 107–108 seems to indicate. It takes the criticisms in the intervening section of the poem to build Persius' version of *verum* in a way that keeps it safe from misappropriation.

This strategy ensures that the didactic narrative of these *Satires* will contrast with Horace's, which begins with *prima elementa* and tracks the development of students into authority figures. Persius makes no attempt to render his students as children at the outset—indeed, he poses as a child himself while his interlocutors speak as adults. The satirist's irreverent laughter at 1.12 is a prelude to his self-portrayal as an impish boy who threatens to piss on society's figurative shrines (1.112–114). The image of the innocent child guilelessly exposing the hypocrisy of the adult world is a device sometimes used in diatribe, and so fits well in Persius.[51] This device gets its power in part from the way that it confounds the dichotomy of *doctores/pueri*, the very idea with which Horace introduced his own brand of didacticism. In Persius, it is the *puer* who acts as teacher, exposing the greater ignorance of those who see themselves as learned (e.g., *quo didicisse*, 24; *doctas . . . figuras*, 86; *didicit*, 93). Persius' satirist figure exploits the special authority of a child as readily as that of a Stoic *sapiens*.

Several rhetorical characteristics of the *Satires* echo the programmatic transformation of the didactic analogy in *Satire* 1. First, Persius destabilizes poetic and moral authority with frequent use of direct discourse that lacks clear transitions. It is often difficult to tell who is speaking at given points in a poem, even when a poem presents arresting *sententiae* that would seem perfect anchors for moral discussion.[52] *Satire* 1 is a notorious example of Persius' difficult dialogic style; another is the vexed *Satire* 3, which begins as an imitation of *Sermones* 2.3 with one speaker lecturing another on madness. The dialogue has been variously interpreted as the poet's lecture to a friend, his own inner dialogue, and a scenario of Horatian inversion with the poet in the target's seat. The uncertainty about the division of lines (and about the very number of speakers involved in the poem) quickly derails the connection with the Horatian model, a disorienting shift that is felt up until the poem's un-Horatian conclusion.[53]

The allusive structure of *Satire* 3 is also a vehicle for Persius' engagement with his predecessor as a past, and passive, author. *Sermones* 2.3 makes a target of Horace, with Damasippus initially chiding him for poor writing and reading habits (1–4, 11–12). The target of the lecture in Persius 3 is also a lazy scholar, whose Horatian habits (sleeping late, blaming his pen) are dramatized vividly in the opening dialogue (1–19). But the obvious parallel in the themes and dramatic scenarios of the two poems only partly offsets a sense of lopsidedness. Persius is not just imitating a Horatian model, but revisiting the scene of criticism *of* Horace. Were the student in Persius 3 more easily identified as the poet himself, the poem might appear to be an imitation of Horace's self-critical strategy in *Sermones* 2 (indeed, editors tend to base their interpretation of the poem's dialogue structure on their assumptions about Persius' allusive intentions). But the uncertainty about the real position of Persius leaves open an interesting possibility: that Persius is taking on Damasippus' role while keeping "Horace" in his old position of target. The scholar bristles at this treatment: "Don't play tutor with me; I buried him long ago, and you're next" (*ne sis mihi tutor. / iam pridem hunc sepeli; tu restas*, 96–97), combining remarks borrowed from Horace's more uncomfortable encounters (in addition to 2.3, the conversation with the pest in 1.9[54]). Even in combination, such retorts make a useless arsenal against the lecture. The new Damasippus wins; new poet keeps old poet in the objectified role that was originally a Saturnalian mask.

Persius apparently declines to practice Horace's quasi-Saturnalian self-criticism, instead scrutinizing Horace's own poem using the lazy scholar figure as a linking device. One effect of this is that Horace's experiment in role-reversal and self-displacement is cast, tendentiously of course, as superficial and incomplete. But the poem cannot logically critique Horatian self-criticism with a repetition of the earlier performance in the same mode. Instead, Persius constructs a didactic authority that is not even located in the single perspective of a lecturing figure. As Hooley puts it, this poem is "on one level . . . nothing but an arrangement of orientations," in which perspective itself is thematized: the reader is made to see the moral topic at different moments through the eyes of recalcitrant student, stern pedagogue, unschooled soldier, and so on.[55] We may observe in addition that the poem's construction of authority plays with time itself. Instead of positing that learning and authority are accumulated in a linear chronological progression, *Satire* 3 undermines that idea. The young man being lectured is described as one who has already studied philosophy (56–57), and his case is compared to those of other individuals—the well-rewarded lawyer (73–76), the confident centurion (77–87)—who despite their material success or complacency are implicitly advised to continue learning.[56]

Education does not propel one on an irreversible path; the other side of this coin is that insight can come from memory as much as from new experience. This seems to be the point of the curious anecdote at 44–47, in which the lecturing figure recalls (*memini*) that as a boy he shirked his declamatory exercises by feigning illness.[57] A calculated didactic strategy is being represented here: the lecturer uses his own checkered past to connect with his interlocutor. This recalls Damasippus' willingness to refer to his former self as an exemplum of madness (*Sermones* 2.3.64–65). But in that context, Damasippus is only quoting the original lecture of Stertinius, aimed at himself; as regards his own case, he declares that he is concerned only with the affairs of others (*aliena negotia*, 19) since his own financial failure. Where Horace's lecturer figure shifts his focus entirely to his target, Persius' blurs the boundary between the two roles. By using a past self to construct a more empathetic style of authority, he can be seen at once as both adult and child, teacher and errant student. This approach recalls Persius' use in *Satire* 1 of the image of the disobedient child to represent his satiric project. Like the boy-satirist who threatens to piss in society's sacred places, the truant in *Satire* 3 might conceivably be seen as a rebellious individualist, resisting a prescribed role ("I didn't want to learn the great words of the dying Cato, which would be praised much by my mad teacher," *nollem morituri verba Catonis / discere non sano multum laudanda magistro*, 45–46). Juvenal will also reminisce jadedly about composing *suasoriae* as a boy, implying that this is conventional training for a poet (1.15–17).[58]

The past of the teacher figure in *Satire* 3 takes on meaning as it is exposed in the present, and contributes to a nonhierarchical didactic scenario. Authority is similarly fragmented, and constructed dynamically, in *Satire* 4. Persius initially anchors this poem's dialogue by figuring the speakers as Socrates and Alcibiades. As Horace's personae evoke the Greek philosopher, this is a fitting experiment for his successor to perform.[59] He also quotes moral attacks by unknown third parties (27–32, 35–41). Persius (via "Socrates") gives a voice to anonymous critics in society even when he may be implying that their outlook is flawed. It is the interpretive activity required by those who hear (or overhear) such criticism that accomplishes satire's didactic work.[60] While he challenges the authority of words and *sententiae*, Persius makes education out of the interactions between players.

By destabilizing didactic authority and scrambling linear time, Persius also manipulates our impression of his role in the didactic satiric tradition. As satirist, Persius absorbs the whole spectrum of images of the teacher figure presented in the *Satires*, from impish child to experienced adult. These images function to keep Persius out of the linear progression that Horace stages in the *Sermones*. Because he does not begin the *Satires* as a monologic diatribist, but rather as an elusive and protean character who nevertheless interacts with his critics from the beginning, Persius resists being seen as a teacher figure with a finite role. This interpretation is reinforced by another deviation from the Horatian strategy, this one concerning the poet's autobiographical self-presentation. Although he participates in or narrates didactic scenarios throughout the *Satires*, Persius withholds information about his own educational credentials until the penultimate *Satire* of the book. *Satire* 5, the "graduation" poem, addresses the poet's Stoic tutor Cornutus with a discussion of freedom.

This discourages the reader from reading the poet's life story and his internal story of satiric teaching as a linear one. Instead, the poet uses the climactic poem of his book to look back into his past. *Satire* 5 at once reveals the human source of Persius' moral standpoint and turns that person into the addressee of a lecture. Cornutus is figured both as teacher (in the highly allusive memory related at 30–51) and as student (in the remaining one hundred and forty lines of the poem). Simultaneously, Persius occupies both roles by volunteering the vivid image of himself as a morally vulnerable youth, even as he begins to transform tutor into pupil. When he met Cornutus, the future poet was just entering young manhood, relinquishing his protective amulet (*bulla*), and eyeing the pleasures offered by his peers and the seedy parts of the city (30–36). Although it represents the future satirist at a slightly later stage, the scene parallels Horace's own memory of his formal schooling at *Sermones* 1.6.71–88. Both memories form part of an address to a father figure whom the poet is thanking, and both represent the future poet in a morally and physically vulnerable state.[61] But for Persius, the memory opens the most authoritative performance of his book, a poem in which the satirist plays the roles of student and teacher at once.

Like the severed formula for satiric didacticism, Persius' own authority-building autobiography is rendered into separate chapters, the confrontation of his own past coming only just prior to his withdrawal from the scene in the epistle-like *Satire* 6. The poem figures Persius as master of an estate, warning his anxious heir that he intends to enjoy rather than hoard his property. *Satire* 6 serves as the poet's departing declaration of immunity to misappropriation. Persius drives poetic heirs away from his text, removing the *Satires* from the "vast commodities exchange" that he has shown to be governing Roman society. His teasing refusal to share his property with heirs may also be read as a metaliterary reference to the poem's allusion-packed finale, where the satirist indulges in the full breadth and depth of his poetic patrimony.[62] Thus the last two *Satires* of the book span Persius' entire satiric autobiography, including his withdrawal and potential replacement, while reorganizing the terms that governed Horace's staged experience. Persius saves the topics of his own past and his teacher to introduce his most ambitious didactic poem, and raises the issue of his own reception only to pretend to resist its inevitability. The march of time is still a concern for the didactic satirist, but the possibility of varying the story of succession has been introduced. Juvenal will take up the task of doing one better than this.

TEACHING VICE, MAKING SATIRE

Like Horace and Persius, Juvenal situates his satire in a didactic context, manipulates the chronological scheme of education, and introduces agents who challenge his authority as satirist. But the landscape of Juvenal's *Satires* transforms these elements of the didactic theme almost beyond recognition. Most significant, whereas Horace and Persius destabilize and decentralize didactic authority, Juvenal transfers it entirely onto others from the beginning. This generates a very different story about satire's connection to teaching, centering not on the satirist figure himself but on other didactic traditions that dominate his environment. Yet Juvenal's abdication of authority is also an aggressive move to reinvent his genre and valorize his role in the tradition.

This process begins with the satirist's programmatic autobiography, which contrasts noticeably with the solemn, extended reminiscences of Horace and Persius. Although Juvenal uses the first person in every poem, his corpus as a whole features very little autobiographical digression. A cynical statement of poetic credentials and a brief glimpse of the young future satirist are rolled into one brief passage in *Satire* 1. Complaining that mediocre poets have held the stage for too long, Juvenal claims that he is prepared to join their enterprise:

> et nos ergo manum ferulae subduximus, et nos
> consilium dedimus Sullae, privatus ut altum
> dormiret.
>
> I too have snatched my hand from under the cane;
> I too have given Sulla the advice to retire
> as a private citizen.
> (1.15–17)

Juvenal refers to two aspects of his education: his experience of corporal punishment and his practice of declamatory exercises such as the advice to Sulla. As a display of credentials, this vignette claims no moral training in the manner of Horace's tributes to his father or Persius' memory of his talks with Cornutus. In the same poem, it also becomes apparent that Juvenal himself is not offering to teach his readers. Neither the past experience of the satirist-to-be nor his introductory promises communicate any didactic agenda. The Horatian *ridentem dicere verum* is not fragmented, as in Persius, but absent. As if already experiencing assaults from an unhappy audience, the young future satirist was subjected to punishment and pain (without receiving the edifying content of Persius' ear-scraping).[63] Laughter is also absent from Juvenal's picture of teaching, and from the other programmatic claims in the poem.

Juvenal's display of his educational credentials previews his style of satire and his version of the satirist figure, one that lacks authority in any conventional sense. But authority can derive from unexpected sources and take unconventional forms. As Juvenal's childhood memory offers a vision of his future satiric style, another fleeting reminiscence—the only other one included in *Satire* 1—establishes the personal perspective that gives this satirist his authority. In his first list of examples of contemporary depravity, Juvenal includes this complaint about the instability of social rank: "[Satire is called for] when one man rivals all the nobility with his wealth, the same man whose clipping made my heavy youthful beard rasp" (*patricios omnis opibus cum provocet unus / quo tondente gravis iuveni mihi barba sonabat*, 24–25). In other words, the satirist's former barber is now a millionaire. This anecdote proclaims Juvenal's outrage at large-scale societal change, as distinct from immorality in general. From the point of view of the poet (although certainly not for his former barber), this individual case of economic progress illustrates a general decline—and, consequently, indicates an urgent need for satire. The evident parody of Vergil *Ecl.* 1.28 in line 25 strengthens the impression that times have changed, in more than one way.[64] First, the passage in the bucolic poem is also about change: the shepherd Tityrus has received his freedom only late in life. But in other respects, the echo draws attention to significant differences between the texts. Juvenal's distance from the Vergil of the *Eclogues*, in both temporal and generic senses, amplifies the retrospective feeling conjured by the allusion. In Juvenal 1 *libertas* has not appeared, but disappeared, along with the imagined simplicity of the country and the past. The complex allusion to Vergil leads us directly to the justification for Juvenal's appearance on the scene.

The specificity of the complaint has a particularly weighty connotation. Juvenal, so briefly that it might go unnoticed, maps the barber's progress—and thus the general societal problem—onto his own life history, from youth (*iuveni mihi*) to the present moment. This comment tendentiously presents Juvenal's lifetime as the backdrop for the decline of Roman values, via the rise of the *nouveaux riches*. The result is that—even as Juvenal gestures to his satiric predecessors as inspiration—*Satire* 1 pretends that moral decline is recent, something that this poet is particularly qualified to treat. The barber anecdote relegates Juvenal's satiric predecessors to a different category from his: they may have developed the genre, but it is Juvenal's age that is really appropriate for satire. The new poet personalizes the material of satire in such a way that it obscures, if not diminishes, the influence of earlier poets: as Juvenal implies, they simply had less shocking material about which to write.

A review of *Satire* 1 reveals that the subtle claim of lines 24–25 is part of a larger pattern familiar to readers of Juvenal. Throughout this programmatic poem, Juvenal argues that vice and crime are a characteristic of his own, modern world. After describing his subject matter as "whatever people do," *quidquid agunt homines*, the satirist declares that vice has reached its peak in his time:

> et quando uberior vitiorum copia? quando
> maior avaritiae patuit sinus? alea quando
> hos animos?

> And when was the crop of vices richer? When
> did the maw of greed gape wider? When did dice
> stir up such passions?
> (1.87–89)

Juvenal goes on to present his trademark barrage of illustrative vignettes (89–146), and finally sums up the conditions of his age:

> nil erit ulterius quod nostris moribus addat
> posteritas, eadem facient cupientque minores,
> omne in praecipiti vitium stetit.

> There will be nothing more for posterity to add to
> our ways; our descendants will do and desire the same things;
> all vice is now standing on a precipice.
> (1.147–149)

With this last grand declaration about the state of vice, Juvenal implies that he faces the greatest challenge in the genre's history. The satirist's project is no longer simply to write better, a task that absorbed the attention of his predecessors, but to rise to the occasion of having better things to write about; the fifteen poems that follow will answer Juvenal's self-imposed challenge. At later points we find more conventional expressions of general moral decline, which sustain the claim made in *Satire* 1. The opening of *Satire* 6 looks back to the innocent Age of Saturn, a time when Chastity still walked the earth.[65] In the first poem of the collection's final book, Juvenal follows Hesiod and Ovid in linking human social and technological evolution to moral decline (13.28–70; cf. the metal ages at Hes. *Op.* 174–201 and Ov. *Met.* 1.127–150). But the satirist's age surpasses those of his models in depravity: Juvenal lives in the "ninth age . . . a generation worse than the age of iron" (*nona aetas . . . peioraque saecula ferri / temporibus*, 28–29).[66]

More significant, in addition to claiming that Roman morals have reached a nadir in his time, Juvenal informs us in the course of *Satire* 1 how this has actually happened. Here again, personal history and satiric material are woven together. Moreover, the vehicle for the development of vice is fundamentally the same as that which has qualified Juvenal and his predecessors to write satire, according to their autobiographical vignettes. Vice develops and spreads because it is taught; the wicked follow principles of training just as the good do. For example, the husband who condones his wife's adultery is "well-trained in gazing at the ceiling, and well-trained in snoring over his cup with wakeful nose" (*doctus spectare lacunar, / doctus et ad calicem vigilanti stertere naso*, 56–57).[67] Scheming wives perfect and share their own arts: one experienced woman "teaches her unskilled neighbor-wives to carry out blackened [i.e. poisoned] husbands for burial in full view" (*instituit . . . rudes melior Lucusta propinquas / per famam et populum nigros efferre maritos*, 71–72). Apparently vice has reached a pinnacle in Juvenal's time because it has essentially become an institution. Since miscreants are willing to pass on their knowledge and methods, wickedness is guaranteed to thrive. This scenario provides unlimited and self-regenerating material for the satirist even if, when it comes to treating well-known figures, he must restrict himself to the dead (170–171).

This connection between Juvenal's brief autobiographical comments and his general description of the state of humanity in *Satire* 1 contributes to the poem's thematic cohesion. But the thematic play on didaxis seen here characterizes the rest of Juvenal's satire as well. In a startling transformation of the didactic theme and context represented in Horace and Persius, Juvenal justifies his own work by pointing to the spread of vice around him. The method of teaching corruption varies: it can be a direct transfer of knowledge (as in the sharing of poisoning techniques), or a training in self-presentation that echoes Roman rhetorical education, or an insidious drawing out of latent tendencies. In *Satire* 2, pathic sexual behavior is a trade taught by Romans to provincials (159–170). Even those who practice it in Rome have to progress through stages: "No one ever became thoroughly foul all at once" (*nemo repente fuit turpissimus*, 83).[68] The tirade of Umbricius in *Satire* 3 culminates in a lament for an earlier Rome that was "content with one prison" (*uno contentam carcere Romam*, 314); the increase in criminals and prisons is a pernicious kind of evolution. In *Satire* 6, women grow into their innate vices just by watching stage performances: "Thymele is transfixed; now the novice Thymele is learning" (*attendit Thymele: Thymele tunc rustica discit*, 66). Mothers, meanwhile, actually teach their married daughters how to carry on adulterous affairs in secret (231–241). In the so-called Oxford fragment of the same poem, the insidious household *cinaedi* are exposed as the real instigators of women's depravity:

> horum consiliis nubunt subitaeque recedunt,
> his languentem animum servant et seria vitae,
> his clunem atque latus discunt vibrare magistris,
> quicquid praeterea scit qui docet.
>
> By the counsels of these men women abruptly marry and divorce,
> to these they entrust their thoughts in leisure and in business,
> and with them as teachers, they learn to wiggle buttocks and hips;
> the one who does the teaching knows what else.
> (6.O17–20)

If there are any characters worse than the women of *Satire* 6, it is these *cinaedi*, lurking in the poem's disrupted center, training Roman wives to turn their households upside down.

Just as Juvenal in particular and the satiric genre in general have undergone growth, training, and refinement, vice has its own evolutionary patterns. We absorb this dire fact throughout the *Satires*, in scenes that give examples of particular vices and explain how they are spread. Juvenal's vignettes of decline give vice the characteristics of a living entity, a beast whose growth is represented in multiplying prisons and lectures on poisoning. By projecting onto his material the theme of education and evolution—in a perverted, pernicious form— Juvenal creates the image of organic, evolving satiric subject matter. He imagines the content of satire, not merely the tradition and its individual representatives, as a living entity. The history of satire thus appears as the history of its subject matter, not simply as the various attempts to represent that subject matter. Juvenal's revision of the teaching theme, then, is also a self-promoting programmatic strategy. While he cannot compete as moral teacher with the didactic traditions of vice, as chronicler he is ensured top-notch material. Each poem is evidence of the societal change, effected by education in immorality, that has supposedly created the need for his labor.

Moral education is only one of satire's didactic concerns; like Horace and Persius, Juvenal also brings issues of literary production and pedagogy into his treatment of the didactic theme. In a world teeming with teachers of vice, Rome's aspiring literary professionals and educators stand for a noble tradition that is nevertheless struggling, as the seventh *Satire* argues. The mundane problems attached to literary, rhetorical, and teaching careers occupy the satirist throughout, although the poem's ostensible occasion is the new ray of hope offered by an emperor interested in literature (1–3, 20–21). In fact, although Juvenal poses as an advisor to younger authors who may look confidently toward the future ("get to work, young men," *hoc agite, o iuvenes*, 20), his attention shifts quickly to the unsympathetic patronage environment that has prevailed until now. Instead of envisioning the new and improved circumstances, the satirist prefers to elaborate on the past, with the result that the poem's original happy occasion is gradually obscured. Juvenal begins to look like a combination between an unhelpful patron, who witnesses but does not remedy his clients' suffering, and a failing teacher.[69]

The poem's catalogue of alternative careers in letters itself feels like a regression; each option is worse than the last in terms of the meager rewards and the disrespect that it reaps. Poets, historians, case pleaders (*causidici*), teachers of declamation (*rhetores*), and finally teachers of literature (*grammatici*) are counted wretched. Even the *grammaticus* whose daily companions are the texts of Vergil and Horace sees those classics degraded from use, smeared with lamp-oil and soot (226–227).[70] The survey of careers is not just a reverse literary *cursus honorum*, but a regression from the pinnacle of mature literary achievement—the production of sublime poems like those of the same Vergil and Horace (53–71)—to boyhood, a condition that the *grammaticus* seems doomed to relive for eternity.[71] This "lowest" profession does have noble associations, of course, which it struggles to retain. Juvenal acknowledges the teacher's importance as a moral influence on his young charges, using the metaphor of the *grammaticus* as sculptor or potter who "fashions tender characters as if with the thumb, as when one makes a face with wax" (*mores teneros ceu pollice ducat, / ut si quis cera voltum facit*, 237–238). The same metaphor adorns Persius' sober address to Cornutus (5.40).[72] In this new context, however, the compliment is hardly allowed to stand. The ennobling metaphor is juxtaposed with a scene of the classroom buzzing with adolescent sexuality, in which hands are put to more literal use. The teacher is reduced to a guard watching over his charges "lest they play dirty games, lest they take turns 'doing it'" (*ne turpia ludant, / ne faciant vicibus*, 239–240).[73] The satirist's advice and the teacher's efforts at discipline are made to seem ineffectual, as Juvenal gives us a glimpse of the boys' success: "It is no easy thing to keep watch over the hands of so many boys, over their eyes that tremble in climax" (*non est leve tot puerorum / observare manus oculosque in fine trementis*, 240–241).

This image of sexual mischief in the classroom is as old as Aristophanes.[74] But this teacher's failure takes on further significance when it is contrasted with the ideal function of the poet in society. After all, considering how this poem begins, the *grammaticus* looks like a would-be poet, demoted to the schools after following the satirist's advice to "break your pen, pitiful one" (*frange miser calamum*, 27[75]) and trying out alternative careers in reverse order of prestige. He is certainly not the ideal poet of Horace's *Epistle to Augustus*, who has an essential role in education and religion (*Epist.* 2.1.126–133), and whose own metaphorical sculpting leads children toward sexual modesty ("the poet molds the child's soft and stammering mouth, and presently turns his ear away from obscene talk," *os tenerum pueri balbumque poeta figurat, / torquet ab obscenis iam nunc sermonibus aurem*, 126–127). The failure of Juvenal's *grammaticus* is particularly spectacular when viewed in the broader context of the traditional moral-didactic associations of poetry. In the satiric tradition, on the other hand, this figure is more at home—and not only because he is essentially a chagrined monitor of indecent behavior. For a year of this service, the *grammaticus* can hope to be paid something equivalent to a victorious gladiator's one-time fee (242–243).[76] This demeaning comparison in the poem's final couplet links the embattled teacher to the underdog satirist figure engaged in performance and violence.

Juvenal's professional teachers are unable to teach, while his immoral characters proceed to spread their knowledge easily. They accomplish their work even as the satirist produces stand-in speakers who replicate his critical function, such as Umbricius (*Satire* 3) and the equally bitter gigolo Naevolus (9). The latter, who is both a social critic and a "disfigurement of *virtus Romana*,"[77] embodies the idea that the satirist's critical function is outdone by the overwhelming climate of vice in Rome. And although Naevolus sees his future as a prostitute threatened by his cooling relations with one patron, Virro, his interlocutor Juvenal assures him that Rome abounds with potential clients ("you'll never want for a friendly pathic as long as these hills are safe and standing," *numquam pathicus tibi derit amicus / stantibus et salvis his collibus*, 130–131). While *Satire* 9 is itself a drama between two artful speakers, it also conveys the idea that another drama is occurring out in Rome, one that has replaced the nobler traditions associated with its seven hills.

The climax of Juvenal's reverse-didactic narrative comes in his final book, a group of texts that pointedly resists narrative closure by focusing again on the perpetuation of vice. Juvenal's framing of his oeuvre with these two books is appropriate in light of his use of the didactic theme. While book 1 announces the constant historical progression of vice that will be perpetuated not through ever-worsening behavior, but only through the institutionalized transfer of knowledge, book 5 constitutes an update and assessment of the impact of this institution on the world. The book's centerpiece, the three-hundred-line *Satire* 14, is devoted to the vices that parents teach their children, knowingly or otherwise. While on the surface the poem looks like an opportunity for the satirist to spin out more exaggerated vignettes of greedy and self-destructive behavior, its general argument has a unique ethical focus. Juvenal begins with the claim that bad example is the cause of most immoral behavior (1–3). The poem abounds with *sententiae* on this topic, such as

> sic natura iubet: velocius et citius nos
> corrumpunt vitiorum exempla domestica, magnis
> cum subeant animos auctoribus.
>
> So Nature decrees it: examples of vice set at home
> corrupt us more swiftly and quickly, since they
> enter our minds on high authority.
> (14.31–33)

Not only are we more impressionable when our parents set the example, but bad examples are particularly effective: "We are all easily taught to imitate foul and crooked deeds" (*dociles imitandis / turpibus ac pravis omnes sumus*, 40–41). Human nature and contemporary vice combine to ensure that the world will continue to be populated with criminals.[78]

Juvenal eventually narrows his focus to the vice of avarice and the frenzied financial ambition that it inspires, a familiar theme from Horace and Persius. One passage playfully alludes to similar treatments by Juvenal's predecessors. At 179–209, continuing to argue that children only become greedy through example, Juvenal dramatizes this didactic scenario. First, he quotes an old-fashioned, honest father, who in a condensed version of the speech of Ofellus in *Sermones* 2.2 exhorts his sons to live simply off the land and avoid the trappings of wealth (179–188). Juvenal's *senex* recommends exercise, rustic food, and a reliable winter wardrobe. "These were the teachings old-time folk gave to their children" (*haec illi veteres praecepta minoribus*, 189), the satirist wistfully concludes. Now, however, fathers urge their sons to pursue riches through careers in forensic speaking, military service, or commerce (189–209). Wealth is the only guiding principle in the new world: "No one asks from where you get it, but you've got to have it" (*unde habeas quaerit nemo, sed oportet habere*, 207).

Vice, as it develops, apparently absorbs and imitates even the rhetoric of moral instruction. But this second speech has a more specific model in its perversion of the ideal of labor: it recalls Persius' personification of greed, *Avaritia*, who shouts at a still-snoring man to rise and load his ships (5.132–153). The Persian passage, in turn, echoes both Persius himself (the opening lecture of *Satire* 3) and other satiric images of life in the city, especially Horace *Sermones* 2.6.23–39 and Lucilius 1145–1151 W.[79] Juvenal thus juxtaposes not just two moral models, but two allusive quotations, the models for which draw heavily on traditional moralist discourse themselves. This nods at the diachronic development of the theme of greed in the satiric tradition, and in particular recalls the earlier poets' use of direct speech in didactic scenes. When Juvenal follows the quote with the complaint "this is what little old nurses teach crawling boys, this is what all little girls learn before their letters" (*hoc monstrant vetulae pueris repentibus assae / hoc discunt omnes ante alpha et beta puellae*, 208–209), his telescoping allusion seems even more purposeful.[80] Horace's schoolboys at 1.1.25–26, eager to learn their ABCs, are also part of this passage's background. Juvenal feeds several generations of satiric discourse into a scene that proves his argument that his age represents the pinnacle of depravity. In Juvenal's world, the *prima elementa* of children are vices.

In other ways, the last two poems of Juvenal's last book also represent the constant reproduction of vice and crime throughout the world. In *Satire* 15, the poet uses the story of Egyptian cannibalism to point out that the Roman effort to spread moral philosophy throughout the world has evidently failed (106–112). Like the poem that precedes it, *Satire* 15 addresses the role of human nature in civilization, painting a superficially positive picture of the human capacity for compassion (131–158). But the Stoic-humanitarian excursus on the social contract ends with a reminder of the Juvenalian historical theme: "But now there is greater concord among serpents [than among humans]" (*sed iam serpentum maior concordia*, 159). The poem communicates the idea that the civilized world has lost control over what happens at its outskirts, in addition to producing increasingly depraved new generations at home. *Satire* 16 reframes the same problem by attacking the sinister legal system of the Roman military. Though the army is what separates Romans from barbarians, Juvenal's army offers no protection at all, and indeed turns back against the Roman people. The didactic agenda of vice itself has allies in Roman culture, in the communities of Others, and everywhere in between.

Juvenal's picture of education is at once absurdly narrow (in its concentration on the subject matter of vice) and startlingly expansive. The teaching that he pretends to document clearly takes place in a Roman context, using methods familiar from traditional education (invoking exempla, emphasizing self-presentation) and with consequences that affect Roman identity and political stability. Juvenal's new use of the didactic theme helps the genre grow into the identity that Quintilian attributes to it, *tota [Romana]*. The basic function of the satirist as teacher has disappeared, so that satire no longer mimes didaxis. But it has developed a new, symbiotic relationship with the didacticism of its subjects.

Juvenal enters his own satiric scene without possessing any didactic influence—unlike Horace who dramatizes his own loss of control, and Persius who reconfigures satiric teaching to depend on alternative notions of authority. Any teaching that Juvenal accomplishes is the teaching about satire's own evolution and its changing relevance, both a self-undermining and a self-promoting strategy. It is self-undermining because this satirist has arrived on the scene too late to change it. It is self-promoting in two respects. First, as is broadly true of the satirists' uses of models, any publicity is good publicity when the agenda is the exhibition of generic functions—a project that is not to be confused with pure self-defense or sanitization. It is also self-promoting in a sense more specific to this case. Juvenal reinvents satire to fit the challenges of his age, and writes the history of the genre as if all its momentum had been building up for his own appearance.

This fits the satiric rhetorical style of Juvenal, the satirist with the least prominent self in any sense other than his speaking voice. By figuring himself as an observer of and commentator on the world in *Satire* 1, Juvenal suggests that he (*qua* satirist) is a product of that world. In view of the conclusions of these four chapters, we may see the *ego* that Juvenal presents not as a dramatic mask constructed only to provide a narrative voice, but as a creation of the society represented in the *Satires*, fascinated with his own origins. On the surface he seems to efface the generic authorial figure, but a closer look reveals that this figure and its poetic project have become so purely reactive that they are entirely defined by their subject matter.

This symbiotic relationship exists on a more basic level from the beginning of the tradition, and underlies satire's adoption of multiple agendas. The genre does not balance its various approaches harmoniously, mitigating malice with moral teaching or punishment with entertainment. Instead, these elements cooperate and even blur into one another. Even the model examined in this chapter, which would appear to represent satire's most altruistic and solemn function, is a form of play just as the others are, and borrows aspects of their identities. The struggles in which the satirists engage in their individual didactic plots represent teaching as a kind of competitive game that overlaps with the arenas of law and violence (though the latter has more subtle manifestations, such as in Juvenal's memory of beatings at school). But no other model is as relevant to satiric teaching as the dramatic analogy. The arrangement and performance of roles, whether in a predictable or a surprising manner, are a fundamental element of didaxis in the world of satire. The struggles enacted between student and teacher figures, at least in Horace and Persius, evoke satire's ancestor comedy, with its agonistic authorial postures and its stock characters. Juvenal's twisting of satiric teaching into a pernicious force out of the satirist's control is one strategy that assimilates his work to tragedy, the genre that narrates the downfall of houses and communities.

But certainly the most fundamentally dramatic element of satiric teaching, and the one that reaches outside the text to satire's real audience, is the mask that the teacher figure must adopt in order to attract attention and elicit cooperation. Our attention is focused on this figure even as he is challenged, mocked, excluded, and frustrated. He first raises our expectations about the genre, devising a compelling interpretive language that we readily absorb. He also acts out satire's agenda in ways that require us to read actively—recalling programmatic claims, denials, or debates; assessing how those provocations are continued and answered in the genre's depictions of society. Satire functions as a mirror in the same way that drama does, by configuring, engaging, and drawing out its readers' expectations. In this way satiric teaching, more than the genre's other functions, reaches the world outside the text. Lessons in reading are Roman satire's lasting didactic legacy.

Conclusion

Observing Romans

It is appropriate to conclude a study of satire's social models with an examination of the didactic analogy, which draws on satire's other models in many ways and reinforces the insights that they provide on satire and society. The special connection between teaching and performance, however, is a reminder of the strong influence of the rhetorical persona approach to satire—one that I have attempted to refine and expand by listening closely to the satirists' own words. The performance of the satirist figure is not simply akin to that of a rhetorician or actor; it is the performance of various Roman male social agents, concentrated in one figure. We may still call the satiric speaker a persona, but should use the term in this broader sense. In this way, we will become increasingly accustomed to regarding satiric speech in the way that we now tend to view other Roman genres, not only as literary experiment but also as modes of cultural discourse.

We will also be able to reformulate another traditional notion about satire, one that is perhaps infrequently invoked but still subtly influential. The figure who practices satire, whose model of the world is fashioned in the satiric mode, has long been viewed as standing at a distance, physically or emotionally, from his society.[1] The material examined in chapter 1 reminds us that even spectatorship is a participatory activity. Yet readers still tend to believe in such a thing as satiric distance. This is due in part to the persona theory, which is still the only theoretical approach used to discuss the whole genre in all its phases.[2] Emphasizing the poets' expressed emotions and attitudes as the site of interpretation encourages readers to imagine the satirist figure in an isolated state, focused only on how to convert the reality before him into a rhetorical performance directed at his readers. A fresh look at this convergence of ideas, and a bit of untangling, is useful at this point. From where does the idea of the satirist as observer originate, and how might it be synthesized with an account of satire as (simulated) social practice?

Each of the Roman satirists, at some point, describes his work as the observation of society. Horace claims to piece his satire together while walking through the city musing about others' behavior (1.4.133–139). The cackle of Persius is a result of his having "inspected" what people do (*cum . . . aspexi . . . facimus quaecumque*, 1.9–10). Juvenal paints himself as a recorder of everyday life, standing at the crossroads (1.63–64). These passages construct satire's authorial stance as reactive. Were they our only set of programmatic gestures, we might infer that the satirist looks but does not participate, recording as if he were watching the activity of an alien culture.

Understanding satire as a composite of various social models requires us to reconsider the traditional idea of the satirist as observer in a new light. As scholars have long recognized, and as I noted in the introduction, the acts of observation and commentary have a self-reflexive dimension and are guided by cultural and generic concerns. This is especially true when a speaker is using a mask constructed by generic tradition and personal erudition. Even the versions of the satiric models studied here that seem on the surface to be passive or neutral modes—spectatorship, fair arbitration, transmission of wisdom—are in practice self-defining activities that engage the agent's moral attitudes, social and educational background, and anxieties.

The currently dominant view of the satirist as a rhetorician gives the observation theme a more Roman flavor, as the subgenres and techniques of Roman rhetoric clearly operate in satiric discourse. But the rhetorical view cannot explain satire's critical agendas, or even satire's articulations of its critical agendas. Programmatic discussions allege that satire has several social missions, and we need an interpretive approach that treats this material as something more than misleading ornamentation. On this issue, the more popular, contemporary associations of the term "rhetoric," as opposed to the specifically Roman associations, may be getting in the way. If we view rhetoric simply as the opposite of reality, as lies and exaggeration, then we will not listen to what the satirists are trying to make us believe—even if what they are telling us might help in the interpretation of their genre.[3] Rather than approaching the discourse of the genre as skeptics, only taking evidence of the poets' rhetorical learning at face value, we would learn more by taking in all that we are given. No social criticism can be completely detached and ironic, after all. Social critics are also products of society.

The inherent complications of satire's social models make fertile ground for the satirists' self-definition and their social criticism alike; they also offer a new way of seeing the observation theme. We may interpret the satirist figure's observational stance as representing his fascination with the culture that defines him. Rather than being alienated from society, he is a self-professed product of it, both miming Roman critical procedures and holding his experiments up for his audience's view. This double agenda accounts for satire's seeming inconsistency in its moral and political positions. The satirists' movements between oppositional and conservative stances are indications not of the genre's detachment from society, but of its exploratory and self-critical agenda.

The tools of this agenda are both diverse and consistent, as the traditional compound definitions of satire show. The nature of the combinations themselves must be properly understood, as well as their appeal and validity as guides for reading the satiric genre. In identifying multiple functions of satire that engage different expectations and desires on the reader's part, we should not be

CONCLUSION

aiming to contain or sanitize the provocative associations of each function. To suggest, for example, that satire attacks, but only with a certain degree of intensity because it is also trying to teach, renders the combination less powerful. Each component exerts a strong influence on its own. It is especially important to perceive the relationships between the models that are brought out in the satiric illustration of their operation. The conventional metaphorical thinking about satire's functions is also reflected in the relationships that exist between them: prosecution is a version of attack, both of those functions are types of performance, teaching has its performative and its agonistic aspects, and so on. This is suggested in the very selection and combination of them in a definition such as Rudd's ("attack, performance, preaching"). The satirist figure's odd assembly of tools has its own powerful logic.

Satire is active, interested, and at times interventional. Yet the notion of the satirist as observer exerts its own peculiar influence even from within the genre, and may help us better understand developments over the tradition. A genre that observes and reacts is logically bound to change, in response to the changing conditions that it encounters. At the same time, this very manner of engagement leads the satirist to a kind of passivity. All three satirists appear to move toward a less active, more distanced stance over the course of their work. Once Horace abandons the pure diatribe mode and becomes more engaged in the world of his poems, he becomes part of a drama in which others have power. In book 2, Horace the character feels external restrictions, retaliation from formerly invisible characters, and the increasing power of comic agents and practitioners of *sermo*. Persius performs a more deliberate retreat, withdrawing into the epistolary mode in *Satire* 6 and creating a sense of distance from his subjects with the poem's dramatic setting. His autobiographical digression in the previous poem enhances the impression of solipsistic retreat. If detached observation is not the poets' method throughout, it does seem to be a mode into which each one grows, in his own way.

Juvenal's progress toward this position begins earlier and so invites a different interpretation of the satirist's retreat, one that is guided by the metaliterary approach of this book. In *Satire* 1, Juvenal's shifting of the didactic role to his subjects revises the satirist's relationship to his poetic material. The genre's energy and functions are transferred onto its narrative subjects. The effects of satiric teaching are no longer limited to the endless replication of alter egos who displace their original teacher, as in Horace, but include the harnessing of teaching itself for criminal purposes. By the same token, Juvenal's pared-down poetic autobiography subordinates the satirist to the phenomena that characterize his model of reality: teaching, violence, competition. Authorial history only matters in the context of a much vaster tradition of vice and corruption.

The integration of the persona theory into Roman satire studies offered a way of interpreting, in literary terms, the diachronic changes in the individual poets' oeuvres and over the course of the tradition. But this view of the satirist's changing stance, with its emphasis on rhetorical style, leaves out other aspects of his performance. The consequences of a purely rhetorical, rather than broadly social, concept of the persona theory are reflected especially in Juvenal studies. That poet's sequence of distinct and colorful personae was a major inspiration in the development of the persona approach in the first place. Anderson's and Braund's analyses of Juvenal's changing persona conclude with outlines of the later books and suggestions for further investigation.[4] But although these scholars aimed to stimulate further study of generic features, results have been slow in coming. The rich oeuvre of Juvenal, beyond the revolutionary first six poems, is not well understood as a site of satire's development.[5] Readers of this book will, I hope, have a new appreciation of Juvenal's work and perspective. Satire's generic definition, although its ingredients are present from the beginning, unfolds over the entire history of the tradition and is thematized energetically by the last satirist.

The persona approach invites investigation of these features, although it leads to conclusions that may seem at odds with the traditional assessment. In Juvenal's later books, where the poet has been said to employ a distanced perspective, his stance involves more engagement than a purely rhetorical reading would imply. Juvenal presents Democritus as satiric alter ego at the opening of book 4 (*Satire* 10.28–53). The laughing philosopher who found an abundance of amusement just outside his doorstep seems a fitting alter ego for the satirist who performs the panoramic tenth *Satire*. The Democritean perspective also informs the two domestic poems that round out the book, featuring a satirist who now contemplates urban mores from his own quiet retreat. But the theatrical associations of the Democritus scene suggest that such observation has its own way of drawing in the viewer. Even Juvenal's detached persona continues to act out satire's social functions.

Similarly, Juvenal begins book 5 by advising his addressee to move beyond his indignation (*Satire* 13), in an apparent repudiation of his own early satiric emotions. But the opposite view gains some support from the arguments made in this study. In book 5, Juvenal can be seen probing the emotions and topics of his own early satire (anger and its consequences, the family, the city, foreigners, the disenfranchisement of the poor citizen) as if confirming their centrality to his satiric program. Juvenal's rhetorical stance with regard to his material may change, but the poems themselves revive the emotional energy and color of his early satire. The programmatic metaphors make a final and influential appearance in book 5. The aporetic narratives of the individual poems highlight key themes: teaching (*Satire* 14), violence evocative of tragedy (15), and law (16). This is a fitting conclusion to the tradition, even a retrospective interpretation of it. Juvenal celebrates satire's dependence on society. It is not surprising that he was beginning his *Satires* at the same time that Quintilian was deeming satire "wholly Roman" (*tota nostra*) in an account that also acknowledges the tradition's continuing evolution (*Inst.* 10.1.93–94). At the height of the Roman Empire, Juvenal plays the part of the quintessential satirist, defining and theorizing the genre's method as well as his own culture's strategies of self-definition.

CONCLUSION

Juvenal's picture of the genre's history and of the external world are designed to justify his own work. But it is also true that throughout the tradition, the satirist figure has been carrying the same apparatus of social models. In this sense, satire was *tota Romana* all along, as Quintilian seems to believe. For the models adopted by the satirists are all key strategies of Roman self-definition, from Republic to Empire. Romans organized (and Romanized) their world using the stage and the theater, the arena and the army, the laws and the courts, the schoolrooms, the libraries, and the didactic process. But the satirist figure is unique in that he can afford to act out both the successes and the more problematic effects of these processes. The picture of social institutions run awry in Juvenal's last book pushes the genre, and the organizational apparatus of Roman culture, to their limits.

Notes

INTRODUCTION

1. Rudd, *Themes in Roman Satire*, 1; cf. Nichols, who emphasizes satire's blend of attack and moral analysis ("indirect aggression against a target or targets which are made to seem blameworthy within a given context"; *Insinuation*, 35), and Feinberg, who describes the satiric mode as "playfully critical distortion" (*Introduction to Satire*, 19).

2. On rhetoric in particular, see Braund, "Declamation and Contestation." Braund calls satire parasitic in *Roman Verse Satire* (3–4). Recent studies of the satirists' allusive strategies include Hooley, *Knotted Thong*, on Persius, and Schmitz, *Das Satirische*, on Juvenal.

3. Thorpe theorizes satire as a primitive version of comic drama ("Satire as Pre-Comedy").

4. Rosen, *Old Comedy*, 15; cf. Cucchiarelli, *La satira e il poeta*, 125–129.

5. This is an assertion of Dryden's, argued more fully in Randolph, "Structural Design."

6. Rudd follows his compound definition of satire with this admission: "Of course 'attack,' 'entertainment,' and 'preaching' are themselves very loose and flexible terms" (*Themes in Roman Satire*, 1).

7. Braund makes useful remarks about the satirist figure's range (*Roman Satirists*, 37–41). Even if we believe that literary satire is a civilized descendent of malevolent spells and curses, the genre still "retains a connection . . . with its primitive past" (Elliott, *Power of Satire*, 129). This point is well illustrated by Hutcheon's chart of various audience reactions to irony (*Irony's Edge*, 46–47). Hutcheon views the range of positive and negative reactions as parts of an ever-present affective spectrum from which the reader chooses an interpretation. This idea of reader participation is relevant to many aspects of the interpretation of satire (a genre full of irony and ambiguity), and poses a significant challenge to the traditional view that the satirists themselves carefully balance opposed qualities or agendas (e.g. "attack" versus "reason" or "humor"; cf. Frye, *Anatomy of Criticism*, 224–225, and Rudd, *Themes in Roman Satire*, 1).

8. "Inquiry and provocation" is Griffin's phrase (*Satire*, 35–39).

9. Braund assembles the apologiae for comparison in *Satires Book I*, 116–119.

10. According to Bogel, "in satire, referentiality and factuality are essential conventions, products of certain rhetorical strategies" (*Difference Satire Makes*, 11). Bogel's focus is English Augustan satire, but this theoretical assertion (especially as it describes a

tradition that explicitly follows the Roman authors) is just as applicable to the Roman genre, including its conventional apologia. Cf. Keane, "Critical Contexts."

11. Keane, "Defining the Art of Blame." On authorial self-presentation in comedy see Hubbard, *Mask of Comedy*; Slater, *Plautus in Performance*, 122–126; and Parker, "Plautus vs. Terence," 601. As chapter 1 will show, this is just one of the strategies that the satirists borrow from drama in their own project of generic construction.

12. Bogel, *Difference Satire Makes*, 29–30. Fitzgerald's discussion of the reception of Catullus is also illuminating: traditionally, readers have exculpated Catullus' obscene or "extreme" poems by privileging his "sympathetic" or "moral" ones, when the collection may actually be better understood as a tension-filled and dynamically evolving system (*Catullan Provocations*, 13–14).

13. Classen regards this last problem as satire's definitive characteristic ("The Elusive Genre").

14. Fishelov views metaphorical conceptions of genre as useful tools for interpretation, if their various implications are explored (*Metaphors of Genre*).

15. Slater, *Plautus in Performance*, examines metatheater in comedy; Hinds, *Allusion and Intertext*, studies the expression of generic theory through intertextuality.

16. On food, see Gowers, *Loaded Table*; on teaching, Henderson, *Writing Down Rome*, 228–248; and on the journey in Horace, *Sermones* 1.5, see Cucchiarelli, *La satira e il poeta*. For another metaliterary reading see Schlegel, "Horace Satires 1.7," and now *Satire and the Threat of Speech*.

17. "Every genre is a model of reality which mediates the empirical world. The text does not work upon the direct presence of 'reality,' but upon a select representation of it" (Conte, *Genres and Readers*, 112). Conte's definition echoes that of Bakhtin and Medvedev: "Every significant genre is a complex system of means and methods for the conscious control and finalization [closure, wholeness] of reality" (*Formal Method*, 133).

18. Wehrle, *Satiric Voice*, 24; cf. Braund and Cloud, "Juvenal—a diptych," 200.

19. The quoted passage helps to define the satirist of Juvenal 1 "as an unusually greedy, undiscriminating poet" (Gowers, *Loaded Table*, 192).

20. Braund cautions against taking the documentary view in the study of social themes in satire (*Satire and Society*, 1–3).

21. Henderson, *Writing Down Rome*, 180.

22. This point is made by Labate ("Il sermo oraziano," 427).

23. Ovid's *Amores* present "a 'romance' . . . in the twofold sense of 'romantic adventure' and 'narrative of romantic adventures' . . . The fusion of 'poetic business' and actually experienced erotic adventures marks the elegiac speaker's twofold role as *poeta* and *amator*" (Holzberg, *Ovid*, 17).

24. Zetzel, "Horace's *Liber Sermonum*."

25. Mack, "Muse of Satire," initiated the persona approach to English satire; cf. Kernan's subsequent seminal work, *Cankered Muse*. Anderson brought the persona into Roman satire studies in a series of essays (later collected in *Essays on Roman Satire*). The nuanced and mutable personae of Horace and Juvenal, respectively, are further explored in Freudenburg, *Walking Muse*; and Braund, *Beyond Anger*.

26. Fitzgerald, *Catullan Provocations*; cf. Miller, *Lyric Texts*. Horace, an author of both lyric and satire, has received the most attention in this type of persona scholarship; see especially Oliensis, *Rhetoric of Authority*. Wray conducts an important critique of persona scholarship in *Catullus*, 161–167; see also Miller, *Subjecting Verses*, 51.

27. Freudenburg, *Satires of Rome*, 3–4. Cf. Ramage, "Juvenal and the Establishment," on the context of Juvenal's portrayal of recent history.

28. Hinds justifies this approach in the closing discussion of *Allusion and Intertext* (144): "The fact is that in authorial subjectivity we have one of our best and most enabling terms to conceptualize the partiality, and interestedness, of any construction of literary tradition, any version of literary history—our own included . . . Without some idea of the poet as aetiologist, as mobilizer of his own tradition, ever tendentious and ever manipulative, *our* accounts of literary tradition will always turn out too flat."

CHAPTER 1

1. Livy 7.2; this tantalizing account has some defenders (e.g., Knapp, "Dramatic Satura"), although Livy's label *satura* does not imply any connection to the later verse genre (for a survey of evidence, see Duckworth, *Nature of Roman Comedy*, 4–10). Scholars interested in the dramatic qualities of satire often mention the dramatic *satura*, but tend to avoid arguing for or against its existence (e.g., Ehlers, "Zur Rezitation," 178).

2. To this list of comic models for satire Plotnick adds the satyr play, in an interpretation of Horace's discussion of the genre at *Ars P.* 220–250 ("Horace on Satyr Drama," 329–335). Although this genre is associated with Athens, Wiseman contends that there may have been a Roman satyr play tradition motivating this passage, in "Satyrs in Rome," 13.

3. Cucchiarelli views this passage as a significant piece of Horace's satiric theory that refers to his revision of Lucilius' Old Comic program in *Sermones* 1.4 and 1.5 (*La satira e il poeta*, 40–43; on the role of comic models in Horace, especially Aristophanes' *Frogs*, see 15–55).

4. Some scholars have also argued that the Plato here mentioned is not the philosopher but the comic poet, which would make for a more generically congruent list of authors; see Fairclough, *Satires, Epistles, Ars Poetica*, 152–153; Morris, *Satires and Epistles*, 171; and Palmer, *Satires of Horace*, 385. But for the opposite, and more common, view see Freudenburg, *Walking Muse*, 107–108; Haight, "Menander," 147–148; Kiessling and Heinze, *Satiren*, 219; Lejay, *Satires*, 392–393; and Muecke, *Satires II*, 133. Kassel and Austin also find this interpretation more plausible (*Poetae Comici Graeci* VII, 432).

5. Horace is certainly exaggerating the resemblance between Old Comedy and Lucilius (Rudd, *Satires of Horace*, 88–89). But some scholars infer that this was the conception of satire prevalent in Horace's day; see Hendrickson, "Horace, Serm. 1 4," 124; Heldmann, "Die Wesenbestimmung"; and LaFleur, "Horace and *Onomasti Komodein*," 1794–1795.

6. Diomedes, *De Arte Grammatica* book 3 (Kiel, *Grammatici Latini* 1, 485 lines 30–32).

7. On Horace's New Comic technique, see Leach, "Horace's *Pater Optimus*"; cf. Fairclough, "Satire and Comedy."

8. Mueller, focusing more narrowly on the Old Comic model, argues that in positioning himself against Lucilius Horace alludes to Aristophanes' criticism of his rival Cratinus ("Aristophanes und Horaz"). In this light Horace appears to be borrowing the agonistic dynamic of the Old Comic poets even as he distances himself from their style of comedy (a strategy discussed more fully in Keane, "Critical Contexts," 23–26).

9. Woodman, "Juvenal 1 and Horace," points out the echoes of Horace's comic

pater in Juvenal's Lucilius, *pater* of the satiric genre. But the view of Horace as Juvenal as "comic" and "tragic," respectively, has a long history; see Weber's examination in "Comic Humor and Tragic Spirit," and Bogel, *Difference Satire Makes*, 29–30. On tragic material in Juvenal see Smith, "Heroic Models," 812, and Schmitz, *Das Satirische*, 38–50. Powell, however, believes that Juvenal genuinely distances himself from tragedy in the *Satire* 6 passage ("Stylistic Registers in Juvenal," 317–318).

10. Horace cites tragedy as the first genre attempted by Roman authors (*Epist.* 2.1.162–167); on this passage and Juvenal see Keane, "Theatre," 265–269.

11. Burns, *Theatricality*, 13; cf. Wilshire, *Role Playing and Identity*.

12. Handbooks describe Horace's technique as "dramatic," especially when speaking of book 2 of the *Sermones*; e.g., Knoche, *Roman Satire*, 85–86. Cf. Musurillo, "Horace and the Bore," 65–69.

13. On the connection between rhetoric and drama see Gotoff, "Oratory." The dramatic technique of impersonation (*prosopopoeia*) is useful for forensic oratory, as Quintilian notes (*Inst.* 6.1.25–26). In the same book, Quintilian advises students to practice debate with one another, and especially to imagine and respond to likely charges from adversaries (*Inst.* 6.4.14); cf. *Rhet. Her.* 4.52–53 on dialogue and *prosopopoeia*. On rhetoric in tragedy, see Goldberg, "Melpomene's declamation," and on comedy, Hughes, "*Inter tribunal et scaenam*." For the scholiast's comment on Persius 1.44, see Jahn, *Satirarum Liber*, 258. The rupture of dramatic illusion is especially common in Athenian Old Comedy and in Plautus; for discussion see Duckworth, *Nature of Roman Comedy*, 132–136, and for references to plot construction, see Plaut. *Cas.* 860–861, *Pseud.* 1240, and the prologues in general.

14. On Persius' style of "acting parts" see Kissel, *Satiren*, 170–172. On the difficult *Satire* 3 see Smith, "Speakers." Ehlers concludes that of all the satirists, Persius would have made the greatest demands on the abilities of a reciter with his multiple speakers lacking clear divisions ("Zur Rezitation," 179).

15. On the case of Crispinus, see Braund, *Satires Book I*, 236–237; cf. Ferguson, *Satires*, 159. The quasi-legal exercises (*suasoriae* and *controversiae*) that were the core of declamatory training required the student to try on other voices, often those of socially liminal characters (Bloomer, "History of Declamation").

16. On dramatic devices in Juvenal, see de Decker, *Juvenalis Declamans*, 90–103; cf. Maier, "Juvenal—Dramatiker und Regisseur."

17. Walters, "Making a Spectacle."

18. Keane, "Theatre," 263–265.

19. Schmitz views the passage as a programmatic assertion of Juvenal's spectacular influences (*Das Satirische*, 20–23).

20. Edwards outlines the functions of and attitudes toward theater and entertainment in Rome (*Politics of Immorality*, 98–136). Such assemblies were sites where the forces of social organization met the forces of political subversion head on: "The theatre was a place where power and hierarchy were displayed; it was in the theatre that they could most easily be subverted" (127). On political communication in the theater in the early Imperial period, see also Bartsch, *Actors in the Audience*.

21. On these intertwined functions of Republican comedy see McCarthy, *Plautine Comedy*, which revises the "comedy as liberation" theory applied to Plautus by Segal (*Roman Laughter*).

22. Arbuscula was active twenty years before Horace' time; Cicero praises a per-

formance of hers at *Att.* 4.15.6. On the popularity of mime see McKeown, "Augustan Elegy and Mime," 73–75.

23. The second prologue of *Hecyra* appeals to "your discernment" (*vostra intellegentia*, 31); see Duckworth, *Nature of Roman Comedy*, 62–65, for other examples.

24. Laberius' story is told at Macrob. 2.7 and Gell. 8.15. On the paradoxical critical license of actors and unwilling performers, see Edwards, *Politics of Immorality*, 131–134.

25. Edwards, *Politics of Immorality*, 123–134.

26. The performing professions are here associated with other ways of life that center around the body and the senses, just like Cicero's disapproving list at *Off.* 1.150 (which includes cooks, fishermen, perfume-sellers, and dancers).

27. Damasippus cleverly synthesizes material from different tragic texts into the dialogue between Ajax and Agamemnon (Muecke, *Satires II*, 153–155). The passage on the lover lingering outside the door (the *exclusus amator*) is "close to a word for word citation of Terence [*Eun.* 46–80]" (Muecke, *Satires II*, 160).

28. Caston, "Fall of the Curtain," surveys comic elements in the *Sermones*. On the *doctor ineptus*, the buffoon, and the adulterer, see Freudenburg, *Walking Muse*, 21–48. The adultery scenes in 1.2 and 2.7 draw both on comedy (cf. Plaut. *Mil.* 1394–1437) and on a popular mime subject (cf. Reynolds, "Adultery Mime"). Davus is the name of the slave in Terence's *Phormio*. On parasites and similar characters, such as the *captator* of 2.5 and the pest of 1.9, see Damon, *Mask of the Parasite*, 108–134.

29. Freudenburg, *Walking Muse*, 48 and 27–34. Horace also has characteristics of a comic parasite (Turpin, "Epicurean Parasite").

30. The label "self-incriminating" is given by Oliensis (*Rhetoric of Authority*, 41–63). The sense of change in Horace may be attributed to the satirist's creation of dramatic time through structural arrangement; cf. Zetzel on book 1 ("Horace's *Liber Sermonum*").

31. Caston argues that 2.8 dramatizes satire's eclipsing of comedy ("Fall of the Curtain"); on the poem's other metapoetic elements, see O'Connor, "Horace's *Cena Nasidieni*."

32. This connection is implied by the fact that actors and prostitutes share certain legal disabilities (Gai. *Dig.* 48.5.25, Suet. *Aug.* 45.3, Tac. *Ann.* 1.77), and argued in depth in Edwards, "Unspeakable Professions."

33. The comparison is made by Freudenburg (*Walking Muse*, 227; cf. 216–217).

34. With its public setting and the sense of role-playing that is added by the animal imagery, Lucilius' work seems to anticipate the spectacular punishments of the Imperial period examined in Coleman, "Fatal Charades." This phenomenon, as well as the animal fable model for Horace's description, are discussed in chapter 2.

35. On this sense of *scaena*, see Muecke, *Satires II*, 112, and cf. Cic. *Amic.* 97, *Ad Brut.* 1.9.2, and *De orat.* 3.177. Cucchiarelli acknowledges the theatrical allusion in the Horatian passage (*La satira e il poeta*, 39 n. 81). Feeney argues that this image of metaphorical public theater is echoed in Horace's examination of theater as a political activity in *Epistle* 2.1 ("*Una cum scriptore meo*," 183–184).

36. The passage draws on *Sermones* 2.3.259–271, Terence's *Eunuch*, and elegiac laments (Hooley, *Knotted Thong*, 111–116).

37. "Have an ear for" is Conington's translation of *audis* (*Satires*, 31).

38. In *Satire* 1, men listening to affected modern poetry seem sexually aroused (19–21 and 80–82); on the poetic associations of these images see Freudenburg, *Satires of Rome*, 162–172.

39. Jenkinson brings out the gastronomic significance of the actor's name by translating it as "Sucré" (*Satires*, 86).

40. Kissel, *Satiren*, 275. Relihan interprets the passage differently: "Persius asks specifically for a *reader* of Aristophanes; this is a call for an antiquary and a pedant, for only these read Old Comedy at this time" ("Confessions of Persius," 155). The description of the Old Comic poets' emotion is certainly conventional (Kissel, *Satiren*, 273–275). But by joining these images with a description of the reader's response, Persius plays up the emotional impact of reading.

41. Smith surveys the different interpretations of the poem at "Speakers," 305 n. 1; cf. Jenkinson, *Satires*, 112–113, and Housman's influential interpretation that Persius is talking with himself ("Notes on Persius," 18). Relihan likens this "inner dialogue" to a convention of Menippean satire ("Confessions of Persius," 152–158).

42. Comparing Persius unfavorably with Horace on this point, Nisbet writes that "like all Persius' characters the centurion [who speaks at 3.78–85] talks like Persius" ("Persius," 56).

43. Freudenburg, *Satires of Rome*, 189–195.

44. Cf. Bartsch's analysis of audience behavior at spectacles in the Principate (*Actors in the Audience*, 1–35).

45. The exact nature of these sources of "entertainment" is uncertain. The "Edict" may be an announcement of legal business or a playbill. Callirhoe may be a character in a poem, a tragedy, or a comedy, or a mime actress (see the ancient commentary in Jahn, *Satirarum Liber*, 277–278; cf. Jenkinson, *Satires*, 76 and Bramble, *Programmatic* Satire, 141 and n. 2).

46. Freudenburg, *Satires of Rome*, 115–117.

47. Bartsch views this passage as evidence of the theatrical political climate of the first century CE (*Actors in the Audience*, 49–50).

48. The motif of the *cena inaequalis* also appears in Martial (2.43, 3.49, 3.60, 4.85, 6.11) and at Plin. *Ep*. 2.6.

49. The performing monkey is an apt symbol of the slavish Trebius, according to Adamietz (*Untersuchungen zu Juvenal*, 95–96). Freudenburg sees the monkey as a degraded satirist figure (*Satires of Rome*, 274–275).

50. The entertainment theme is noted by Braund (*Satires Book I*, 301); cf. Ferguson on 5.26 (*Satires*, 175).

51. Parker ("Crucially Funny") analyzes the social function of this aspect of the comic slave's role.

52. Cic. *Off*. 1.150, Quint. *Inst*. 1.10.31, Plin. *Pan*. 46.5.

53. The *trechedipna* ("dinner-runners," probably slippers) named in line 67 as the new attire of Romans may refer to the shoes of comic parasites (Courtney, *Satires*, 165), which would enhance the sense of theatricalized social life in Rome.

54. Burns, *Theatricality*, 151.

55. Quintilian discusses this all-important aspect of Roman rhetoric at *Inst*. 6.2. Cf. *Inst*. 11 for his instructions on counterfeiting emotions, discussed in Anderson, *Essays on Roman Satire*, 425–428.

56. Rhetorical questions are used at 38, 49–50, 81–85, and 126–130; overgeneralizations using forms of *nullus* and *omnis* appear at 22, 109, 125, 183, 211, 247, and 308. Umbricius' speech brings to mind the formulaic address to a departing traveler (*syntaktikon*; cf. Braund, *Satires Book I*, 231). It also resembles the standard declama-

tory exercise comparing town and country life (cf. Quint. *Inst.* 2.4.24); for more on this character's rhetorical techniques see Anderson, *Essays on Roman Satire*, 293–361; cf. Anderson, "Rustic Urbanity"; Braund, "City and Country," 26–39; and *Satires Book I*, 234.

57. Winkler concludes that "the boorish, reactionary satirist is just as much a target of Juvenalian satire as the people, objects, or attitudes which he attacks" and that the purpose of Juvenal's satire "is one of liberal didacticism" (*Persona*, 223 and 227). Anderson, "Juvenal Satire 15," makes similar suggestions. Both discussions imply that we should dissociate the speaker from the real poet because the former's attitudes are clearly bigoted. But we should do this simply because the speaker is a poetic construct, not because we want to believe that the poet holds particular values.

58. Kirby, "On Acting and Not-Acting," 47 and 51.

59. Henderson, *Figuring Out Roman Nobility*, 39–41.

60. The echo of *Hecyra* 1–57 is noted by Brink (*Epistles Book II*, 219–220).

61. On Democritus as alter ego for Juvenal, see Bellandi, *Etica Diatribica*, 66–101; on the allusion to Horace, see Braund, *Beyond Anger*, 189.

62. Juvenal's description of the *pompa circensis* may be compared to other ancient accounts; see Versnel, *Triumphus*, 58–59. Schmitz, *Das Satirische*, 27–28, further analyzes the spectacular aspects of the Juvenalian scene.

63. Keane, "Theatre," 272–273. Parker argues that Roman elites on view had to assert such control over spectators in order to avoid being seen as vulgar performers themselves: "[The elite] must be the giver of images, never the object of others' interpretations" ("Observed of All Observers," 168).

64. At *Ann.* 1.15.1–5, Tacitus describes the transfer of elections from the Campus Martius to the senate in 14 CE as liberation from "the partiality of the tribes" (*studiis tribuum*) and a source of relief for senators, who no longer needed to bribe and campaign. He adds, "nor did the people protest that their right was being taken away, except in idle talk" (*neque populus ademptum ius questus est nisi inani rumore*). That the elections change was followed by a request by the tribunes of the plebs to put on games in honor of Augustus (1.15.6–11) helps Tacitus to press the idea that the people were ready to turn from politics to shows. But the real point of view of the populace—the real nature of their "idle talk"—is obscured. Furneaux (*Annalium Libri I–IV*, 26) glosses Tacitus' account by citing the Juvenalian passage, and thus seems to accept the accuracy of both. But evidence shows that the urban plebs was a considerable political force with motivations other than *panem et circenses* (Rowe, *Princes and Political Cultures*, 85–101).

65. *Circenses* may broadly connote all sport here (Ferguson, *Satires*, 260).

66. Juvenal may allude more cryptically to the connection between spectatorship and the lost vote of the *populus* at 8.211, where he imagines that Seneca would be chosen emperor over the performer Nero "if the people were given a free vote" (*libera si dentur populo suffragia*).

67. Freudenburg perceives another connection in that both Juvenal and the theatergoing women mistake myth for reality (*Satires of Rome*, 254–255), but the passage in *Satire* 6 does not seem to me to support this view; the women's passion for performances is not a sign of naiveté.

68. Juvenal portrays the rustic spectators as wearing dark blue hoods (*veneto cucullo*, 170), a garment associated with the stock paupers of comedy (Courtney, *Satires*,

178; cf. Freudenburg, *Walking Muse*, 219). This strengthens the impression the audience is playing a dramatic role.

69. Freudenburg, *Satires of Rome*, 64 and 259.

CHAPTER 2

1. Elliott, *Power of Satire*; cf. the similar argument of Kernan, "Aggression and Satire."

2. Freud, *Jokes*, especially 114–121 and 171–193. Cf. Richlin's application of Freud to a Roman context in *Garden of Priapus*, 59–63.

3. Robinson, "Art of Violence," 99.

4. Bogel, *Difference Satire Makes*, 41–42.

5. Richlin, *Garden of Priapus*, 57–63.

6. Henderson, *Writing Down Rome*, 173–201.

7. Bogel, *Difference Satire Makes*, 44–46, drawing on two key anthropological studies: Girard's *Violence and the Sacred*, and Douglas, *Purity and Danger*. Seidel applies these anthropological theories to satire (*Satiric Inheritance*, 16–20). He argues that satirists aim to create order by first embracing and examining disorder; they are "ready to risk exposure to dirt and disorder for the power such a risk transfers to them" (16). Braund notes this source of power as well (*Roman Satirists*, 40–41).

8. Cic. *De or.* 2.239; orators exploited opponents' physical flaws to suggest flaws in character. See Corbeill, *Controlling Laughter*, 14–56, and Grant, *Ancient Rhetorical Theories*, 79–81.

9. "Public violence . . . constituted what was finally a conservative apotropaic political ceremony channeling aggression in manageable directions" (Plass, *Game of Death*, 9; cf. 56–77). Cf. Barton, *Sorrows of the Ancient Romans*, and Coleman, "Fatal Charades," especially 69–70.

10. Bogel, *Difference Satire Makes*, 46.

11. Hipponax is especially known for enacting violence in his poems (see frs. 120–121 in West, *Iambi et Elegi Graeci* I), but his fellow iambographer Archilochus has a similar image in ancient criticism (e.g., Pind. *Pyth.* 2.54–56, Cic. *Nat. D.* 3.91, Hor. *Ars P.* 79). For more images of iambic verses as weapons, cf. Catull. 36.5, Ov. *Rem.* 377–378, *Ib.* 53–54 and 521–524, Stat. *Silv.* 2.2.115. Cucchiarelli, *La satira e il poeta*, 125–129, assembles relevant images for comparison with Horace.

12. The verb *differre* has two different senses in 1085 and 1086 W (Warmington, *Remains of Old Latin* III), as Nonius' glosses indicate: in 1085 it means "to defame, publish a bad report on" (*diffamare, divulgare*, Nonius 284.13), in 1086 the more literal "to divide or cleave" (*dividere vel scindere*, 284.17).

13. "A sustained metaphor, in which the salt cleanses and causes pain in the victims, as well as amusing the reader," Brown, *Satires I*, 184.

14. For the fable, see Babrius 139 in Perry, *Babrius and Phaedrus*, 182–183; Muecke, however, views the fable's moral as insignificant to Horace (*Satires II*, 110).

15. Persius represents satiric violence as diminishing between Lucilius and Horace: Lucilius bit while Horace only touches (*tangit*, 1.117; cf. Freudenburg, *Satires of Rome*, 179).

16. Cucchiarelli describes Horace's self-positioning in the *Epodes* and *Sermones* as play with "una doppia personalità poetica" (*La satira e il poeta*, 120).

17. Freudenburg, *Satires of Rome*.

18. Horace *Epod.* 6.12 represents the iambic poet as an angry bull ("I raise my

ready horns," *parata tollo cornua*). But Hipponax played on the name of his victim Boupalus as evoking a bull (Rosen, "Hipponax").

19. Cucchiarelli notes that *urbanitas* is a quality of Horace's comic model Terence (*La satira e il poeta*, 114). A Lucilian parallel to this accusation appears in 1085 W, quoted above.

20. Horace uses traditional images even when he revises his program at the beginning of book 2 (Shero, "Satirist's Apologia," 156 n. 8; cf. Hendrickson, "Horace, Serm. I," 127–128).

21. Freudenburg, "Satires 2.1," 195–196.

22. The violence in the Persius passage recalls Horace's persona in the *Epodes*, thus playfully merging the generic agendas that Horace himself (also playfully) separates throughout the two collections (Cucchiarelli, *La satira e il poeta*, 197–198). The interlocutor's reference to a barking dog at Persius 1.109–110 also recalls the canine poet and his adversary in *Epod*. 6.

23. Randolph examines the medical associations of English Renaissance satire ("Medical Concept"). Her list of common metaphors used to describe the genre (142) resembles the one presented in this chapter's opening discussion.

24. Rome is full of critics with asses' ears (1.121) while the ears of Persius' ideal reader have been cleansed and inspired by Old Comedy (1.126), cf. the Stoic at 5.86. On the motif see Reckford, "Studies in Persius," 476–483, and Bramble, *Programmatic Satire*, 26–27.

25. Jenkinson's translation, "[you are] qualified to slice away sick habits and to pin down vice in a sport beyond reproach" (*Satires*, 41), conveys some of the complexity of the images. Anderson finds the tensions difficult to accept (*Essays on Roman Satire*, 172). Cucchiarelli, in contrast, argues that Persius deliberately merges generic images that Horace presents as opposed in the *Sermones* (*La satira e il poeta*, 199).

26. On the possible corruption of the text here, see Courtney, *Satires*, 116–117 and Braund, *Satires Book I*, 108 (the subject of *deducit* is most likely the burned corpse).

27. On historical instances of this kind of spectacle, cf. Gell. 3.14.19 (among the Carthaginians) and Tac. *Ann*. 15.44; cf. Braund's note (*Satires Book I*, 108). Such a punishment was reserved for the lowest members of society and thus degrades the satirist figure in the Juvenalian passage (Freudenburg, *Satires of Rome*, 243–245). It seems right to distinguish these burnings from the deadly mythological reenactments of the arena, in which the lowly victims were transformed by their disguises into suitable offerings (Coleman, "Fatal Charades," 69–70).

28. Freudenburg sees metaliterary significance in the line drawn in the sand: *deducit* evokes the neoteric aesthetic, and the mark is a pale imitation of the literary legacy of the powerful Lucilius (*Satires of Rome*, 245 and n. 58).

29. Bogel, *Difference Satire Makes*, 10.

30. Oliensis, *Rhetoric of Authority*, 18; cf. Schlegel, "Horace and his Fathers," and Henderson, *Writing Down Rome*, 202–227.

31. Novara points out that while the concepts of necessity and utility are common to a number of ancient theories of human progress, Horace relates these concepts primarily to the early humans' tendency to violence; see *Les idées romaines* II, 788–789.

32. Fish, *Doing What Comes Naturally*, 504.

33. Gowers, "Fragments of Autobiography," 74–76; for Horace, fingernails, at least bitten ones, are signs of thoughtful editing (*Serm*. 1.10.71).

34. "Give meaning to": Var. *Ling.* 7.110, Cic. *Tusc.* 3.10, Lucr. 1.914; "censure, stigmatize": Cic. *Brut.* 224, Ov. *Her.* 9.20; cf. *Sermones* 1.3.24, where Horace plays the censor.

35. For justification of a reading of the two passages in sequence, see Zetzel ("Horace's *Liber Sermonum*," 63): "The only significant chronology in a *liber* of this sort is that of unrolling the book . . . The order of reading creates its own dramatic time."

36. As related briefly at *Epist.* 2.2.46–52; cf. Fraenkel, *Horace*, 9–13, and DuQuesnay, "Horace and Maecenas," 24–26.

37. Rudd calls 1.5, 1.7, 1.8, and 1.9 "entertainments" (*Horace*, 54–85).

38. On the staging of political struggle in 1.7, see Henderson, "Getting Rid of Kings." Gowers sees an allusion to proscription in the transition between 1.7 and 1.8 ("Blind Eyes and Cut Throats"); cf. "Fragments of Autobiography" (on autobiographical allusions throughout book 1).

39. Cucchiarelli compares this distance with the more central role that Horace's iambic persona plays in conflict (*La satira e il poeta*, 124).

40. Horace begins by invoking the Muse (51–53) and giving miniature genealogies of the performers (53–56). The buffoons' names evoke Atellan farce (*sarmentum*= "the stick;" *kikirros* "the cock;" see Kiessling and Heinze, *Satiren*, 98).

41. On Messius as a reminder of Horace's bull persona (*Epod.* 6.11–12), see Cucchiarelli, *La satira e il poeta*, 145. On Horace's position as *scriba* following the battle of Philippi, see Oliensis, *Rhetoric of Authority*, 29–30 and 30 n. 13; Gowers, "Horace, Satires 1.5," 59; and Armstrong, "*Horatius eques et scriba*," 263–277. Cucchiarelli writes that "La contesa dei due buffoni ha un'altra, ironica evidenza per la satira di Orazio, come in un gioco di specchi" (*La satira e il poeta*, 98).

42. Messius had "the Campanian disease" (62), which, according to the scholiast, produced growths that had to be surgically removed.

43. The iambic associations are noted by Cucchiarelli (*La satira e il poeta*, 144).

44. Horace calls Lucilius "tough in his composition of verses" (*durus componere versus*, 1.4.8) and adds that he "flowed muddily" (*flueret lutulentus*, 1.4.11). On the similarity to Persius' invective see Schlegel, "Horace Satires 1.7," 341, and Buchheit, "Homerparodie und Literarkritik," 544–545.

45. Schlegel, "Horace Satires 1.7," 351, seconded by McGinn, "Satire and the Law," 95. Schlegel views the conflict between the litigants in a Girardian framework as a battle between increasingly equivalent and vehement "twins" (344).

46. Hallett compares the poem's ironic ending with other Priapic poems ("*Pepedi / diffissa nate ficus*," 346–347); cf. Richlin, *Garden of Priapus*, 57–63 and 177.

47. Welch, "*Est locus uni cuique suus*," 184–189; on other aspects of the persona relevant to Horace see Habash, "Priapus: Horace in Disguise." Canidia's adverse sexual and poetic influence on Horace in the *Epodes* and *Sermones* is discussed in Oliensis, "Canidia;" cf. *Rhetoric of Authority*, 68–101.

48. Tupet, *La magie* I, 318–329.

49. Cucchiarelli sees hints of Horace's iambic side in the chaotic endings of 2.6, 2.7, and 2.8 (*La satira e il poeta*, 156–163).

50. Fitzgerald, exploring the ways in which master and slave merge in the poem, sees an anagram of *servus* in *versus* (*Slavery*, 18–24).

51. On Persius' use of dominant metaphors in his poems, see Dessen, *Iunctura Callidus Acri*, 12. On connections between the body and the mind in particular, see Bramble, *Programmatic Satire*, 35. Cf. Reckford, "Reading the Sick Body."

52. Cf. Henderson's study of the "Care of the Self" recommended in the *Satires* as an alternative to conformity or rebellion (*Writing Down Rome*, 228–248).

53. Similarly, the fashionable poetry makes "your clean-shaven dandy jump about on the bench" (*trossulus exultat tibi per subsellia levis*, 82). In 1.19–21, the body of the reciting poet is painted as effeminate and degenerate; see Bramble, *Programmatic Satire*, 73–79; Richlin, *Garden of Priapus*, 187; and Freudenburg, *Satires of Rome*, 162–172.

54. On this sense of *patranti fractus ocello* (18), see Bramble, *Programmatic Satire*, 76–77; cf. Adams, *Latin Sexual Vocabulary*, 143; Miller, "Bodily Grotesque," 267; and Freudenburg, *Satires of Rome*, 162–166. Sen. *Ep.* 114 discusses the effeminate style; Jenkinson (*Satires*, 68) notes additional sources on stylistic matters.

55. Although this line brings to mind Persius' description of the Stoic's ear washed with vinegar (5.86), the ancient commentary paraphrases *mordaci vero auriculas radere* as "to grate on or rend" (*id est perstringere vel lacerare*; Jahn, *Satirarum Liber*, 273).

56. Dessen, *Iunctura Callidus Acri*, 46, on lines 64–67; cf. Gowers, *Loaded Table*, 182, and Flintoff, "Food for Thought," 352, on Persius' merging of animal and human flesh.

57. Cf. Hor. *Carm.* 3.23 and Juvenal 10.346–366. On Persius' use of the motif see Hooley, *Knotted Thong*, 183–201.

58. Cf. Girard, *Violence and the Sacred*, 1–38.

59. Reckford, "Reading the Sick Body," 340. Reckford suggests that the scholar character's utterance "I am bursting!" (*findor*, 9) may be construed not simply as a giving in to anger, but as a splitting of self or personality (349–350 and n. 23).

60. Dessen adds that Persius links physical torments (the bronze Sicilian bull in which victims were roasted, 39, the sword of Damocles, 40–41) with the spiritual agony brought on by guilt (42–43; *Iunctura Callidus Acri*, 54).

61. Dessen sees "the politician as prostitute" as the poem's dominant metaphor (*Iunctura Callidus Acri*, 66), although Miller ("Bodily Grotesque," 268–269) emphasizes the sterility of Alcibiades' body. The man's buttocks have been heated (*elixas*) and depilated with a curved forceps (*forcipe adunca*, 40); which is either a cosmetic or a medical procedure (on the latter, see Baldwin, "Persius' Boiled Buttocks").

62. It is unclear who speaks the lines. Jahn (*Satirarum Liber*, 41) and Gildersleeve (*Satires*, 54) assign them to the Socrates figure, Jenkinson to Alcibiades (*Satires*, 39). On the possible reference to a ball game, see Jahn (*Satirarum Liber*, 177) and Jenkinson (*Satires*, 84), who cite Isid. *Orig.* 18.69.2 and Plut. *Cic.* 17.2.

63. Jahn, *Satirarum Liber*, 237–238.

64. E.g., Richlin: "He rejects the crude audience that mocks the crippled" (*Garden of Priapus*, 187); this echoes the judgments of Wehrle (*Satiric Voice*, 35), Bramble (*Programmatic Satire*, 140), and Kissel (*Satiren*, 279), who remarks that such jokes went beyond the bounds of the "natürlichen Spottlust" of the Greeks and Romans. The relevance of an alleged work of invective by Nero called *Luscio* (cf. Suet. *Dom.* 1) is unproven (Kissel, *Satiren*, 280).

65. Grant notes that the Ciceronian passage brings Persius 1.128 to mind (*Ancient Rhetorical Theories*, 79).

66. In Freud's theory of humor there must be three parties to a tendentious joke (*Jokes*, 175–178).

67. Cf. *poetas* at 3.9 and other examples noted by Braund (*Satires Book I*, 26) and Schmitz (*Das Satirische*, 117–121).

68. Cf. Barton, *Sorrows of the Ancient Romans*, and Plass, *Game of Death*.

69. The first item in Kernan's list of satire's metaphorical tools is a medical instrument: "The surgeon's knife, the whip, the purge, the rack, the flood, and the holocaust" (*Cankered Muse*, 33).

70. Braund (*Satires Book I*, 200) makes note of the metaphors.

71. Several of the urban scenes in *Satire* 3 are modeled on scenes of epic violence; the motif and specific allusions are explored by Staley ("Juvenal's Third Satire") and Baines ("Umbricius' *Bellum Civile*").

72. As Braund notes (*Satires Book I*, 282); cf. Petron. 67.11, Mart. 3.68.6 and 4.66.12.

73. Juvenal exposes the euphemistic nature of the language of *amicitia* by using it in this ugly poem (Braund, *Satires Book I*, 33, 304, and 307).

74. Barton, *Sorrows of the Ancient Romans*, 141–142 and 145–172.

75. Gowers (*Loaded Table*, 198–200) sees the cannibalism theme as mirroring Rome's own self-destructive practices identified in earlier *Satires*. On the poem's subtle criticisms of Roman imperialism, see Anderson, "Juvenal Satire 15," and more generally on its wit see Singleton, "Juvenal's Fifteenth Satire."

76. It is especially telling to compare Juvenal's opening and the Ciceronian passage on which it is clearly modeled: "Who is unaware of the ways of the Egyptians? Their minds are so steeped in the errors of their perversity that they'd rather face torture than violate an ibis, an asp, a cat, a dog, or a crocodile" (*Aegyptiorum morem quis ignorat? quorum imbutae mentes pravitatis erroribus quamvis carnificinam prius subierint quam ibim aut aspidem aut faelem aut canem aut crocodilum violent, Tusc.* 5.78). Cicero is including the Egyptians among examples of great courage motivated by beliefs or natural instincts. Juvenal inverts Cicero's point to emphasize the Egyptians' religious perversity and downplay their courage.

77. Girard, *Violence and the Sacred*, 14; cf. Seidel, *Satiric Inheritance*, 18, and Bogel, *Difference Satire Makes*, 44.

78. "Canopus . . . was notorious as a resort not for rich Egyptians but for Greeks and Romans" (McKim, "Philosophers and Cannibals," 63; cf. Courtney, *Satires*, 599).

79. This sequence represents a "capsule history of man's progress in warfare" (McKim, "Philosophers and Cannibals," 69).

80. On this characterization of *sermo*, which is both typical and disingenuous coming from Horace, see Rudd, *Epistles Book II*, 117–118.

81. I owe this formulation of the poem's theme to Susanna Braund (e-mail, February 16, 2003).

CHAPTER 3

1. Kiel, *Grammatici Latini* I, 486; cf. Coffey, *Roman Satire*, 11–18, and Van Rooy, *Studies in Classical Satire*, 1–29.

2. Knight, "Imagination's Cerberus," 142.

3. See de Decker, *Juvenalis Declamans*; cf. Braund, "Declamation and Contestation."

4. Knight, "Imagination's Cerberus," 143–144.

5. As discussed in Freudenburg, *Satires of Rome*, and with regard to Horace in particular, Mazurek, "Legal Terminology," and McGinn, "Satire and the Law."

6. These phrases are chapter titles in Posner, *Law and Literature*; cf. Ward, *Law and Literature*; and Weisberg and Barricelli, "Literature and Law," 150–175. Ziolkowski

examines similar issues, though he asserts that Roman texts never question the sanctity of the law (*Mirror of Justice*, 64).

7. On legal discourse as play, see Huizinga, *Homo Ludens*, 78–88; on its literary qualities, see Fish, *Doing What Comes Naturally*, and Weisberg and Barricelli, 161–174.

8. Cloud catalogues such distortions ("Satirists and the Law").

9. Smith, "Law of Libel," and LaFleur, "Horace and *Onomasti Komodein*," 1817–1819 n. 73. For the law (Table VIII.1a–1b in Warmington, *Remains of Old Latin* III, 474–475) see Cic. *Rep.* 4.12 and Plin. *HN* 28.18. Another relevant passage is Hor. *Epist.* 2.1.139–155, which describes the inflammatory Fescennine verses and the law that evolved forbidding "anyone from being described in abusive song" (*malo . . . carmine quemquam / describi*, 153–154); see discussion below and Rudd, *Epistles Book II*, 100.

10. See Dio Cass. 56.27.1 and Sen. *Controv.* 10 pref. 5 (on Augustan cases), Tac. *Ann.* 4.35 and Sen. *Dial.* 6.1.3 (on the historian Cremutius Cordus, under Tiberius), and Tac. *Ag.* 2.1 (on cases under Domitian). Historical accounts of such cases influence Juvenal's representation of his "belated" satire (Freudenburg, *Satires of Rome*, 215–248).

11. Griffith, "Juvenal's First *Satire*," 69, and Fredricksmeyer, "Programmatic Satires." For the argument that book 1 also featured an apologia, see Shero, "Satirist's Apologia," 165–167.

12. So Hooley has recently argued regarding the literary and moral construction of satire in Horace *Sermones* 1.4; see "Horace Sat. 1.4."

13. As Lejay observes, the term when used at 3.24 evokes the censor's *nota* (*Satires*, 76); Freudenburg believes that the same is true at 1.4.5, though the association of the *censura* with fifth-century Athens is "anachronistic and far-fetched, to say the least" (*Satires of Rome*, 17).

14. On the link between Lucilius and the elder Horace (addressed again in chapter 4), see Schlegel, "Horace and His Fathers," 94–107.

15. Cf. McGinn ("Satire and the Law," 98) on *Sermones* 2.1: "In this satire, whatever the play of dialogue, the poet is effectively engaged in dialectic with no one other than himself."

16. Oberhelman and Armstrong, "Satire as Poetry;" cf. Freudenburg, *Walking Muse*, 119–128.

17. Kiessling and Heinze point out that 1.10 returns to literary matters (*Satiren*, 78), although Lejay (*Satires*, 121) reads the comment at 1.4.63–64 as a false promise.

18. *Licentia*, "license," has negative connotations for the Romans, in contrast to *libertas*, which implies recognition of law's positive value; see Ducos, *Les Romains et la loi*, 80–81 and 171. On the echoes between the *Epistles* passage and Horace's satiric apologiae, especially the ending of 2.1, see Brink, "Horace and Varro," 194–195.

19. So Feeney observes: "The history of Roman literature . . . is for all intents and purposes co-extensive with the history of the state's regulation with it" ("*Una cum scriptore meo*," 182). Braund, however, gives more weight to the first step in the account, when social censure alone kept the verses in check ("*Libertas* or *Licentia*," 414–415).

20. Horace uses legal themes to engage in literary play throughout his oeuvre, as discussed in Ducos, "Horace et le droit."

21. Kiessling and Heinze (*Satiren*, 79) and Brown (*Satires I*, 133) understand Horace to be using *libellus* in two clearly different senses in 1.4. But Freudenburg, writing on Horace's reference to his own *libellus* at 1.10.92, believes that the poet is milking the ambiguity of the term (*Satires of Rome*, 67 n. 85).

22. Cucchiarelli (*La satira e il poeta*, 150 n. 117) identifies 1.4.100–101 as an iambic image, comparable to Canidia's black poison (1.8.23).

23. See Introduction, n. 7, and Hutcheon, *Irony's Edge*, 47.

24. For a survey of the debate (and a case for a strictly legal reading of *ultra legem*), see Muecke, "Law, Rhetoric, and Genre," 205–206, which follows the interpretation of Leeman ("Rhetorical Status," 159). For further metaphorical and critical senses of the debate in the poem, see Freudenburg, "Horace Satires 2.1."

25. McGinn argues that Horace makes a subtle demand for similar accommodation from the legal system ("Satire and the Law," 99).

26. Leeman connects Horace's arguments to the legal strategies available to defendants ("Rhetorical Status").

27. Cf. *Carm.* 1.1 and Pind. *Ol.* 1.1–7. Horace will take a similar stance (*quid faciam?*) when explaining his *inability* to write at *Epist.* 2.2.57.

28. Leeman notes that Horace's appeal to nature and to others' tendency to self-defense is an attempt to construct *status qualitatis*, or a case of justified transgression ("Rhetorical Status," 161). The animals and Canidia have iambic associations (see *Epod.* 6 and Cucchiarelli, *La satira e il poeta*, 149).

29. Braund, "City and Country," 39–44; Anderson, "Rustic Urbanity," 112–114.

30. Freudenburg, *Satires of Rome*, 107; a more optimistic reading of the reference to Caesar's influence is presented in Tatum, "*Ultra legem*," 695–699.

31. This transition is announced with the same flourish ("in short," *ne longum faciam*, 57) that Horace uses to round out the last of his earlier diatribe poems (1.3.137).

32. On these lines, Muecke (*Satires II*, 109) writes that Horace's tone "changes from that of apology to defiance," and like Kiessling and Heinze (*Satiren*, 187) notes that this effect is enhanced by the high-flown description of Death in line 58.

33. Warmington assigns the fragment to book 30 and suggests that it refers to the anti-alien *lex Junia Penni* from 126 BCE (*Remains of Old Latin* III, 331). Cf. Raschke, "*Arma pro amico*," 313–314, for a discussion of the evidence.

34. One might consider as an example the image of bandit societies as legally bound, a phenomenon discussed in Shaw, "Bandits in the Roman Empire," and Habinek, *Politics of Latin Literature*, 69–87.

35. Plotnick argues that this passage of *Ars* alludes to Horatian *satura* ("Horace on Satyr Drama"; cf. chapter 1).

36. Hooley, *Knotted Thong*, 55.

37. Duret, "Juvénal réplique à Trébatius," 205–206.

38. Coleman analyzes the punitive spectacles of the Imperial period as a method of social control that stands outside normal legal process ("Fatal Charades," 44–49).

39. Like Persius, Martial uses the phrase "*hic est*" of famous poets (1.1.1, 5.13.3, 9.97.3–4); Juvenal's accusing use of it thus stands out all the more, as noted by Gérard, "Des droits et des deviors," 269–270 n. 5.

40. On the truth value and conventionality of this claim see Lutz, "Any Resemblance," 115–120; cf. Fredricksmeyer, "Programmatic Satires."

41. Mazurek, "Legal Terminology," 19.

42. See also 1239 W, on the fictional *lex Tappula* from a poem by Valerius Valentinus.

43. McGinn, "Satire and the Law," 85–86; Zetzel, "Horace's *Liber Sermonum*," 69–70; and Freudenburg, *Walking Muse*, 23–24.

44. My survey is selective; for more extensive examination of the legal coloring of the diatribe poems, see Mazurek, "Legal Terminology," 37–53, and McGinn, "Satire and the Law," 85–89 (who is less convinced that all legal references are significant to generic construction).

45. See e.g. Van Rooy, "Satires 1–4"; Zetzel, "Horace's *Liber Sermonum*," 65; and now Knorr, *Verborgene Kunst*, 98–104.

46. Galba is a jurist, an adulterer, or both: on the various interpretations see Mazurek, "Legal Terminology," 42 n. 10, and Brown, *Satires I*, 106.

47. Similarly, Juvenal appeals to the fears of a parent whose handsome son may one day become an adulterer (10.311–317). Like Horace, he lists the ways in which cuckolded husbands retaliate ("the sword . . . lashes . . . even the mullet," *ferro . . . verberibus . . . et mugilis*, 316–317). He also remarks that a husband's resentment (*dolor*) often exceeds legal bounds (315–316).

48. Horace takes on the adulterer's role to make his point at his own expense (Brown, *Satires I*, 114).

49. "Because the current legal system is in such disarray, the satirist must start from scratch to devise a new and better way of dispensing justice" (Mazurek, "Legal Terminology," 50).

50. The parent of law is *utilitas* (1.3.98); for the opposite Stoic belief that laws come from Nature see, e.g., Diog. Laert. 7.128, citing Chrysippus *On the Good* (discussed in Kiessling and Heinze, *Satiren*, 62–63).

51. Armstrong, *Horace*, 41; Fraenkel, *Horace*, 112 and 124; Braund, "Declamation and Contestation," 161–162; and Schlegel, "Horace *Satires* 1.7."

52. Mazurek, "Self-Parody," 13–15.

53. Musurillo, "Horace and the Bore," 68.

54. Oliensis, *Rhetoric of Authority*, 41–63; cf. Freudenburg, *Satires of Rome*, 108–117, and Gowers, *Loaded Table*, 130–179.

55. Oliensis, *Rhetoric of Authority*, 44. Cf. Kiessling and Heinze, *Satiren*, 187: the threat of exile has real relevance "in dem Stürmen dieser Revolutionsjahre" of 31–30 B.C.

56. On the practice see Cic. *Caecin.* 100: "Exile is not a punishment, but a refuge and a harbor from punishment" (*exsilium enim non supplicium est, sed perfugium portusque supplici*). Cf. Bauman, *Crime and Punishment*, 13–18.

57. On Horace's puns on the term *ius* ("sauce" or "right") see Gowers, *Loaded Table*, 128, 131, 133–135, 140, and 175. Berg, "Mystery Gourmet," sees book 2 as a narrative of Horace's rivalry for authority with Nasidienus the gourmet.

58. This idea is developed in Bernstein, "'O Totiens Servus.'"

59. The suggestive juxtaposition is discussed again in chapter 4.

60. The free Roman's enjoyment of Saturnalian *libertas* was symbolized in his wearing of the freedman's cap, *pila*; see Sen. *Ep.* 18.3, Mart. 11.6.4 and 14.1.2.

61. As Bernstein points out, Horace's formal gesture is a reminder of this "lawless" holiday's grounding in the normal social order ("'O Totiens Servus,'" 462).

62. Bernstein, "'O Totiens Servus,'" 469.

63. For comic references to this punishment, see e.g. Plaut. *Epid.* 121, *Mostell.* 19 (in wording similar to Horace's), and Ter. *Phorm.* 249.

64. Freudenburg, *Satires of Rome*, 151–172.

65. The scale (*trutina*) appears in 5–7, critical nails (*severos unguis*) and the straight drawn *rubrica* in 63–66, and "shaved antitheses" (*rasis antithetis*) in 85–86.

66. Freudenburg understands the second *hic* to be alluding to the first (*Satires of Rome*, 180).

67. The ancient biography of Persius reports that 1.121 originally read "King Midas has the ears of an ass," *auriculas asini Mida rex habet*, and was later altered by Cornutus to read "who doesn't have the ears of an ass?" *auriculas asini quis non habet*, "lest Nero think this was said about himself" (*ne hoc in se Nero dictum arbitraretur*; Jahn, *Satirarum Liber*, 238). This story offers the only external evidence that Persius' satire struck his contemporaries as risky.

68. Gildersleeve first made the comparison (*Satires*, xxvii), as discussed in Hooley (*Knotted Thong*, 10–11), who sees said "thong" as an apt metaphor for Persius' compositional and allusive style as well.

69. Cloud, "Satirists and the Law," 52.

70. Kissel (*Satiren*, 668–670) regards the two terms *publica lex hominum* and *natura* as synonymous; that is, as coming from the Stoic list of interchangeable terms for the force governing the world (a list which includes *ratio* in line 96). Cf. Villeneuve, *Satires*, 133, and Hooley, *Knotted Thong*, 96.

71. Hooley identifies the echo of Persius' satiric style in the listener's "private ear" (*secretam . . . aurem*, recalling *secrete loquimur* at 5.21; *Knotted Thong*, 96, citing Dessen, *Iunctura Callidus Acri*, 78).

72. E.g., at Persius 2.73; cf. *fas* contrasted with *leges* at Cic. *Mil.* 43.

73. Persius finishes the thought later in the poem with *auriculas asini quis non habet?* (121), though Freudenburg points out that it is foreshadowed by *quis non a si* in line 8 (*Satires of Rome*, 158–159).

74. Criminals' impunity is the obsession of the indignant satirist; cf. Braund, *Beyond Anger*, 6, and Jensen, "Crime, Vice and Retribution," 158–160.

75. These three cases are highlighted by the bursts of *indignatio* that frame them: "Why should I tell how great a rage burns my dry liver, when . . . " (*quid referam quanta siccum iecur ardeat ira, cum* . . . , 45–46) and "should I not think this [material] worthy of the Horatian [i.e. satiric] lamp?" (*haec ego non credam Venusina lucerna?* 51).

76. Freudenburg, *Satires of Rome*, 258–264. Also on the poem's oblique criticism see Sweet, "Juvenal's *Satire* 4," 283–303. The focus on "trifles" (*nugis*, 150) in *Satire* 4 may be compared to the passage in 8 on Nero's stage performances, which the satirist claims were the emperor's real crimes (215–223).

77. Interpretations of Juvenal's reference to Domitian's "working-class" assassins (*cerdonibus*) are discussed by Courtney (*Satires*, 228–229).

78. Braund, "A Passion Unconsoled," 76.

79. Juvenal's case poses a particular challenge to Cloud's claim that the law "does not play a major part in the world which the . . . Roman satirists have constructed for their readers" ("Satirists and the Law," 49). It is certainly true, however, that "reference to Roman law enhances the Romanness of [Horace's] *Satires*" (65); this point applies equally to Juvenal.

80. Braund, *Satires Book I*, 105. Both tales expand the Horatian vignette that likens the effect of funerals on passersby to the effect of the elder Horace's *exempla* on his son (*Sermones* 1.4.126–127; cf. chapter 2).

81. Housman's suspicion that line 124 is inauthentic may be countered by other examples of "over-long lists" in Juvenal (Courtney, *Satires*, 403 and 48).

82. Fishelov explores the differences between Persius 2 and Juvenal 10 ("Vanity of the Reader's Wishes," 372–375).

83. Fish, *Doing What Comes Naturally*, 504.

84. Anderson, *Essays on Roman Satire*, 281–283; cf. Braund, *Beyond Anger*, 189–191. The physiology of Calvinus' anger, a sign of his *simplicitas*, is described at 13–15 and 35; Juvenal attributes *simplicitas* to earlier satire at 1.151–153, and portrays Lucilius as "burning" effectively at 1.165.

85. Highet believes the entire poem was an attack on military ambition (*Juvenal the Satirist*, 154–160 and 288–289 n. 6). On the poem as it stands see Anderson, *Essays on Roman Satire*, 283, Braund, *Beyond Anger*, 196, and Clark, "Juvenal, *Satire* 16."

86. While Juvenal speaks from the perspective of the wronged civilian (37, 47), he also mocks this character's misfortune throughout.

87. Clark calls the Illyrian boot (14) "a menacing symbol of impersonal cruelty" ("Juvenal, *Satire* 16," 116).

88. Clark, "Juvenal, *Satire* 16," 119.

89. Courtney, *Satires*, 619.

90. Posner's chapter on "Literary Indictment of Legal Injustice" weighs the benefits and (in his opinion more serious) drawbacks of many critics' assumption that literature takes the side of the weak against the strong (*Law and Literature*, 132–175). Satire 16 is the sort of complex text that Posner might use to support his argument: while it explores "issues relating to the connection between the legal outlook and the sense of justice, between legalism and civilization, and between law and other forms of institutionalized morality" (174–175), it does not assert the superiority of the second category over the first.

CHAPTER 4

1. Rudd, *Themes in Roman Satire*, 1.

2. The allusion is an appropriate beginning to Horace's Epicurean diatribes (Knorr, *Verborgene Kunst*, 109).

3. Oltramare, *La diatribe romaine*, 138–152, and Freudenburg, *Walking Muse*, 8–21 and 81–82. Cf. Anderson on the poet's "Socratic" persona (*Essays on Roman Satire*, 13–49).

4. The label "doctrinaire poet" is Witke's (*Latin Satire*, 79–112); cf. Ramage, Sigsbee, and Fredericks, *Roman Satirists*, 114–135. Henderson presents a more nuanced view of the poet's didacticism (*Writing Down Rome*, 228–248).

5. Winkler, "Function of Epic."

6. Horace describes Lucilius as employing a less subtle autobiographical mode than the one that he himself cultivates, as argued in Harrison, "Confessions of Lucilius." DuQuesnay notes the authentic feel of Horace's own self-portrait in *Sermones* I: "Nowhere . . . does [Horace] adopt any conventional poetic stance such as those adopted in *Epodes* 7 and 16 . . . Nothing is done which would allow the reader to feel conscious of any gap between the image presented in the poems and reality" ("Horace and Maecenas," 26). Even so, DuQuesnay stresses that this effect is intended and created by Horace's art.

7. This relationship is examined in Oliensis, *Rhetoric of Authority*, and Cucchiarelli, *La satira e il poeta*; cf. Anderson, *Essays on Roman Satire*, 50–73.

8. Keane, "Satiric Memories."

9. Bloom, *Anxiety of Influence*.

10. Freudenburg understands the satirists' responses to Lucilius as being "both

conditioned by, and expressive of, specific pressures felt in the separate political and social worlds that they inhabit" (*Satires of Rome*, 4).

11. "Ancient education still preserved some of the features of oral culture. Those who pursued *paideia* may have acquired their linguistic competence in literary dialect initially by reading, but they had to display it by speaking" (Gleason, *Making Men*, xxiv). One potential aspect of adult male social performance was forensic performance; thus declamation, a core element of education in the early Imperial period, played a role in the socialization process. Declamatory exercises engaged students in "fantasies of transgression and reparation," and so constituted "rehearsals of the real drama of Roman subjectivity" (Gunderson, *Declamation*, 19). Cf. Bloomer, "History of Declamation," on the social context of the "ludic version of forensic conflict" that was declamatory training.

12. Fraenkel, *Horace*, 96; Knorr, *Verborgene Kunst*, 105–115.

13. So Lejay translates *velint* ("consentent à"; *Satires*, 14).

14. "La natura del poeta può essere satiricamente rappresentata come ragione della poesia, e la poesia a sua volta come effetto del poeta, per un processo di rispecchiamento che talvolta chiameremo 'circolazione'" (Cucchiarelli, *La satira e il poeta*, 11); cf. Gowers, "Fragments of Autobiography."

15. Hooley, "Generic Modeling," is a good discussion of the poem's tendentious dramatization of the development of literature, cf. Freudenburg, *Walking Muse*, 92–108 on the poem's comic theory, and Oberhelman and Armstrong, "Satire as Poetry," on Horace's equally tendentious self-presentation as a nonpoet.

16. Horace's inward turn may also be taken as setting an example for readers, as Brown sees it (*Satires I*, 138).

17. On memories as part of Horace's authority, see Oliensis, *Rhetoric of Authority*, especially 17–41. On Horace's vulnerability in particular, see Keane, "Satiric Memories," 217–221.

18. The brilliance of Horace's comedy-influenced picture of his father lies in the fact that their relationship is "free of the notorious tensions which Roman comedy so boisterously exploits" (Schlegel, "Horace and his Fathers," 117).

19. "To put it brutally, the father is just another of the obstacles Horace has got past" (Gowers, "Fragments of Autobiography," 72).

20. Gowers includes 1.9 as a cryptically autobiographical account: "[*Sermones* 1.7–1.9] can be seen with a leap of the imagination to be playing out Horace's evolution through displaced activity of various kinds . . . this life-history works in parallel with the civilizing of satire" ("Fragments of Autobiography," 82).

21. Welch, "*Est locus uni cuique suus*," 167–184; cf. Henderson: "[The pest's] grammar proposes that they become a 'we,' indeed they already 'are a we'" (*Writing Down Rome*, 209).

22. Knorr, *Verborgene Kunst*, 152. The anxiety that Horace expresses later in his career, in *Epist*. 1.20, is understandably amplified: "A classic in his own lifetime, his reception out of his control, he is imitated by the others, pawed over by the uncomprehending, the object of envy, plagiarism, and inevitable misreading" (Feeney, "*Una cum scriptore meo*," 175; cf. Oliensis, *Rhetoric of Authority*, 174–175).

23. Scodel, "Horace, Lucilius, and Callimachean Polemic," 207–212.

24. DuQuesnay notes that in discrediting Lucilius' admirers, Horace undermines the poet's epithet *doctus* (e.g., Cic. *De or.* 1.72, 2.25) ("Horace and Maecenas," 28). The

doctus motif of *Sermones* 1.10 is also reflected in the reference to an editor as *grammaticorum equitum doctissimus* in the probably spurious prologue (8).

25. On Lucilius' readership (especially in 635 W) and Horace's inversion of his poetic request, see Brown, *Satires I*, 192. Warmington's reconstruction (*Remains of Old Latin* III, 201) follows Cichorius.

26. On the culinary metaphor, see Gowers, *Loaded Table*, 130–135.

27. The speakers in book 2 are "men displaced, declassed, or dispossessed by the vicissitudes of the civil wars, men on the make, men scrambling to repair their fortunes" (Oliensis, *Rhetoric of Authority*, 56).

28. For Horace as would-be host (*quaerenti convivam*, 2.8.2) see Lejay, *Satires*, 589, and Muecke, *Satires II*, 91, although Gowers interprets the phrase as meaning that Horace has been trying to dine out (*Loaded Table*, 132).

29. Oliensis, *Rhetoric of Authority*, 52–53. Ofellus is a boyhood neighbor of Horace (112) who shared in the fate of expropriation with many others (Muecke, *Satires II*, 116).

30. "Everything that happens in this book is Horatian *sermo* and nothing else . . . But knowing precisely how to figure it as his talk is a problem with no automatic solution" (Freudenburg, *Satires of Rome*, 112).

31. Muecke, *Satires II*, 130–131 and 141; cf. Bond, "Horace on Damasippus," for a full analysis of the parody of Stoic doctrine.

32. Boll first identified this pattern ("Die Anordnung").

33. Muecke, *Satires II*, 9.

34. Oliensis points out the contrast (*Rhetoric of Authority*, 57).

35. Freudenburg, *Satires of Rome*, 99.

36. Leach, "Horace's Sabine Topography," 285–287; Frischer, "La Villa ercolanese dei Papiri," 224–226; and Oliensis, *Rhetoric of Authority*, 50.

37. "In contrast to the looser construction of *Sat.* 2.3, *Sat.* 2.7 has an allegorical coherence of character, theme, and setting" (Muecke, *Satires II*, 214).

38. Muecke finds elements to criticize in Davus' speech (such as occasional lack of clarity; see *Satires II*, 219 on line 45), but also notes (214) that he his accusations are particularly striking after Horace's "charming self-portrait" in 2.6. If we may imagine this dramatic character as cognizant of the book's structure, we may say that Davus successfully exploits his context.

39. This displacement occurs on a fictional level; the reverse of this "succession" appears to be happening if we focus on the real Horace's manipulation of Fundanius' narrative (Caston, "Fall of the Curtain").

40. Henderson, *Writing Down Rome*, 243–244. Reckford challenged the "doctrinaire Stoic" view much earlier ("Studies in Persius," 490–498).

41. "The prologue is . . . a complexly coherent, small-scale masterwork of volatile counterpositions addressing fundamental issues in artistic composition" (Hooley, *Knotted Thong*, 236).

42. This is not to say that Persius does not draw ingeniously on aspects of satiric theory presented in *Sermones* 1, as Cucchiarelli shows (*La satira e il poeta*, 189–203).

43. *quis leget haec?* is understood to be an adaptation of Lucilius 632–635 W; see Marx, *Lucilii Carminum Reliquiae* II, 220–221. Lines 2–3 on the prospect of a small readership also generally recall the end of *Sermones* 1.10 and Seneca *Ep.* 7.11. On the relevance of the last allusion, see Bramble, *Programmatic Satire*, 68, and Hooley, *Knotted Thong*, 37.

44. Nisbet, "Persius," 56. Contrast Horace's characters: in *Sermones* 1.1, for instance, speakers complain to the satirist that spending a penny will lead to utter poverty (43) and that drawing from a large pile is simply more pleasing (51); such foolish contentions seem designed to be knocked down.

45. On problems pertaining to the unclear attribution of lines in the literary-critical discussion, see Jenkinson, *Satires*, 97–111. On the Horatian stylistic precepts exchanged there, see Hooley, *Knotted Thong*, 42–56.

46. Kissel, *Satiren*, 127–128. For instances of *cachinnus* emphasizing sound and physical effort, see Persius 3.87, Ovid *Ars am.* 3.287, and perhaps Lucilius 683 W (where the word supplements *risus*).

47. Juvenal borrows the image from Sen. *Dial.* 9.15.2, although Seneca's philosopher only laughs (*ridebat*). For the ancient note on Persius' *cachinnus*, see Jahn, *Satirarum Liber*, 250.

48. Bramble does notice the echo, and cites the Horatian line in order to defend the reading *vero* over *verbo* (*Programmatic Satire*, 132 n. 3). On the iambic associations of *mordax* see Cucchiarelli, *La satira e il poeta*, 216.

49. This complements the other, well-known rhetorical delay around which *Satire* 1 is structured. Persius interrupts his own question "Who at Rome does not . . . " (*Romae quis non*, 8), returning to it at the climactic line 121: "Who does not have the ears of an ass?" (*auriculas asini quis non habet?*)

50. Hooley, *Knotted Thong*, 26–63, focusing on *Satire* 1.

51. On the child figure, a flexible symbol in diatribe, see Bramble, *Programmatic Satire*, 185–189. Cf. Keane, "Satiric Memories," 221–225, on Persius' authorial image as child.

52. Hooley, *Knotted Thong*, 134–138 (on *Satire* 4).

53. On the division of lines, see chapter 1 and Jenkinson, *Satires*, 112–113. On the conclusion, see Hooley, *Knotted Thong*, 226–229.

54. "Don't play the uncle with me" is a response Damasippus/Stertinius imagines receiving from his target (*ne sis patruus mihi*, *Sermones* 2.3.88). The exchange "I've buried all [my family];" "That leaves me" occurs between the pest and Horace at 1.9.27–28.

55. Hooley, *Knotted Thong*, 222.

56. The patron's pantry is full of gifts from grateful clients (73–76), and the centurion dismisses learning and earns a laugh (77–87). When the scholar speaks again after the baths vignette he still protests (in vain) that he is not sick (107–109).

57. Jenkinson (*Satires*, 31 and 112–113) assigns these lines to the student (whom he identifies as Persius), but most editors, including Jahn (*Satirarum Liber*, 32) and Gildersleeve (*Satires*, 49), accept them as the lecturer's, which appears to be the interpretation of the ancient scholiast (Jahn, *Satirarum Liber*, 300).

58. Juvenal's *suasoria* urged the dictator Sulla to retire; Henderson speculates that the generic topic is significant, alluding to the satirist's hatred of tyrants (*Writing Down Rome*, 269).

59. Anderson, *Essays on Roman Satire*, 13–49.

60. Freudenburg argues, with reference to this poem, that reading satire for cryptic historical references "diagnoses" the reader's own desires (*Satires of Rome*, 191).

61. Keane, "Satiric Memories," 222.

62. These two interpretations are offered by Malamud ("Out of Circulation," 61), and Freudenburg (*Satires of Rome*, 205–206).

63. Keane, "Satiric Memories," 226–227.

64. "Freedom, which looked back for me, albeit late, after my beard was falling whiter at the barber's hand—still, freedom looked back for me and came, after a long time" (*libertas, quae vera tamen respexit inertem / candidior postquam tondenti barba cadebat / respexit tamen et longo post tempore venit, Ecl.* 1.27–29). Braund (*Satires Book I*, 82) notes another motivation for the allusion: the "low" status shared by satire and bucolic.

65. Here Juvenal embeds another allusion to his project; see Keane, "Juvenal's Cave-Woman."

66. The "ninth age" (cf. Luc. 7.387) may have had specific prophetic associations in the early Imperial period; for the evidence see McGann, "Juvenal's Ninth Age."

67. With the ironic term *doctus*, Juvenal "indicates the total overthrow of Roman *virtus* by transferring terms of moral approval to the description of immorality" (Anderson, *Essays on Roman Satire*, 201).

68. As suggested by Nappa's reading of the poem, the satirist also attempts to "catch up" with the moral degradation of his subjects by shifting from target to target as new associations arise; Juvenal's attack resembles "a motion picture [and not] a snapshot" ("Praetextati mores," 92).

69. In this sense *Satire* 7 foreshadows the breakdown of moral teaching among the nobility in *Satire* 8; cf. Henderson, *Figuring Out Roman Nobility*, 94. Bartsch discusses the poem as an example of doublespeak reminiscent of Tacitus' *Dialogue on Orators* (*Actors in the Audience*, 125–147); Braund examines its allusive and ironic techniques (*Beyond Anger*, 24–68).

70. The survey of professions travels down the literary ladder, even tainting the quintessential noble poets in the end: the *grammaticus* is "at the bottom of the pile . . . with his faded Horace and begrimed Virgil" (Henderson, *Figuring Out Roman Nobility*, 95). The "inglorious and ridiculous position" of the *grammaticus* and the primary position of the poet in *Satire* 7 appear to reverse the order of careers examined in Suetonius' *De viris illustribus* (Townend, "Literary Substrata," 152).

71. The *rhetor* may at least console himself with the thought that he is training future poets, to judge from 1.15–17.

72. Cf. Persius 3.20–24, which describes the lazy student first as a leaking, flawed pot and then as wet clay needing to be shaped, a labored comparison that "points up the urgency of Stoic education" (Reckford, "Reading the Sick Body," 341).

73. On the various sexual connotations of *facio* see Adams, *Latin Sexual Vocabulary*, 204, and cf. Catull. 110.2 and 5; Lucr. 4.1112 and 1195; Petron. 45.8; and Mart. 1.46.1. Juvenal's schoolboys take turns either at masturbation (like those at *Nub.* 966; see Sommerstein, *Clouds*, 207) or at penetrating one another (Adams, *Latin Sexual Vocabulary*, 166 n. 2).

74. *Nub.* 966 and 973–980. Cf. Sen. *Controv.* 4 pr. 11, Quint. *Inst.* 1.2.2–5, 2.2.3–4, 14, and 15; Plin. *Ep.* 3.3.3. Braund notes that after Juvenal's reference to the boys' behavior, the term *coetus*, used to refer to the "class" at 239, takes on sexual overtones in retrospect (*Beyond Anger*, 134).

75. Although Juvenal's command most closely echoes Mart. 9.73.9 (*frange leves calamos*), it has special impact when viewed next to the complaints of Horace and of Persius' scholar character about faulty *calami* (*Sermones* 2.3.7, Persius 3.19). Where the earlier satirists mocked such excuses, Juvenal urges poets to embrace them.

76. "Brains are dragged down to the level of brawn" (Courtney, *Satires*, 380).

77. According to Henderson, Naevolus represents the worst effects of the decline chronicled in book 3 (*Figuring Out Roman Nobility*, 96). Naevolus' discourse on secret vice, and Juvenal's relaying of his words to his own audience, also makes the poem a fitting "allegory for the procedure of satire" (Braund, *Beyond Anger*, 170).

78. For the argument that the poem is controlled by the theme of Nature's laws rather than that of education, see Corn, "'Thus Nature Ordains'," 309–322. The theme of example is common in ancient treatises on moral education; a contemporary text is Ps-Plutarch *De liberis educandis* (*Moralia* 1a–14c).

79. Hooley discusses the set of allusions (*Knotted Thong*, 106–110). The Persius passage also recalls Horace's criticisms of the financial preoccupation in education at *Ars P.* 325–332 and *Epist.* 1.1.53–69, where the god Janus is imagined exhorting Romans: "Citizens, citizens, money's the first thing to seek; virtue after money" ('*o cives, cives, quaerenda pecunia primum est; / virtus post nummos,*' 53–54). Horace points out that this sentiment is opposed to the simple wisdom of children, the *pueri ludentes* described at 59–60; the literary descendants of these children are struggling to follow their better instincts in Juvenal 14. On the motif of children's wisdom see Mayer, *Epistles Book I*, 100.

80. Lines 208–209 may be out of place, according to Courtney (*Satires*, 580) and Duff (who nevertheless calls them "excellent;" *Saturae*, 429).

CONCLUSION: OBSERVING ROMANS

1. Persius' solipsistic pose has invited the most explicit characterizations of the satirist as isolated observer: see especially Anderson's description of Persius as the original "angry young man" (*Essays on Roman Satire*, 169–193, echoed in Braund, *Roman Verse Satire*, 33). While these studies emphasize the unique contribution of Persius, the view of his "isolation" spills out into the persona approach to the genre. By giving the most attention to the poets' rhetorical styles and emotional attitudes, we cultivate the view of satire as observation and reaction, ignoring the possibility that even spectatorship is a participatory activity.

2. Freudenburg's *Satires of Rome* presents a theoretical approach that is not based solely on the persona theory, and so takes satire studies into new territory. But as Freudenburg notes (10–11), the book does not address all of Juvenal's oeuvre, concentrating on the striking debut performance of *Satires* 1–6.

3. Braund explains simply and forcefully why we need to abandon modern notions of rhetoric as insincerity in the study of satiric rhetoric: to say about a speech "'it's just rhetoric' [is] a way of dismissing that speech without engaging with it" (*Roman Satirists*, 9).

4. Anderson, *Essays on Roman Satire*, 281–284, and Braund, *Beyond Anger*, 189–196.

5. The comprehensive studies of Juvenal that have appeared since 1988 should not be ignored, but they do not explicitly integrate the preceding theoretical shift toward the persona. Schmitz, *Das Satirische*, is concerned with poetics and allusion, but not with generic theory per se. Wehrle's study of Juvenal and Persius concentrates on issues of language and meaning, and deliberately steers around current theoretical approaches (*Satiric Voice*, 2–4). Cucchiarelli, however, examines the development of satiric theory in Juvenal (and Persius) in the last chapter of *La satira e il poeta* (187–217).

Bibliography

EDITIONS AND COMMENTARIES

Braund, Susanna. *Juvenal: Satires Book I*. Cambridge: Cambridge University Press, 1996.
Brown, P. Michael. *Horace: Satires I*. Warminster: Aris & Phillips, 1993.
Clausen, W. V. *A. Persi Flacci et D. Iuni Iuvenalis Saturae*. 2nd ed. Oxford: Oxford University Press, 1992.
Conington, John. *The Satires of A. Persius Flaccus*. Edited by Henry Nettleship. Oxford: Clarendon, 1893.
Courtney, Edward. *A Commentary on the Satires of Juvenal*. London: Athlone, 1980.
Duff, J. D. *Iuni Iuvenalis Saturae XIV*. New ed. Introduction by Michael Coffey. Pitt Press Series. Cambridge: Cambridge University Press, 1970.
Fairclough, H. Rushton. *Horace: Satires, Epistles, Ars Poetica*. Loeb Classical Library No. 194. Cambridge, MA: Harvard University Press, 1991.
Ferguson, John. *Juvenal: The Satires*. New York: St. Martin's, 1979.
Furneaux, Henry. *Cornelii Taciti Annalium Libri I–IV*. 2nd ed. Oxford: Clarendon, 1897.
Gildersleeve, Basil L. *The Satires of A. Persius Flaccus*. New York: Harper & Brothers, 1875.
Jahn, Otto. *Auli Persii Flacci Satirarum Liber cum Scholiis Antiquis*. Leipzig: Breitkopf and Hertel, 1843.
Jenkinson, J. R. *Persius: The Satires*. Warminster: Aris & Phillips, 1980.
Kassel, R. and C. Austin. *Poetae Comici Graeci*. Vol. 7. Berlin: Walter de Gruyter, 1989.
Kiel, Heinrich. *Grammatici Latini*. Vol. 1. Leipzig: Teubner, 1857. Reprint, Hildesheim: Olms, 1961.
Kiessling, Adolf and Richard Heinze. *Q. Horatius Flaccus: Satiren*. Berlin: Weidmann, 1977.
Kissel, Walter. *Aules Persius Flaccus Satiren*. Heidelberg: Carl Winter, 1990.
Lejay, Paul. *Oeuvres d'Horace: Satires*. Paris: Hachette, 1911.
Marx, Friedrich. *Lucilii Carminum Reliquiae*. Vol. 2. Leipzig: Teubner, 1904.
Mayer, Roland. *Horace: Epistles Book I*. Cambridge: Cambridge University Press, 1994.
Morris, Edward P. *Horace: The Satires and Epistles*. American Book Company, 1939. Reprint, Norman, OK: University of Oklahoma Press, 1968.
Muecke, Frances. *Horace: Satires II*. Warminster: Aris & Phillips, 1993.
Palmer, Arthur. *The Satires of Horace*. London: MacMillan; New York: St. Martin's, 1955.
Perry, Ben E. *Babrius and Phaedrus*. Loeb Classical Library No. 436. London and Cambridge, MA: Harvard University Press, 1965.
Rudd, Niall. *Horace: Epistles Book II and Epistle to the Pisones ('Ars Poetica')*. Cambridge: Cambridge University Press, 1989.
Sommerstein, Alan. *Aristophanes: Clouds*. Warminster: Aris & Phillips, 1982.

Villeneuve, François. *Les Satires de Perse*. Paris: Hachette, 1918.
Warmington, E. H. *Remains of Old Latin*. Vol. 3: *Lucilius; The Twelve Tables*. Rev. ed. Loeb Classical Library No. 329. Cambridge, MA: Harvard University Press, 1967.
West, M. L. *Iambi et Elegi Graeci*. Vol. 1. 2nd ed. Oxford: Oxford University Press, 1989.
Wickham, Edward C. *Q. Horati Flacci Opera*. 2nd ed. Edited by H. W. Garrod. Oxford: Oxford University Press, 1922.

BOOKS AND ARTICLES

Adamietz, Joachim. *Untersuchungen zur Juvenal*. Wiesbaden: F. Steiner, 1972.
Adams, J. N. *The Latin Sexual Vocabulary*. Baltimore: Johns Hopkins University Press, 1982.
Anderson, W. S. *Essays on Roman Satire*. Princeton, NJ: Princeton University Press, 1982.
———. "Rustic Urbanity: Satirists In and Out of Rome." *CO* 61 (1984): 111–117.
———. "Juvenal Satire 15: Cannibals and Culture." *Ramus* 16 (1987): 203–214.
Armstrong, David. *"Horatius eques et scriba: Satires* 1.6 and 2.7." *TAPA* 116 (1986): 255–288.
———. *Horace*. New Haven, CT: Yale University Press, 1989.
Baines, Victoria. "Umbricius' *Bellum Civile:* Juvenal, Satire 3." *G & R* 50 (2003): 220–237.
Bakhtin, Mikhail and P. Medvedev. *The Formal Method in Literary Scholarship: A Critical Introduction to Sociological Poetics*. Translated by A. J. Wehrle. Baltimore: Johns Hopkins University Press, 1977. (Originally published 1928 by P. Medvedev.)
Baldwin, Barry. "Persius' Boiled Buttocks." *AClass* 38 (1995): 94–97.
Barton, Carlin A. *The Sorrows of the Ancient Romans: The Gladiator and the Monster*. Princeton, NJ: Princeton University Press, 1993.
Bartsch, Shadi. *Actors in the Audience: Theatricality and Doublespeak from Nero to Hadrian*. Cambridge, MA: Harvard University Press, 1994.
Bauman, Richard A. *Crime and Punishment in Ancient Rome*. London and New York: Routledge, 1996.
Bellandi, Franco. *Etica Diatribica e Protesta Sociale nelle Satire di Giovenale*. Bologna: Pàtron, 1980.
Berg, Deena. "The Mystery Gourmet of Horace's *Satires* 2" *CJ* 91 (1996): 141–151.
Bernstein, Michael André. "'O totiens servus:' Saturnalia and Servitude in Augustan Rome." *Critical Inquiry* 13 (1987): 450–474.
Bloom, Harold. *The Anxiety of Influence: A Theory of Poetry*. Oxford: Oxford University Press, 1973.
Bloomer, W. Martin. "A Preface to the History of Declamation: Whose Speech? Whose History?" In *The Roman Cultural Revolution*, edited by Thomas Habinek and Alessandro Schiesaro, 199–215. Cambridge: Cambridge University Press, 1997.
Bogel, Fredric. *The Difference Satire Makes: Rhetoric and Reading from Jonson to Byron*. Ithaca, NY and London: Cornell University Press, 2001.
Boll, Franz. "Die Anordnung im zweiten Buch von Horaz' Satiren." *Hermes* 48 (1913): 143–145.
Bond, Robin P. "Horace on Damasippus on Stertinius on . . ." *Scholia* 7 (1998): 82–108.
Bramble, J. C. *Persius and the Programmatic Satire*. Cambridge: Cambridge University Press, 1974.
Braund, S. H. (Susanna) *Beyond Anger: A Study of Juvenal's Third Book of Satires*. Cambridge: Cambridge University Press, 1988.
———, ed. *Satire and Society in Ancient Rome*. Exeter Studies in History No. 23. Exeter: Exeter University Publications, 1989.
———. "City and Country in Roman Satire." In Braund, *Satire and Society*, 23–47.

———. *Roman Verse Satire*. Greece & Rome New Surveys in the Classics No. 23. Oxford: Oxford University Press, 1992.

———. *The Roman Satirists and Their Masks*. Classical World Series. London: Bristol Classical Press, 1996.

———. "Declamation and Contestation in Satire." In Dominik, *Roman Eloquence*, 147–165.

———. "A Passion Unconsoled? Grief and Anger in Juvenal 'Satire' 13." In *The Passions in Roman Thought and Literature*, edited by Susanna Braund and Christopher Gill, 68–88. Cambridge: Cambridge University Press, 1997.

———. "*Libertas* or *Licentia*? Freedom and Criticism in Roman Satire." In *Free Speech in Classical Antiquity*, edited by Ineke Sluiter and Ralph Rosen, 409–428. Leiden and Boston: Brill, 2004.

Braund, Susan (Susanna), and J. D. Cloud. "Juvenal: A diptych." *LCM* 6 (1981): 195–208.

Brink, C. O. "Horace and Varro." In *Varron: Six Exposés et Discussions*, edited by Olivier Reverdin, 173–200. Entretiens sur l'Antiquité Classique 9. Geneva: Fondation Hardt, 1963.

———. *Horace on Poetry: Epistles Book II*. Cambridge: Cambridge University Press, 1982.

Buchheit, Vinzenz. "Homerparodie und Literarkritik in Horazens Satiren I 7 und I 9." *Gymnasium* 75 (1968): 519–555.

Burns, Elizabeth. *Theatricality: A Study of Convention in the Theatre and in Social Life*. New York: Harper and Row, 1973.

Caston, Ruth Rothaus. "The Fall of the Curtain (Horace S. 2.8)." *TAPA* 127 (1997): 233–256.

Clark, Mark Edward. "Juvenal, Satire 16: Fragmentary Justice." *ICS* 13 (1988): 113–125.

Classen, Carl Joachim. "Satire—The Elusive Genre." *SO* 63 (1988): 95–121.

Cloud, J. Duncan. "Satirists and the Law." In Braund, *Satire and Society*, 49–67.

Coffey, Michael. *Roman Satire*. London: Methuen; New York: Barnes & Noble, 1976.

Coleman, K. M. "Fatal Charades: Roman Executions Staged as Mythological Enactments." *JRS* 80 (1990): 44–73.

Conte, Gian Biagio. *Genres and Readers: Lucretius, Livy, Pliny's Encyclopedia*. Translated by Glenn Most with a foreword by Charles Segal. Baltimore: Johns Hopkins University Press, 1994.

Corbeill, Anthony. *Controlling Laughter: Political Humor in the Late Roman Republic*. Princeton, NJ: Princeton University Press, 1996.

Corn, Alan M. "'Thus Nature Ordains': Juvenal's Fourteenth Satire." *ICS* 17 (1992): 309–322.

Cucchiarelli, Andrea. *La satira e il poeta: Orazio tra* Epodi *e* Sermones. Pisa: Giardini, 2001.

Damon, Cynthia. *The Mask of the Parasite: A Pathology of Roman Patronage*. Ann Arbor: University of Michigan Press, 1997.

Decker, Josué de. *Juvenalis Declamans: Étude sur la Rhétorique Declamatoire dans les Satires de Juvénal*. Ghent: E. van Goethem, 1913.

Dessen, Cynthia S. *Iunctura Callidus Acri: A Study of Persius' Satires*. Urbana: University of Illinois Press, 1968.

Dominik, William J., ed. *Roman Eloquence: Rhetoric in Society and Literature*. London: Routledge, 1997.

Douglas, Mary. *Purity and Danger: An Analysis of the Concepts of Pollution and Taboo*. London: Routledge and Kegan Paul, 1978.

Duckworth, George E. *The Nature of Roman Comedy: A Study in Popular Entertainment*.

2nd ed. Foreword and bibliographical appendix by Richard Hunter. Norman: University of Oklahoma Press, 1994.
Ducos, Michèle. *Les Romains et la loi: Recherches sur les rapports de la philosophie grecque et de la tradition romaine à la fin de la République*. Collection d'Études Anciennes. Paris: Société d'Édition Les Belles Lettres, 1984.
———. "Horace et le droit." *REL* 72 (1994): 79–89.
DuQuesnay, I. M. "Horace and Maecenas: The Propaganda Value of *Sermones* I." In *Poetry and Politics in the Age of Augustus*, edited by A. J. Woodman and David West, 19–58. Cambridge: Cambridge University Press, 1984.
Duret, Luc. "Juvénal réplique à Trébatius." *REL* 61 (1983): 201–226.
Edwards, Catharine. *The Politics of Immorality in Ancient Rome*. Cambridge: Cambridge University Press, 1993.
———. "Unspeakable Professions: Public Performance and Prostitution in Ancient Rome." In *Roman Sexualities*, edited by Judith Hallett and Marilyn Skinner, 69–82. Princeton, NJ: Princeton University Press, 1997.
Ehlers, Widu-Wolfgang. "Zur Rezitation der Satiren des Persius." In *Strukturen der Mündlichkeit in der römischen Literatur*, edited by Gregor Vogt-Spira, 171–181. ScriptOralia 19. Tübingen: Gunter Narr, 1990.
Elliott, Robert C. *The Power of Satire: Magic, Ritual, Art*. Princeton, NJ: Princeton University Press, 1960.
Fairclough, H. Rushton. "Horace's View of the Relation Between Satire and Comedy." *AJP* 34 (1913): 183–193.
Feeney, Denis. "*Una cum scriptore meo:* Poetry, Principate and the Traditions of Literary History in the Epistle to Augustus." In *Traditions and Contexts in the Poetry of Horace*, edited by A. J. Woodman and Denis Feeney, 172–187. Cambridge and New York: Cambridge University Press, 2002.
Feinberg, Leonard. *Introduction to Satire*. Ames: Iowa State University Press, 1967.
Fish, Stanley. *Doing What Comes Naturally: Change, Rhetoric, and the Practice of Theory in Literary and Legal Studies*. Durham, NC: Duke University Press, 1989.
Fishelov, David. "The Vanity of the Reader's Wishes: Rereading Juvenal's *Satire* 10." *AJP* 111 (1990): 370–382.
———. *Metaphors of Genre: The Role of Analogies in Genre Theory*. University Park: Pennsylvania State University Press, 1993.
Fitzgerald, William. *Catullan Provocations: Lyric Poetry and the Drama of Position*. Classics and Contemporary Thought. Vol. 1. Berkeley: University of California Press, 1995.
———. *Slavery and the Roman Literary Imagination*. Roman Literature in its Contexts. Cambridge: Cambridge University Press, 2000.
Flintoff, Everard. "Food for Thought: Some Imagery in Persius' Satire 2." *Hermes* 110 (1982): 341–354.
Fraenkel, Eduard. *Horace*. Oxford: Clarendon, 1957.
Fredricksmeyer, Hardy. "An Observation on the Programmatic Satires of Juvenal, Horace, and Persius." *Latomus* 49 (1990): 792–800.
Freud, Sigmund. *Jokes and Their Relation to the Unconscious*. Translated and edited by James Strachey with a biographical introduction by Peter Gay. New York: W. W. Norton, 1960.
Freudenburg, Kirk. "Horace's Satiric Program and the Language of Contemporary Theory in *Satires* 2.1." *AJP* 111 (1990): 187–203.
———. *The Walking Muse: Horace on the Theory of Satire*. Princeton, NJ: Princeton University Press, 1993.

———. *Satires of Rome: Threatening Poses from Lucilius to Juvenal*. Cambridge: Cambridge University Press, 2001.
Frischer, Bernard. "Fu la Villa ercolanese dei Papiri un modello per la Villa Sabina di Orazio?" *Cronache Ercolanesi* 25 (1995): 211–229.
Frye, Northrop. *Anatomy of Criticism: Four Essays*. Princeton, NJ: Princeton University Press, 1957.
Gérard, Jean. "Des droits et des deviors du poète satirique à l'âge d'argent de la latinité." *ICS* 14 (1989): 265–284.
Girard, René. *Violence and the Sacred*. Translated by Patrick Gregory. Baltimore: Johns Hopkins University Press, 1977.
Gleason, Maud. *Making Men: Sophists and Self-Presentation in Ancient Rome*. Princeton, NJ: Princeton University Press, 1995.
Goldberg, Sander M. "Melpomene's Declamation (Rhetoric and Tragedy)." In Dominik, *Roman Eloquence*, 166–181.
Gotoff, H. C. "Oratory: The Art of Illusion." *HSCP* 95 (1993): 289–313.
Gowers, Emily. *The Loaded Table: Representations of Food in Roman Literature*. Oxford: Clarendon, 1993.
———. Horace, *Satires* 1.5: An Inconsequential Journey." *PCPhS* 39 (1993): 48–66.
———. "Blind Eyes and Cut Throats: Amnesia and Silence in Horace *Satire* 1.7." *CP* 97 (2002): 145–161.
———. "Fragments of Autobiography in Horace *Satires* 1." *CA* 22 (2003): 55–92.
Grant, Mary. *The Ancient Rhetorical Theories of the Laughable: The Greek Rhetoricians and Cicero*. University of Wisconsin Studies in Language and Literature 21. Madison: University of Wisconsin, 1924.
Griffin, Dustin. *Satire: A Critical Reintroduction*. Lexington: University Press of Kentucky, 1994.
Griffith, John G. "The Ending of Juvenal's First Satire and Lucilius Book III." *Hermes* 98 (1970): 56–72.
Gunderson, Erik. *Declamation, Paternity, and Roman Identity: Authority and the Rhetorical Self*. Cambridge: Cambridge University Press, 2003.
Habash, Martha. "Priapus: Horace in Disguise?" *CJ* 94 (1999): 285–297.
Haight, Elizabeth. "Menander at the Sabine Farm, *Exemplar Vitae*." *CP* 42 (1947): 147–155.
Habinek, Thomas. *The Politics of Latin Literature: Writing, Identity, and Empire in Ancient Rome*. Princeton, NJ: Princeton University Press, 1998.
Hallett, Judith P. "*Pepedi/ diffissa nate ficus*: Priapic Revenge in Horace's *Satires* 1.8." *RhM* 124 (1981): 341–347.
Harrison, Geoffrey. "The Confessions of Lucilius (Horace *Sat.* 2.1.30–34): A Defense of Autobiographical Satire?" *CA* 6 (1987): 38–52.
Heldmann, K. "Die Wesenbestimmung der Horazischen Satire durch die Komödie." *A & A* 33 (1987): 122–139.
Henderson, John. "On Getting Rid of Kings: Horace, Satires 1.7." *CQ* 44 (1994): 146–170.
———. *Figuring out Roman Nobility: Juvenal's Eighth Satire*. Exeter: University of Exeter Press, 1997.
———. *Writing Down Rome: Satire, Comedy, and Other Offences in Latin Poetry*. Oxford: Oxford University Press, 1999.
Hendrickson, G. L. "Horace, Serm. 1 4: A Protest and a Programme." *AJP* 21 (1900): 121–142.
Highet, Gilbert. *Juvenal the Satirist*. Oxford: Clarendon, 1954.
Hinds, Stephen. *Allusion and Intertext: Dynamics of Appropriation in Roman Poetry*. Roman Literature in its Contexts. Cambridge: Cambridge University Press, 1998.

Holzberg, Nicholas. *Ovid: The Poet and his Work*. Ithaca, NY: Cornell University Press, 2002.
Hooley, Daniel M. *The Knotted Thong: Structures of Mimesis in Persius*. Ann Arbor: University of Michigan Press, 1997.
———. "'What? Me A Poet?' Generic Modeling in Horace Sat. 1.4." In *Ancient Journeys: Festschrift for Eugene Numa Lane*, edited by Cathy Callaway. Online Webschrift, published at the Stoa Website, University of Kentucky, 2002. Available: http://zeno.stoa.org/cgi-bin/ptext?doc=Stoa%3Atext%3A2001.01.0005. July 8, 2005.
Housman, A. E. "Notes on Persius." *CQ* 7 (1913): 12–32.
Hubbard, Thomas. *The Mask of Comedy: Aristophanes and the Intertextual Parabasis*. Ithaca, NY and London: Cornell University Press, 1991.
Hughes, Joseph J. "*Inter tribunal et scaenam*: Comedy and Rhetoric in Rome." In Dominik, *Roman Eloquence*, 182–197.
Huizinga, Johan. *Homo Ludens: A Study of the Play Element in Culture*. Boston: Beacon Press, 1955.
Hutcheon, Linda. *Irony's Edge: the Theory and Politics of Irony*. London: Routledge, 1994.
Jensen, B. Fruelund. "Crime, Vice and Retribution in Juvenal's Satires." *C & M* 33 (1981–1982): 155–168.
Keane, Catherine. "Satiric Memories: Autobiography and the Construction of Genre." *CJ* 97 (2002): 215–231.
———. "The Critical Contexts of Satiric Discourse." *CML* 22 (2002): 7–31.
———. "Juvenal's Cave-Woman and the Programmatics of Satire." *CB* 78 (2002): 5–20.
———. "Theatre, Spectacle, and the Satirist in Juvenal." *Phoenix* 57 (2003): 257–275.
———. "Defining the Art of Blame." in *Companion to Satire*, edited by Ruben Qunitero. Oxford: Blackwell, forthcoming.
Kernan, Alvin B. *The Cankered Muse: Satire of the English Renaissance*. New Haven, CT: Yale University Press, 1959. Reprint: Hamden, CT: Archon Books, 1976.
———. "Aggression and Satire: Art Considered as a Form of Biological Adaptation." In *Literary Theory and Structure: Essays in Honor of William K. Wimsatt*, edited by Frank Brady, John Palmer, and Martin Price, 115–129. New Haven, CT: Yale University Press, 1973.
Kirby, Michael. "On Acting and Not-Acting." In *Acting (Re)Considered: Theories and Practices*, edited by Philip B. Zarilli, 43–58. London: Routledge, 1995.
Knapp, Charles. "The Sceptical Assault on the Roman Tradition Concerning the Dramatic Satura." *AJP* 33 (1912): 125–148.
Knight, Charles A. "Imagination's Cerberus: Satire and the Metaphor of Genre." *Philological Quarterly* 69 (1990): 131–151.
Knoche, Ulrich. *Roman Satire*. Translated by Edwin S. Ramage. Bloomington: Indiana University Press, 1975.
Knorr, Ortwin. *Verborgene Kunst: Argumentationsstruktur und Buchaufbau in den Satiren des Horaz*. Beiträge zur Altertumswissenschaft 15. Hildesheim: Olms-Weidmann, 2004.
Labate, Mario. "Il sermo oraziano e i generi letterari." In *Zeitgenosse Horaz: Der Dichter und seine Leser seit zwei Jahrtausenden*, edited by Helmut Krasser and Ernst A. Schmidt, 424–441. Tübingen: Gunter Narr, 1996.
LaFleur, Richard. "Horace and *Onomasti Komodein*: The Law of Satire." *ANRW* 2.31.3 (1981): 1790–1826.
Leach, Eleanor W. "Horace's *Pater Optimus* and Terence's Demea: Autobiographical Fiction and Comedy in *Sermo* 1.4." *AJP* 92 (1971): 616–632.
———. "Horace's Sabine Topography in Lyric and Hexameter Verse." *AJP* 113 (1993): 271–302.
Leeman, Anton Daniel. "Rhetorical Status in Horace, *Serm*. 2,1." In *Rhetoric Revalued*:

Papers From the International Society for the History of Rhetoric, edited by Brian Vickers, 159–163. Medieval and Renaissance Texts and Studies 19. Binghamton, NY: Center for Medieval and Renaissance Texts and Studies, 1982.

Lutz, Cora E. "Any Resemblance . . . Is Purely Coincidental." *CJ* 46 (1950): 115–120.

Mack, Maynard. "The Muse of Satire." *Yale Review* 61 (1951): 80–92.

Maier, Barbara. "Juvenal—Dramatiker und Regisseur: Am Bespiel der zehnten Satire." *AU* 26 (1983): 49–53.

Malamud, Martha. "Out of Circulation? An Essay on Exchange in Persius' Satires." *Ramus* 25 (1996): 39–64.

Mazurek, Tadeusz. "Legal Terminology in Horace's *Satires*." Ph.D. diss., University of North Carolina at Chapel Hill, 1997.

———. "Self-Parody and the Law in Horace's Satire 1.9." *CJ* 93 (1997): 1–17.

McCarthy, Kathleen. *Slaves, Masters, and the Art of Authority in Plautine Comedy*. Princeton, NJ: Princeton University Press, 2000.

McGann, M. J. "Juvenal's Ninth Age (13, 28ff.)." *Hermes* 96 (1968): 509–514.

McGinn, Thomas A. J. "Satire and the Law: The Case of Horace." *PCPhS* 47 (2001): 81–102.

McKeown, J. C. "Augustan Elegy and Mime." *PCPhS* 25 (1979): 71–84.

McKim, Richard. "Philosophers and Cannibals: Juvenal's Fifteenth Satire." *Phoenix* 40 (1986): 58–71.

Miller, Paul Allen. *Lyric Texts and Lyric Consciousness: The Birth of a Genre from Archaic Greece to Augustan Rome*. London: Routledge, 1994.

———. "The Bodily Grotesque in Roman Satire: Images of Sterility." *Arethusa* 31 (1998): 257–283.

———. *Subjecting Verses: Latin Love Elegy and the Emergence of the Real*. Princeton, NJ and Oxford: Princeton University Press, 2003.

Muecke, Frances. "Law, Rhetoric, and Genre in Horace, *Satires* 2.1." In *Homage to Horace: A Bimillenary Celebration*, edited by S. J. Harrison, 203–218. Oxford: Clarendon, 1995.

Mueller, Carl Werner. "Aristophanes und Horaz: Zu einem Verlaufsschema von Selbstbehauptung und Selbstgewißheit zweier Klassiker." *Hermes* 120 (1992): 129–141.

Musurillo, Herbert. "Horace and the Bore: *Character Dramaticus* of *Sat*. 1.9." *CB* 40 (1964): 65–69.

Nappa, Christopher. "*Praetextati mores*: Juvenal's Second Satire." *Hermes* 126 (1998): 90–108.

Nichols, J. W. *Insinuation: The Tactics of English Satire*. De Proprietatibus Litterarum, Series Maior 22. The Hague: Mouton, 1971.

Nisbet, R. G. M. "Persius." In *Satire*, edited by J. P. Sullivan, 39–71. Critical Essays on Roman Literature 2. Bloomington: Indiana University Press, 1963.

Novara, Antoinette. *Les idées romaines sur le progrès d'après les écrivains de la République*. Vol. 2. Paris: Les Belles Lettres, 1983.

Oberhelman, Steven and David Armstrong. "Satire as Poetry and the Impossibility of Metathesis in Horace's *Satires*." In *Philodemus and Poetry: Poetic Theory and Practice in Lucretius, Philodemus, and Horace*, edited by Dirk Obbink, 233–254. New York and Oxford: Oxford University Press, 1995.

O'Connor, Joseph. "Horace's *Cena Nasidieni* and Poetry's Feast." *CJ* 86 (1991): 23–34.

Oliensis, Ellen. "Canidia, Canicula, and the Decorum of Horace's *Epodes*." *Arethusa* 24 (1991): 107–138.

———. *Horace and the Rhetoric of Authority*. Cambridge: Cambridge University Press, 1998.

Oltramare, André. *Les origins de la diatribe romaine*. Lausanne: Payot, 1962.
Parker, Holt. "Crucially Funny or Tranio on the Couch: The *Servus Callidus* and Jokes About Torture." *TAPA* 119 (1989): 233–246.
———. "Plautus vs. Terence: Audience and Popularity Re-examined." *AJP* 117 (1996): 585–617.
———. "The Observed of All Observers: Spectacle, Applause, and Cultural Poetics in the Roman Theater Audience." In *The Art of Ancient Spectacle*, edited by Bettina Bergmann and Christine Kondoleon, 163–179. Washington, D.C. and New Haven, CT: Yale University Press, 1999.
Plass, Paul. *The Game of Death in Ancient Rome: Arena Sport and Political Suicide*. Madison: University of Wisconsin Press, 1995.
Plotnick, Joan. "Horace on Satyr Drama." *CW* 72 (1979): 329–335.
Posner, Richard A. *Law and Literature: A Misunderstood Relation*. Cambridge, MA: Harvard University Press, 1988.
Powell, J. G. F. "Stylistic Registers in Juvenal." In *Aspects of the Language of Latin Poetry*, edited by J. M. Adams and R. G. Mayer, 311–334. Proceedings of the British Academy 93. Oxford and New York: Oxford University Press, 1999.
Ramage, Edwin S. "Juvenal and the Establishment: Denigration of Predecessor in the 'Satires'." *ANRW* 2.33.1 (1989): 640–707.
Ramage, Edwin S., David L. Sigsbee, and Sigmund C. Fredericks. *Roman Satirists and Their Satire: The Fine Art of Criticism in Ancient Rome*. Park Ridge, NJ: Noyes Press, 1974.
Randolph, Mary Claire. "The Medical Concept in English Renaissance Satiric Theory: Its Possible Relationships and Implications." *Studies in Philology* 38 (1941): 125–157.
———. "The Structural Design of Formal Verse Satire." *Philological Quarterly* 21 (1942): 368–384.
Raschke, Wendy J. "*Arma pro amico*—Lucilian Satire at the Crisis of the Roman Republic." *Hermes* 115 (1987): 299–318.
Reckford, Kenneth J. "Studies in Persius." *Hermes* 90 (1962): 476–504.
———. "Reading the Sick Body: Decomposition and Morality in Persius' Third *Satire*." *Arethusa* 31 (1998): 337–354.
Relihan, Joel. "The Confessions of Persius." *ICS* 14 (1989): 145–167.
Reynolds, R. W. "The Adultery Mime." *CQ* 40 (1976): 77–84.
Richlin, Amy. *The Garden of Priapus: Sexuality and Aggression in Roman Humor*. Rev. ed. New York: Oxford University Press, 1992.
Robinson, Ken. "The Art of Violence in Rochester's Satire." In *English Satire and the Satiric Tradition*, edited by Claude Rawson, 93–108. Oxford: Blackwell, 1984.
Rosen, Ralph M. *Old Comedy and the Iambographic Tradition*. American Classical Studies 19. Atlanta, GA: Scholars Press, 1988.
———. "Hipponax, Boupalos, and the Conventions of the *Psogos*." *TAPA* 118 (1988): 29–41.
Rowe, Greg. *Princes and Political Cultures: The New Tiberian Senatorial Decrees*. Ann Arbor: University of Michigan Press, 2002.
Rudd, Niall. *The Satires of Horace*. Cambridge: Cambridge University Press, 1966. Reprint, Berkeley: University of California Press, 1982.
———. *Themes in Roman Satire*. Norman, OK: University of Oklahoma Press, 1986.
Schlegel, Catherine. "Horace Satires 1.7: Satire as Conflict Irresolution." *Arethusa* 32 (1999): 337–352.
———. "Horace and His Fathers: Satires 1.4 and 1.6." *AJP* 121 (2000): 93–119.
———. *Satire and the Threat of Speech in Horace's* Satires, *Book I*. Madison: University of Wisconsin Press, 2005.

Schmitz, Christine. *Das Satirische in Juvenals Satiren*. Untersuchungen zur antiken Literatur und Geschichte 58. Berlin and New York: Walter de Gruyter, 2000.
Scodel, Ruth. "Horace, Lucilius, and Callimachean Polemic." *HSCP* 91 (1987): 199–215.
Segal, Erich. *Roman Laughter*. 2nd ed. Oxford: Oxford University Press, 1987.
Seidel, Michael. *Satiric Inheritance: Rabelais to Sterne*. Princeton, NJ: Princeton University Press, 1979.
Shaw, Brent D. "Bandits in the Roman Empire." *Past and Present* 105 (1984): 3–52.
Shero, Lucius R. "The Satirist's Apologia." *University of Wisconsin Studies in Language and Literature* 15 (1922): 148–167.
Singleton, David. "Juvenal's Fifteenth Satire: A Reading." *G & R* 30 (1983): 198–207.
Slater, Niall. *Plautus in Performance: The Theatre of the Mind*. Rev. ed. Amsterdam: Hardwood Academic Publishers, 2000.
Smith, R. E. "The Law of Libel in Rome." *CQ* 45 (1951): 169–179.
Smith, Warren S. "Speakers in the Third Satire of Persius." *CJ* 64 (1969): 305–308.
———. "Heroic Models for the Sordid Present: Juvenal's View of Tragedy." *ANRW* 2.33.1 (1989): 811–823.
Staley, Gregory A. "Juvenal's Third Satire: Umbricius' Rome, Vergil's Troy." *MAAR* 45 (2000): 85–98.
Sweet, David. "Juvenal's *Satire* 4: Poetic Uses of Indirection." *CSCA* 12 (1979): 283–303.
Tatum, W. Jeffrey. "*Ultra legem*: Law and Literature in Horace, *Satires* II 1." *Mnemosyne* 51 (1998): 688–699.
Thorpe, Peter. "Satire as Pre-Comedy." *Genre* 4 (1971): 1–17.
Townend, Gavin B. "The Literary Substrata to Juvenal's Satires." *JRS* 63 (1973): 148–160.
Tupet, Anne-Marie. *La magie dans la poésie latine*. Vol. 1. Des origines à la fin du règne d' Auguste. Paris: Les Belles Lettres, 1976.
Turpin, William. "The Epicurean Parasite: Horace, Satires I.1–3." *Ramus* 27 (1998): 127–140.
Van Rooy, C. A. *Studies in Classical Satire and Related Literary Theory*. Leiden: E. J. Brill, 1965.
———. "Arrangement and Structure of Satires in Horace, *Sermones*, Book 1, with More Special Reference to Satires 1–4." *AClass* 11 (1968): 38–72.
Versnel, H. S. *Triumphus: An Inquiry into the Origin, Development and Meaning of the Roman Triumph*. Leiden: Brill, 1970.
Walters, J. "Making a Spectacle: Deviant Men, Invective, and Pleasure." *Arethusa* 31 (1998): 355–367.
Ward, Ian. *Law and Literature: Possibilities and Perspectives*. Cambridge: Cambridge University Press, 1995.
Weber, H. "Comic Humor and Tragic Spirit: The Augustan Distinction Between Horace and Juvenal." *Classical and Modern Literature* 1 (1981): 275–289.
Wehrle, William. T. *The Satiric Voice: Program, Form and Meaning in Persius and Juvenal*. Altertumswissenschaftliche Texte und Studien 23. Hildesheim: G. Olms, 1992.
Weisberg, Richard and Jean-Pierre Barricelli. "Literature and Law." In *Interrelations of Literature*, edited by Jean-Pierre Barricelli and Joseph Gibaldi, 150–175. New York: Modern Language Association of America, 1982.
Welch, Tara. "*Est locus uni cuique suus*: City and Status in Horace's *Satires* 1.8 and 1.9." *CA* 20 (2001): 165–192.
Wilshire, Bruce. *Role Playing and Identity: The Limits of Theatre as Metaphor*. Bloomington: Indiana University Press, 1982.

Winkler, Martin. *The Persona in Three Satires of Juvenal*. Hildesheim: G. Olms, 1983.

———. "The Function of Epic in Juvenal's Satires." In *Studies in Latin Literature and Roman History*, vol. 5, edited by Carl Deroux, 414–443. Brussels: Latomus Revue d'Études Latines, 1989.

Wiseman, T. P. "Satyrs in Rome? The Background to Horace's *Ars Poetica*." *JRS* 78 (1988): 1–13.

Witke, Charles. *Latin Satire: The Structure of Persuasion*. Leiden: E. J. Brill, 1970.

Woodman, A. J. "Juvenal 1 and Horace." *G & R* 30 (1983): 81–84.

Wray, David. *Catullus and the Poetics of Roman Manhood*. Cambridge and New York: Cambridge University Press, 2001.

Zetzel, James E. G. "Horace's *Liber Sermonum*: The Structure of Ambiguity." *Arethusa* 13 (1980): 59–77.

Ziolkowski, Theodore. *The Mirror of Justice: Literary Reflections of Legal Crises*. Princeton, NJ: Princeton University Press, 1997.

Index

Index includes locorum for satires discussed.

Accius, 25. *See also* literary genres: tragedy
actors/actresses, 4, 9, 17–23, 31, 85–86. *See also* drama
adultery, 21–22, 39, 53, 77, 86–88, 95–99, 130–131. *See also* sexual behavior
alter egos/stand-in satirists, 9–11, 20, 23, 28, 30, 33, 60, 64–65, 78–79, 111, 115–118, 139–140
amicitia, 66, 81, 90, 109
analogy, 11, 13–14, 16–17, 19, 28, 33, 40, 48–49, 60, 70, 74, 95–96, 99–103, 105–108, 121, 124, 136–137. *See also* metaphor; metaphors for satire
animals (aggression of), 46–47, 52–54, 80–81
apologia/defense of satire, 5–6, 10–12, 22, 26, 42, 45–47, 51, 60, 76–79, 83–84
arena, 3, 18, 44, 51, 68, 76, 105, 141
Archilochus, 14, 22, 150n.11. *See also* literary genres: iambography
Aristophanes, 14–15, 133. *See also* literary genres: Old comedy
  Clouds, 163n.72
  Frogs, 145n.3
audiences (of performance, of text), 11, 25–26, 28, 32, 34–40, 58, 68, 69, 96, 107–108, 117, 123

Babrius, *Aesopica*, 150n.14. *See also* literary genres: fable
barbarians, 68–72, 95, 101, 135

Callimachus, 81, 111, 160n23
Catullus, *Carmina*, 150n.11, 163n.72

children, 38, 106, 108, 124, 126
Chrysippus, *On the good*, 157n.50
Cicero, 19, 99. *See also* literary genres: oratory
  De Amicitia, 147n.35
  Ad Atticum, 19, 146n.22
  Brutus, 147n.35, 152n.34
  Pro Caecina, 157n.56
  De Oratore, 62, 75, 147n.35, 150n.8, 153n.65, 160n.24
  De Legibus, 75
  Pro Milone, 158n.72
  De Natura Deorum, 150n.11
  De Officiis, 147n.26, 148n.52
  De Republica, 155n.9
  Tusculanae Disputationes, 152n.34, 154n.76
circus, 33, 36–37
clients. *See* patronage
country/rustic life, 8, 37–40, 81, 89–90, 116, 118, 129, 131, 134. *See also* eating
court, 3, 55, 79, 84–85, 88, 96–97, 99–103, 111, 141. *See also* law; metaphors for satire
  trial, 79, 84, 88, 90, 92, 101–102
Cratinus, 14–15, 25. *See also* literary genres: Old comedy
crime/criminals, 5, 9, 15, 25, 29, 33–34, 40, 43, 46, 52–53, 57, 67, 74–87, 90, 93, 95–96, 97–99, 101, 103, 129, 131, 134–135, 139

declamation, 3, 15, 17, 32, 73, 106, 125–126, 128, 132
deformity/disfigurement, 12, 43–44, 54, 58, 62–64, 68, 69

Demosthenes, 99. *See also* literary genres: oratory
deviants, 11, 17, 42–43, 56. *See also* Others; sexual behavior
diatribe, 5, 22–23, 81, 85, 87, 99, 105–109, 113–117, 122–124, 139
Dio Cassius, *Roman History*, 99, 155n.10. *See also* literary genres: historiography
Diogenes Laertius, *De Clarorum Philosophorum Vitis*, 157n.50
Diomedes, *Ars Grammatica*, 14–15, 73, 145n.6, 154n.1–2. *See also satura*
drama, 3, 4–5, 9–11, 17–20, 33, 72, 89, 100, 103–105, 108, 120, 133, 139, 141. *See also* metaphors for satire
dramatic illusion, 17, 39–40

eating, 7, 8, 26, 34, 36, 37, 60, 89, 119–121
  cannibalism, 26–31, 68–69, 135
  cena, 18, 22, 30–31, 34, 54, 66, 69, 97, 119–120
  convivium, 114, 117, 119
  culinary principles/gastronomy, 26–27, 89, 90, 115–116
  gluttony, 60, 97
  rustic/simple food, 81, 117, 134
emotions, 7, 10, 32–33, 35, 37, 39–40, 70–71, 100, 137, 140
  anger, 7, 14, 25, 32, 70–71, 96–100, 140
  envy, 91
  fear, 7
  hatred, 69–71
  indignation, 34, 83, 96–97
  sympathy, 24, 43, 67–68, 71, 86, 102, 122
Eupolis, 14–15, 25, 27. *See also* literary genres: Old comedy
execution, 34, 83, 95, 98
exile, 81–82, 89–90, 95
exposure, 3, 5, 18–19, 29–31, 45–46, 58, 68, 72, 84, 105, 119

foreigners, 140

Gaius, *Digesta*, 147n.32
Gellius, *Noctes Atticae*, 147n.24, 151n.27

Hesiod, *Works and Days*, 130
Hipponax, 150n.18. *See also* literary genres: iambography

Homer, 112
  Iliad, 67
  Odyssey, 116–117, 161n.34
Horace
  Ars Poetica, 80, 82, 83, 124, 145n.2, 150n.11, 156n.35, 164n.79
  Carmina, 153n.57, 156n.27
  Epistles, 70, 78, 133, 147n.35, 152n.36, 155n.9, 156n.27, 160n.22, 164n.79
  Epodes, 46, 55, 150n.16, 150n.18, 151n.22, 152n.41, 156n.28, 159n.6
  Sermones
    book 1: 8, 120–121
    book 2: 22, 28, 57, 85, 89, 120–122, 139, 146n.12
    1.1: 34, 105–106, 108–109, 112, 123
    1.1–1.3: 22, 85, 108
    1.1.9–12: 88
    1.1.24: 123
    1.1.24–26: 4, 105, 108
    1.1.25–26: 135
    1.1.27: 108
    1.1.41–99: 21
    1.1.66–67: 23
    1.1.120: 119
    1.2: 73, 85–86
    1.2.1–3: 21
    1.2.4–22: 21
    1.2.24: 86
    1.2.37–46: 21, 86
    1.2.37–63: 86
    1.2.119: 86
    1.2.127–133: 21
    1.2.134: 86
    1.3: 57, 72–73, 75, 86, 94, 96
    1.3.24: 86–87, 155n.13
    1.3.29–32: 21
    1.3.43–48: 54
    1.3.98: 157n.50
    1.3.99–106: 52–53, 87–88, 91
    1.3.103–106: 99
    1.3.105–106: 73
    1.3.111: 77
    1.3.112: 96
    1.3.119: 93
    1.3.137: 156n.31
    1.3.139: 119
    1.4: 76–77, 81, 85–87, 108–109, 111
    1.4.1–5: 77
    1.4.1–7: 4, 14, 24, 28, 77, 109

INDEX

1.4.3–5: 53
1.4.5: 25
1.4.8–11: 55
1.4.14: 119
1.4.33: 40, 48, 57, 78
1.4.34: 4, 47
1.4.42: 77
1.4.48–56: 21
1.4.63–64: 76–77
1.4.66: 79
1.4.69–71: 78–79, 82
1.4.78–79: 47, 50
1.4.93–101: 79
1.4.103–109: 109
1.4.105–120: 21
1.4.106: 77
1.4.126–127: 60, 158n.80
1.4.130–131: 119
1.4.133–139: 137
1.4.138–139: 79
1.4.139–140: 110
1.5: 56, 62, 87, 108, 144n.16, 145n.3
1.5.51–70: 54
1.6: 87, 108, 111
1.6.62–70: 109
1.6.71–88: 106, 109, 127
1.6.76–83: 109
1.6.85–89: 110
1.6.104: 61
1.6.123: 79
1.7: 56, 61, 88, 111, 144n.16,
1.7.3: 88
1.7.33–35: 54
1.8: 111, 114
1.8.1: 54
1.8.19–45: 88
1.8.23: 156n.22
1.8.46–47: 56, 88
1.9: 88, 114, 125, 147n.28
1.9.7: 111–112
1.9.27–28: 162n.54
1.9.75: 111
1.10: 22, 26, 76, 108, 114, 118, 155n.17, 161n.43
1.10.3–4: 45
1.10.5–6: 20
1.10.12: 77
1.10.14–15: 108
1.10.14–17: 14, 28
1.10.19: 112
1.10.39: 19
1.10.40–42: 19, 120

1.10.40–49: 111–112
1.10.52–57: 112
1.10.71: 151n.33
1.10.74: 82
1.10.76–77: 4, 17–19, 22–23, 34, 35
1.10.76–90: 122
1.10.81–88: 112
1.10.92: 113
2.1: 76, 83, 116–117, 155n.18, 156n.24
2.1.1: 113
2.1.1–4: 48, 75, 79–80
2.1.5–20: 80
2.1.12–15: 48
2.1.18: 115–116
2.1.21–23: 80, 89
2.1.24–29: 48–49, 80
2.1.30–34: 106
2.1.39–42: 4, 47–48, 57, 80
2.1.44–46: 91
2.1.52–53: 47, 80
2.1.59–60: 81, 89
2.1.60–62: 123
2.1.62–65: 23, 30, 45, 80
2.1.62–70: 89
2.1.64–65: 119
2.1.71: 24, 80
2.1.71–74: 90, 117
2.1.74–78: 48
2.1.81: 94
2.1.82–83: 75, 79–80, 92
2.1.83–86: 81–82
2.1.194–198: 35
2.1.197: 36
2.2: 89–90, 114, 116–117, 134
2.2.2: 122
2.3: 22, 27, 89, 90, 114, 116, 124–125
2.3.1–4: 125
2.3.1–16: 114–115, 118
2.3.4–5: 90, 115
2.3.7: 163n.75
2.3.11–12: 14, 22, 27, 125
2.3.13–14: 91
2.3.19: 126
2.3.26–36: 115
2.3.60–62: 21, 80
2.3.64–65: 126
2.3.77–81: 115
2.3.88: 162n.54
2.3.132–141: 21
2.3.259–271: 21, 147n.36

Horace, *Sermones* (continued)
    2.3.300–302: 118–119
    2.3.303–304: 21
    2.3.323: 118
    2.3.326: 115
    2.4: 89, 90, 114–116
    2.4.92: 119
    2.4.95: 119
    2.5: 73, 89, 90, 114, 116–117, 147n.28
    2.5.20: 117
    2.6: 89, 90, 114, 116–117, 152n.49
    2.6.1: 117
    2.6.23–39: 134
    2.6.63–71: 117
    2.6.68–69: 90
    2.6.71: 89
    2.6.71–117: 117–118
    2.7: 22, 89, 91, 114, 116, 152n.49
    2.7.1: 118
    2.7.4–5: 22, 57, 91, 118
    2.7.21–37: 118
    2.7.32–42: 21–22
    2.7.41–42: 119
    2.7.43–46: 118–119
    2.7.46: 22
    2.7.53–67: 21, 22
    2.7.112–113: 57, 119
    2.7.116: 57
    2.7.116–118: 91
    2.8: 89, 90, 114, 116, 152n.49
    2.8.1–2: 119
    2.8.21–24: 21
    2.8.32–33: 120
    2.8.79: 18, 34
humor/laughter, 3, 12, 36, 42, 44, 50, 62, 64–71, 83, 97, 105, 108, 123–124, 128, 140

immigrants, 31–32, 67–68
iniuria, 75–76
injuries/wounds, 55–56, 61–62, 65–66
Isidore of Seville, *Origines sive Etymologiae*, 153n.62

Juvenal, *Satires*
  book 1 (*Satires* 1–5): 66, 67, 99, 133, 140
  book 4 (*Satires* 10–12): 35, 140
  book 5 (*Satires* 13–16): 67, 68, 71, 99, 101, 133, 140
  1: 36, 37, 67, 98–99, 136, 139, 144n.19
  1.1: 50, 83, 95
  1.1–18: 29
  1.15–17: 106, 128, 163n.71
  1.19–20: 46
  1.24–25: 128–129
  1.30–31: 29, 39, 50
  1.32–36: 96
  1.32–48: 29
  1.45: 39
  1.45–46: 158n.75
  1.46–50: 95
  1.50: 98
  1.51: 158n.75
  1.56–57: 130
  1.63–64: 29, 34, 39, 50, 137–138
  1.71–72: 130
  1.73–74: 95
  1.79: 34, 39, 83
  1.85–86: 7, 100
  1.87: 4
  1.87–146: 129
  1.95–126: 29
  1.132–146: 96–97
  1.147–149: 4, 129–130
  1.151–153: 159n.84
  1.155–157: 4, 18, 50–51, 63, 76, 83, 95
  1.157: 102
  1.158–159: 4, 29
  1.161: 83
  1.165: 159n.84
  1.165–167: 4, 15, 40, 46
  1.168–171: 51
  1.170–171: 83, 130
  2: 17, 67
  2.1–15: 29
  2.11–13: 64
  2.29–33: 29
  2.83: 131
  2.137–142: 95
  2.159–170: 130
  3: 67, 69, 71, 133
  3.9: 153n.67
  3.67–68: 31, 63
  3.78: 31
  3.92–97: 31
  3.100–106: 31–32
  3.126–130: 29
  3.147–151: 65, 154n.70
  3.153–158: 37
  3.172–178: 37–38
  3.175: 40
  3.199–301: 65–66
  3.314: 131

4: 67, 95–96, 158n.76
4.1–2: 4, 17
4.15–17: 17
4.47–48: 96
4.72–75: 29
4.150: 158n.76
4.153–154: 96
5: 32–33, 67, 71, 97, 99, 154n.73
5.5: 96
5.26–27: 66, 69
5.26–29: 30
5.37–39: 30
5.49: 30
5.120–121: 34
5.153–158: 30
5.170–173: 66
6: 40, 130
6.53–54: 63
6.61–75: 38–39
6.63–81: 31
6.66: 131
6.70: 40
6.231–241: 131
6.O17–20: 131
6.396–397: 31
6.634–638: 4, 15–18, 75
7: 132–133
7.12: 29
7.13–14: 96
7.72–73: 29
7.87: 29
7.148–149: 96
8: 73
8.1–20: 34
8.49–50: 96
8.80–84: 96
8.87–124: 97–98
8.124: 158n.81
8.183–210: 33–34
8.198–199: 23
8.211: 149n.66
8.215–221: 28
8.215–223: 158n.76
8.221–223: 34
8.266–268: 98
9: 29, 32, 133
9.64–65: 63, 164n.77
10: 98, 158n.82
10.28–51: 35–37
10.28–53: 140
10.29–30: 26
10.31: 123

10.69–72: 99
10.77–81: 36–37
10.120–132: 99
10.158: 63
10.227–228: 63
10.311–317: 98–99, 157n.47
10.317: 95
10.346–366: 153n.57
11.4: 33
11.179–202: 37
12.93–130: 29
13: 32, 67, 71, 73, 96, 99, 104, 140
13.13–15: 159n.84
13.28–70: 130
13.35: 159n.84
13.75–119: 29
13.110: 34
13.137: 102
13.143–161: 100
13.167–173: 67, 71
13.210–249: 100
14: 101, 133–135, 140
14.31–37: 95
14.256–264: 4, 18, 28
15: 68–71, 101, 140
15.29–31: 15, 17, 28
15.106–112: 135
15.131–159: 135
15.131–174: 95
16: 101–103, 135, 140
16.12: 63, 66, 71–72
16.47: 159n.86

law, 11, 52–53, 62, 71–72, 84, 98–99, 102, 105, 136, 140. *See also* court; metaphors for satire
   generic law (*lex operis*), 16, 75–76, 80–81, 89, 92, 103–104
   exlex, 82–83, 85, 87, 90–93, 95, 100–102
   lex per saturam, 73. *See also* satura
libertas, 9, 14–15, 25, 46, 53, 91, 94, 107, 118, 128–129, 163n.64
literary genres (other than satire)
   bucolic, 111, 129. *See also* Vergil
   comedy, 6, 13–14, 111, 115
      Old comedy, 4, 6, 14–15, 26–28, 53, 62, 77, 122. *See also* Cratinus; Eupolis; Aristophanes
      New comedy, 14, 15. *See also* Menander
      Roman comedy, 6, 7, 15. *See also* Plautus; Terence

literary genres (other than satire), (*continued*)
  elegy, 8, 25, 58. *See also* Ovid
  English satire, 43, 49
  epic, 8, 48, 54–55, 111, 116–117. *See also* Homer; Lucan; Ovid; Vergil
  epyllion, 25, 58
  fable, 45–46. *See also* Babrius
  farce, 21, 38–39, 54
  historiography, 8. *See also* Livy, Tacitus
  iambography, 5, 14, 22, 45–46, 54–55, 57, 79, 123. *See also* Archilochus; Hipponax
  lyric, 9
  mime, 13, 17–21, 30, 34
  oratory, 32, 58, 99
  panegyric, 80
  satyr play, 82
  tragedy, 4, 13–16, 25, 58, 111, 112, 136, 140. *See also* Accius; Pacuvius
Livy, *Ab Urbe Condita*, 14, 82, 98, 145n.1. *See also* literary genres: historiography
Lucan, *Bellum Civile*, 163n.66. *See also* literary genres: epic
Lucilius, *Satires* (fragments), 4, 23–24, 42, 48–50, 64, 77, 80–85, 89–90, 99, 109
  5–47W: 84
  53–93W: 84
  64–65W: 82
  303–307W: 84
  599W: 84
  632–636W: 76, 112–113, 122
  635W: 82
  1017W: 82, 85
  1075W: 45, 76
  1078W: 76
  1083–1089W: 76
  1085–1086W: 45
  1088W: 45
  1145–1151W: 84, 134
Lucretius, *De Rerum Natura*, 105, 152n.34, 163n.72

Macrobius, *Saturnalia*, 147n.24
magic, 42, 56, 88, 111
Martial, *Epigrams*, 75, 148n.48, 154n.72, 156n.39, 156n.60, 163n.72, 163n.75
Menander, 14. *See also* literary genres: New comedy

metaphor, 3–8, 34, 42, 45–46, 73–75, 88–89, 92–95, 104, 106–107, 113, 132–133, 139–140. *See also* analogy; metaphors for satire
metaphors for satire
  drama/theater, 3–12, 13–41, 103–104, 107, 120, 140–141
  legal process, 3–12, 40–41, 62, 73–104, 107, 120, 140–141
  medical or surgical procedure, 45–52, 53, 61–62
  physical violence, 3–12, 40–41, 42–72, 79, 88, 103, 107, 120, 141
  sexual aggression, 48, 58–59
  teaching, 3–12, 105–136, 140–141
mimicry, 3–4, 6, 10, 31–34, 59–61, 79, 81, 96, 99, 121, 135
miserliness, 21, 23, 34, 94
myth, 21, 26, 28, 34, 70, 89, 116–117

noble mime (*mimus nobilis*), 23, 33–34
Nonius, *De Compendiosa Doctrina*, 82, 150n.12

Others, 11, 31, 43–44, 53, 55–56, 63–64, 67–71, 135. *See also* barbarians; deviants; foreigners; immigrants
Ovid: *See also* literary genres: elegy; epic
  Amores, 144n.23
  Ars Amatoria, 38, 162n.46
  Heroides, 152n.34
  Ibis, 150n.11
  Metamorphoses, 130
  Remedia Amoris, 150n.11

Pacuvius, 25. *See also* literary genres: tragedy
patronage, 8, 13, 19–20, 29–34, 55–56, 66–67, 81, 88, 90, 97–99, 109–110, 117, 132–133
Persius
  Choliambics, 121
  Satires
    1: 92, 94, 121
    1.1–2: 122
    1.1–3: 161n.43
    1.2–3: 25–26
    1.2–7: 82–83
    1.5–7: 157n.65
    1.7: 27, 121
    1.8: 158n.73, 162n.49
    1.8–9: 82, 94

1.9–10: 137
1.9–11: 122–123
1.12: 50, 83, 123, 124, 163n.47
1.13–106: 123
1.18: 153n.54
1.19–21: 147n.38, 153n.53
1.20–21: 58
1.24: 124
1.28: 83
1.44: 4, 24, 26, 146n.13
1.49: 58
1.55: 124
1.63–66: 58, 157.65
1.76–78: 25
1.80–82: 147n.38
1.82: 153n.53
1.85–86: 157n.65
1.86: 124
1.92: 58
1.93: 124
1.107–108: 4, 49, 58, 65, 94, 123, 124
1.107–110: 82–83
1.108–109: 92
1.109–110, 151n.22
1.112–114: 4, 61–62, 92, 124, 126
1.114–115: 46, 82, 92
1.116–117: 61, 83, 92
1.117: 150n.15
1.119–120: 26, 82–83, 92, 153n.66
1.121: 151n.24, 158n.67, 158n.73, 162n.49
1.122: 50, 83, 123
1.123–125: 15, 24–25, 27, 122
1.126: 27, 123, 151n.24
1.128: 153n.65
1.127–128: 62
1.134: 27
2: 27, 59–60, 69, 94, 158n.82
2.73: 158n.72
3: 26, 61, 94, 124–125, 134, 164n.79
3.1–7: 60
3.1–19: 125
3.9: 153n.59
3.19: 163n.75
3.20–24: 163n.72
3.22: 148n.56
3.38: 148n.56
3.39–43: 153n.60
3.44–47: 125–126
3.49–50: 148n.56
3.56–57: 125

3.73–76: 162n.56
3.73–78: 125
3.77–87: 162n.56
3.81–85: 148n.56
3.87: 162n.46
3.88–106: 97, 124
3.96–97: 125
3.107–109: 162n.56
3.107–118: 60
3.109: 148n.56
3.125–130: 148n.56
3.183: 148n.56
3.211: 148n.56
3.247: 148n.56
3.308: 148n.56
4: 60–61, 94, 126, 162n.52
4.1–3: 17
4.23: 27, 109
4.27–32: 126
4.35–41: 126
4.40: 153n.61
4.52: 27, 60–61
5: 4, 94, 121
5.8–9: 26, 29
5.14: 124
5.14–16: 49, 50, 58
5.21: 158n.71
5.30–36: 127
5.30–51: 106, 127
5.40: 132
5.52–192: 127
5.73–90: 93
5.86: 49, 151n.24, 153n.55
5.88–90: 93
5.96–99: 93–94
5.126–131: 94
5.132–153: 134, 164n.79
5.161–174: 24
5.181–191: 93
6: 94–95, 121, 127, 139
persona/mask, 5, 9–11, 13–41, 99–100, 106, 136–140
Petronius, *Satyricon*, 154n.72, 163n.72
Pindar
  Olympians, 156n.27
  Pythians, 150n.11
Plato, 14
Plautus. *See also* literary genres: Roman comedy
  Casina, 146n.13
  Epidicus, 157n.63
  Miles Gloriosus, 147n.28

Plautus (*continued*)
  Mostellaria, 157n.63
  Pseudolus, 146n.13
Pliny the Elder, *Historia Naturalis*, 155n.9
Pliny the Younger
  Panegyricus, 148n.52
  Epistles, 75, 148n.48, 163n.74
Plutarch, *Cicero*, 153n.62
Pseudo-Plutarch, *De liberis educandis*, 164n.78
populus/crowd, 15, 33–37
prayer, 7, 59
prostitution, 21, 23, 85–86, 119, 133

Quintilian, *Institutio Oratoria*, 3, 9, 77, 135, 140, 141, 146n.13, 148n.52, 148n.55–56, 163n.74

recusatio, 48, 80
revenge/retaliation, 11, 34, 50–51, 57, 63, 65, 74, 83, 86, 88, 94, 95–100, 108, 115, 139
Rhetorica ad Herennium, 76, 77, 143n.13
Roman history
  Brutus, Tarquins, 98
  Caesar, 54–55, 99, 115–116
  civil wars, Octavian-Antony, 9, 54, 89
  Domitian's assassination, 96
  early principate, 47
  elections moved to senate, 36–37
  extortion (Dolabella, Antonius, Verres), 97–98
  Nero, 9, 33–34, 76
  Republican context of Lucilian satire, 107
  proscriptions, 54
  Sejanus' conspiracy against Tiberius, 99
  triumviral expropriations, 114

sacrifice, 11, 42–44, 59–60, 69. *See also* prayer
satura, 7, 14, 73, 82, 113
Saturnalia, 22, 28, 89–90, 93, 113–116, 118–119, 125
Seneca the Elder, *Controversiae*, 155n.10, 163n.74
Seneca the Younger
  Dialogues, 35, 155n.10, 162n.47
  Epistles, 153n.34, 157n.60, 161n.43
sexual behavior, 8, 43, 85–86, 132–133. *See also* adultery
  pathic behavior, 29, 64–65, 131, 133, 130
  sexual aggression, 48, 88
  sexual deviance, 43, 56

slavery, 21, 22, 30, 57, 63, 66–67, 91, 92–93, 94–95, 114, 118–119
social theater, 24, 40
spoudaiogeloion, 105, 123
Statius, *Silvae*, 150n.11
Suetonius
  Augustus, 147n.32
  Domitian, 153n.64
  De Viris Illustribus, 163n.70

Tacitus. *See also* literary genres: historiography
  Annales, 36, 147n.32, 149n.64, 151n.27, 155n.10
  Agricola, 155n.10
  Dialogus de Oratoribus, 163n.69
teaching, 3, 12, 105–106, 121, 131, 139–141. *See also* metaphors for satire
  students, 4, 26, 94, 105–110, 120–122, 124–127
  teachers, 106–110, 115, 119–124, 126–127, 131–132, 136
Terence, 15, 20, 24, 35. *See also* literary genres: Roman comedy
  Eunuchus, 147n.27, 147n.36
  Hecyra, 35, 147n.23, 149n.60
  Phormio, 148n.28, 157n.63
theater. *See* drama; actors/actresses
Twelve Tables, 75, 81, 155n.9

urbanitas, 6, 9, 47

Varro of Atax, 112
Varro
  De Lingua Latina, 152n.34
  Saturae Menippeae, 82
Vergil, 111, 132, 163n.70. *See also* literary genres: bucolic; epic
  Aeneid, 98
  Eclogues, 129, 163n.64
violence, 10, 42, 45, 54, 65, 68–69, 82, 87, 91, 96, 98–99, 103, 105, 133, 136, 139–140. *See also* metaphors for satire
  victims of violence, 5, 9, 11, 18, 30–31, 43, 50–51, 57–58, 66, 71, 79, 83, 96, 98–99, 102–103, 105
vigilantism, 4, 74, 84

Weapons, 4, 42, 46–48, 51–53, 55, 57, 61, 64, 66, 70, 91, 98–99, 101